AF479262

Mathias Braschler & Monika Fischer / China

Mathias Braschler
Monika Fischer

CHINA

中

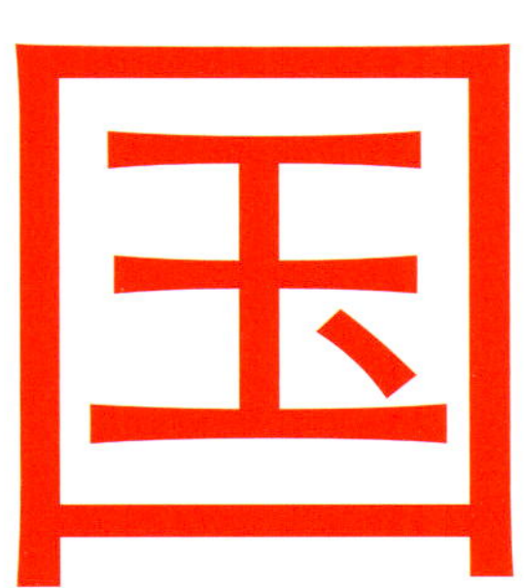

HATJE
CANTZ

Mit Unterstützung von/With the support of:

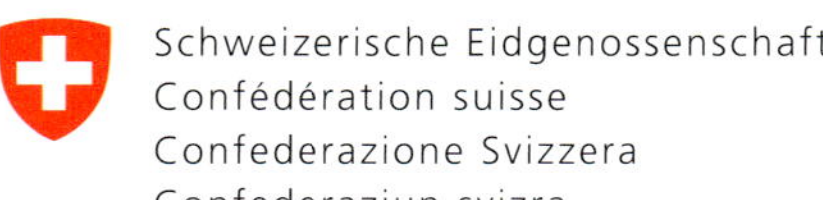

Eidgenössisches Departement des Innern EDI
Bundesamt für Kultur BAK

Mathias Braschler
Monika Fischer
China

Konzept/Concept: Peter Zimmermann
Texte/Texts: Jonathan Watts und/and Braschler & Fischer
Mitherausgeber/Co-Editor: Roger Zoller
Grafische Gestaltung und Satz/Graphic design and typesetting: Peter Zimmermann
Schrift/Typeface: Helvetica LT
Übersetzung/Translation: Christel Klink, Marcus R. A. Endres, www.translate-me.info
Korrektorat/Proofreading: Michael Brewer, Sabine Walter, Word+Image AG
Herstellung/Production: Christine Stäcker, Hatje Cantz
Papier/Paper: Galaxi Keramik, 170 g/m²
Druck/Printing: Memminger MedienCentrum Druckerei und Verlags-AG
Buchbinderei/Binding: Lachenmaier GmbH, Reutlingen

Die Ausgabe für die Schweiz erscheint
in der Edition Stephan Witschi.
ISBN 978-3-9523619-5-5
edition@stephanwitschi.ch

The edition for Switzerland is available
by Edition Stephan Witschi.
ISBN 978-3-9523619-5-5
edition@stephanwitschi.ch

Unveränderte Neuauflage erschienen im/Unrevised new edition published by
Hatje Cantz Verlag
Zeppelinstrasse 32
73760 Ostfildern
Deutschland/Germany
Tel. +49 711 4405-200
Fax +49 711 4405-220
www.hatjecantz.de

Hatje Cantz books are available internationally at selected bookstores. For more information
about our distribution partners please visit our homepage at www.hatjecantz.com

ISBN 978-3-7757-3336-6

Printed in Germany

Umschlagabbildung/Cover illustration: Qin Lingling (5), Zirkusakrobatin/Circus acrobat, Hukou, Shanxi

Die möglicherweise bemerkenswerteste der vielen Leistungen von Mathias Braschler und Monika Fischer auf ihrer 30.000 Kilometer langen fotografischen Reise durch China war wohl die Tatsache, dass sie sich nur einmal verfuhren.

Ich war damals gerade mit ihnen unterwegs. Um für meine Zeitung über ihre Reise zu berichten, schloss ich mich den Schweizer Fotografen auf den Straßen von Yunnan an, dieser fruchtbaren Provinz im Süden des Landes, die sich vom Fuß des Himalajas bis hinunter zu den tropischen Dschungeln an der Grenze zu Burma, Laos und Vietnam erstreckt.

Diese Reise hat sich mir tief ins Bewusstsein eingeprägt, sowohl aufgrund der Einblicke, die sie mir in den Alltag der Menschen gewährte, die in diesem sich rapide modernisierenden Staat leben, als auch im Hinblick auf die intensive Arbeit, die hinter jedem der Portraits in diesem Band steckt.

Wir hatten einige der großartigsten Landschaften Chinas durchfahren: tropische Bergwälder, von Nebelschwaden durchzogene Täler mit den typischen Hütten am Rande der Reisfelder und abgelegene Dörfer aus strohgedeckten Häusern, zwischen denen sich golden die Getreideernte auftürmte.

Sie hatten sich ein Portrait pro Tag zum Ziel gesetzt – kein leichtes Unterfangen, noch dazu wenn man dabei Hunderte von Kilometern zurücklegt, Menschen zum ersten Mal begegnet, ein mobiles Studio aus- und wieder einpacken, eine Unterkunft suchen und sich mit unterschiedlichen Dialekten und einem tief verwurzelten Misstrauen gegenüber fremden Fotografen auseinandersetzen muss.

Morgens brachen sie meist auf, ohne zu wissen, wen sie an diesem Tag treffen und fotografieren würden. Dieses Vertrauen in zufällige Begegnungen macht ihre Arbeit so einzigartig. Sie ist eine Mischung aus Portraitfotografie, Journalismus und Entdeckungsfahrt gleichermaßen.

Jeder Tag brachte wahre Marathonfahrten mit sich, oft genug unterbrochen von Drama und Stress. Da war Mathias knietief im Wasser und fotografierte einen Bauern, der eine schwere Ladung Mist durch das reißende Wasser manövrierte, und am nächsten Tag versuchte Monika die Standbesitzer eines chaotischen ländlichen Markts zu beruhigen, wobei die Menge der Neugierigen so groß wurde, dass der Fotoshoot abgebrochen werden musste.

Solch widrige Umstände wurden aber durch Glücksmomente und Bezeugungen menschlicher Wärme mehr als kompensiert und zwar oft da, wo man es am wenigsten erwartet hätte. Generell verhielten sich die Menschen selten wie erwartet: Eine Abtreibungsärztin, deren Aufgabe es war, Chinas Ein-Kind-Politik rigoros durchzusetzen, stellte sich als eines der schönsten und würdevollsten Motive heraus. Der Offizier einer paramilitärischen Polizeieinheit zur – oft brutalen – Niederschlagung von Aufständen, war ein Ausbund an Charme.

Mit Hilfe einer mittel- und einer großformatigen Kamera, sowie ausgeklügelter Beleuchtung verleihen die beiden den Portraitierten so viel Glanz und Farbe, als handle es sich um Aufnahmen von Hollywoodgrößen. Die Opulenz der Portraits erinnert an die

Among the many achievements of Mathias Braschler and Monika Fischer's 30,000-kilometre photographic journey through China, perhaps the most striking was that they only made one wrong turn. I was with them on that occasion. To record their travels for my newspaper, I joined the Swiss photographers on the road in Yunnan, the lush southern province that stretches from the foothills of the Himalayas down to the tropical jungles along the border with Burma, Laos and Vietnam.

That trip is etched on my mind both for the insights it provided about the everyday lives of people in this rapidly modernising nation, as well as the intensity of the work that went into each of the portraits on the pages of this book.

We had driven through some of the most spectacular scenery in China: lush mountain forests, misty valleys bordered by paddies and remote villages of thatched houses stacked high with the golden corn harvest.

Their goal was to take one portrait each day – no easy feat while they were also covering hundreds of kilometres, meeting people for the first time, packing and unpacking a mobile studio, looking for hotels and dealing with language differences and deep-rooted suspicions about foreign photographers.

Most mornings, they set off without knowing who they would meet and photograph during the day. This reliance on chance encounters is what makes their approach unique. It is part portraiture, part journalism and part exploration.

Each day brought marathon road trips punctuated with sharp bursts of drama and stress. One day, Mathias was up to his knees in water photographing a farmer carrying a heavy load of manure through a fast-moving river. The next, Monika was trying to pacify stallholders in a chaotic rural market that thronged with such a large, curious crowd that the shoot had to be abandoned.

Such frustrations were more than compensated by flashes of fortune and displays of human warmth, often in the most unexpected places. People rarely lived up to their stereotypes. An abortionist who ensured China's family planning policy was rigorously enforced proved to be one of the most beautiful and dignified of subjects. An officer in the paramilitary police, who are used – often brutally – to put down riots, was a model of charm.

Using medium and large-format cameras and elaborate lighting systems, the duo lends their subjects the lustre and colour of a Hollywood celebrity shoot. The richness of the portraits brings to mind the rosy-cheeked propaganda pictures of the Cultural Revolution, whilst the range of shots, which run the gamut from the successful super rich to street beggars, provides an overall image of China that is anything but idealised. Despite the state's constant claims of a "harmonious society" and the "One World, One Dream" slogan of the 2008 Olympics, income inequality, cultural diversity and environmental destruction come across very powerfully in these photographs.

The week before I joined them, Mathias, Monika and their assistant Yuan passed close to the rocket base in Sichuan province where China launched its first lunar probe – part of the country's

rotbackigen Propagandaaufnahmen der Kulturellen Revolution, doch die Bandbreite an Sujets – von den Erfolg- und Superreichen bis hin zu Bettlern – verschafft ein Gesamtbild von China, das keinesfalls idealisierend ist. Trotz der ständigen Betonung einer „harmonischen Gesellschaft" seitens der Mächtigen und dem Slogan der Olympiade 2008, „Eine Welt, ein Traum", bringen diese Bilder ganz deutlich die Einkommensunterschiede, die kulturelle Unterschiedlichkeit und die Zerstörung der Umwelt zum Ausdruck. In der Woche, bevor ich zu ihnen stieß, kamen Mathias, Monika und ihr Assistent Yuan nahe der Raketenbasis in der Provinz Sichuan vorbei, von der aus China im Rahmen eines ambitionierten Weltraumprogramms seine erste Mondsonde abgeschickt hatte. Kaum eine halbe Stunde Fahrtzeit entfernt hingegen fotografierten sie Zhang Weng Xiang, der mit zwei Wasserbüffeln und einem winzigen Feld 5.000 Yuan (540 Euro) im Jahr verdient.

Ihre Bilder zeigen klar, wie unmöglich es ist, dieses riesige, vielseitige und sich schnell entwickelnde Staatsgebilde auf einen Nenner zu bringen. Zwei Arbeiter im Ölterminal von Dalian – Yang Jianguo und Sun Yongyi – könnten als Modelle für ein Bild im Stil des Sozialistischen Realismus dienen. Andere Bilder sind zeitlos: trainierende Kinder an der Akrobatenschule der Provinz Shandong, Kleinkinder als Mitglieder in einem Reisezirkus nahe den Wasserfällen von Hukou, die Baumwollpflücker von Hami in Xinjiang oder ein paar Bauern und Bergleute, deren Werkzeuge und Kleidung direkt dem 19. Jahrhundert entnommen schienen. Einige entlegene Gegenden sind noch ganz unberührt von der neuen Zeit. In der Inneren Mongolei wusste die junge Nomadin Wuluchua weder, was die Olympischen Spiele sind, noch kannte sie den Namen des Präsidenten ihres Landes.

Am eindrucksvollsten sind die Bilder schneller, dramatischer Veränderungen: der kommunistische Parteisekretär Wang Wei inmitten der verwüsteten Ruinen der Porzellanmanufaktur Boshan, die einst seine Arbeitsstätte war. Wie viele andere Staatsbetriebe konnte auch dieser mit den wirtschaftlichen Reformen der letzten Jahre nicht Schritt halten. Dann sind da die neuen Reichen bei Arbeit und Spiel: Xia Yang, Planer und Bauunternehmer, der versucht, Polo in China wieder aufleben zu lassen, Yin Mingshan, der Industrielle aus Chongqing, der eine der größten Autofirmen des Landes aufbaut, und Ma Jing, Tochter eines Generals, die zusammen mit ihrem Mann Li Haifeng gerade einen Hotelkomplex in Penglai in der Provinz Shandong errichtet. Am anderen Ende des sozialen Spektrums stehen die analphabetischen Bauern wie Sun Xuejiang, Bettler wie Bao Keshun, der seinem Gewerbe mit Hilfe eines einbeinigen Affen nachgeht, und die 81-jährige Huang Shufen, die am Tag weniger als 20 Cent verdient, indem sie die am Rande der Schnellstraße liegenden Plastikflaschen aufsammelt. Monika erzählte mir, dass die Frau vor Dankbarkeit in Tränen ausbrach, als sie ihr eine Polaroidaufnahme, etwas Geld und eine Schweizer Glocke als Zeichen ihres Danks überreichte.

Nur wenigen erschließt sich China in dieser Breite. In der Provinz Gansu wurden sie zu Ehrengästen einer riesigen Hochzeit, als die im sechsten Monat schwangere Braut Bin Bin spontan entschied,

ambitious space programme. Less than half an hour's drive away, they photographed Zhang Weng Xiang, who makes 5,000 Yuan (USD 700) a year from two water buffalos and a tiny field.

As their images show, it is impossible to pigeonhole this vast, diverse, fast-moving nation. In Dalian, two oil terminal workers – Yang Jianguo and Sun Yongyi – could be model workers in a socialist realist painting. Other images are timeless: children training at the acrobat school in Shandong province; infant members of the travelling circus near Hukou Falls; the cotton pickers of Hami in Xinjiang; and several farmers and coal miners, whose tools and clothes could easily have come from the 19th century. Some remote areas are still untouched by development. In Inner Mongolia, one young nomad woman, Wuluchua, did not know what the Olympics were, nor could she name the president of her country.

Most striking are the images of sudden, dramatic change: Wang Wei, the Communist party secretary, stands among the rubble and desolation of the porcelain factory in Boshan that once employed him. The company went bankrupt, like many other state-owned enterprises, during the economic reforms of the past 20 years. Then there are the new rich at work and play: Xia Yang, the developer and entrepreneur who is trying to resurrect polo in China; Yin Mingshan, the Chongqing industrialist who is building one of the country's biggest car companies; and Ma Jing, the daughter of a general, who is now building a hotel complex in Penglai, Shandong with her husband, Li Haifeng. At the other end of the social spectrum, there are illiterate subsistence farmers, such as Sun Xuejiang, beggars like Bao Keshun, who plied his trade with a one-legged monkey, and 81-year-old Huang Shufen who earns less than 20 cents a day collecting plastic bottles from the side of a motorway. Monika told me the woman cried with gratitude when they gave her a Polaroid, some money and a Swiss bell as a token of thanks.

Few people get to view such a breadth of China. In Gansu province, they became the guests of honor at a huge wedding after the six months' pregnant bride, Bin Bin, decided that the foreigners would bring luck to the nuptials. Among the most spectacular and poignant shots is the portrait of window cleaner Zhou Huajing perched hundreds of meters above the cityscape of Chongqing on land that he used to farm before it was planted with skyscrapers.

The road brought many challenges, including three detentions by the police, three cases of food poisoning, a gastrointestinal infection, a respiratory infection and a running battle with diarrhoea. They got one speeding ticket (the amount of which was open to negotiation like, it seems, everything else in China), bumped the car once and almost got stuck on a rusty cargo ship on the Yangtze. They crossed a military zone near a nuclear test site in the Taklimakan desert, where they had to bed down secretly in a hotel that was forbidden to foreigners. They drove up to an altitude of 4,500 metres, where the conditions played havoc with the Polaroids. They crisscrossed the Yellow River 10 times, and suffered from the 38°C Beijing summer heat and the early onset of winter on the Qinghai plateau, where the mercury dropped to -6°C.

dass die Fremden bei der Hochzeit Glück bringen würden. Eine der spektakulärsten und ergreifendsten Aufnahmen ist die des Fensterputzers Zhou Huajing Hunderte von Metern über der Stadt Chongqing und über dem Stück Land, das er einst bewirtschaftete, bevor Hochhäuser darauf emporschossen.

Auf der Fahrt hatten sie mit vielen Schwierigkeiten zu kämpfen. So wurden sie dreimal von der Polizei verhaftet, erlitten drei Lebensmittelvergiftungen, eine Magen-Darm-Infektion, eine Atemwegsinfektion und mussten sich unentwegt vor Durchfall in Acht nehmen. Einmal wurden sie auch wegen einer Geschwindigkeitsübertretung angehalten (wobei die Höhe der Strafe, wie so ziemlich alles in China, Verhandlungssache war). Sie hatten einen Auffahrunfall und steckten vorübergehend auf einem alten Frachter auf dem Jangtsekiang fest. Sie durchquerten ein militärisches Schutzgebiet neben einem Atomversuchsgelände in der Wüste Taklamakan, wo sie heimlich in einem Hotel übernachten mussten, das für Fremde eigentlich verboten war. Sie fuhren bis auf 4.500 Meter Höhe hinauf, wo sich Testaufnahmen mit Polaroidbildern aufgrund der Bedingungen schwierig gestalteten. Sie überquerten zehnmal den Gelben Fluss und litten bei 38 Grad unter der Sommerhitze Pekings sowie unter dem frühen Wintereinbruch auf der Qinghai-Tibet-Hochebene, als die Quecksilbersäule auf minus sechs Grad sank.

Doch trotz all dieser Schwierigkeiten haben sie sich nur einmal verirrt. Auf der Rückfahrt von einer entlegenen Gefängniskolonie, deren Wärter ihnen verwehrt hatten, einen Gefangenen zu portraitieren, befanden wir uns auf dem Weg zur Provinzhauptstadt Kunming. In dieser Region mit ihren Bergen und Wäldern gibt es nur wenige Straßen, und einige davon sind in äußerst schlechtem Zustand. Um schneller voranzukommen, wollten wir uns zur nächsten Überlandstraße durchschlagen, was für die beiden ungewöhnlich war, da sie sonst ihre Motive entlang der kleinen Landstraßen suchten. Aus den Straßenkarten war nicht genau ersichtlich, wo wir abbiegen mussten, also fragten wir ein paar Dörfler, die uns den Weg zu einer „nahe gelegenen" Schnellstraße wiesen. „Nah" war sie jedoch nur, wenn man chinesische Maßstäbe anlegt. Diese falsche Abzweigung verlängerte unsere Reise um dreihundert Kilometer, also etwa um die Breite der Schweiz.

Fehler, Erfolge, einfach alles scheint in China viel größer, und deshalb sind diese Portraits einzelner Menschen aus diesem Milliardenvolk so außergewöhnlich.

Jonathan Watts
Ostasien-Korrespondent für den Guardian

Despite these hardships, they got lost only once. We were heading to the provincial capital of Kunming from a remote prison colony, where the wardens had turned down a request for a portrait of an inmate. It was a region of mountains and forests with very few roads, some of which were in very poor condition. To save time, the decision was made to head for the nearest highway, which was unusual as they preferred to look for subjects along small back roads. The maps were a little unclear about where to turn so we asked a couple of villagers, who pointed us towards a "near expressway." Unfortunately, it was "near" only on a Chinese scale. Our wrong turn added 300 kilometres to the journey, equivalent to the size of Switzerland.

Mistakes, successes, everything, it seems is magnified in China. That is what makes these one-in-a-billion portraits of ordinary life so extraordinary.

Jonathan Watts
East Asia Correspondent for the Guardian

刘天佑

Liu Tianyou (91)
Älteste noch lebende Teilnehmerin am Langen Marsch
Oldest living participant of the “Long March”
Yan'an, Shaanxi

Liu Tianyou war gerade erst 18 Jahre alt, als der 12.500 Kilometer lange Marsch im Jahre 1934 seinen Anfang nahm. Während dieses gewaltigen Unterfangens arbeitete sie als Krankenschwester. Heute lebt sie in Chinas einzigem Seniorenheim für Rote-Armee-Veteranen in Yan'an, dem Zielort des Langen Marsches.

Liu Tianyou was just 18 when Mao's 12,500 km Long March started in 1934. She practiced as a nurse during this strenuous endeavor. Today she lives in China's only retirement home for non-commissioned veterans of the Red Army in Yan'an, the final destination of the Long March.

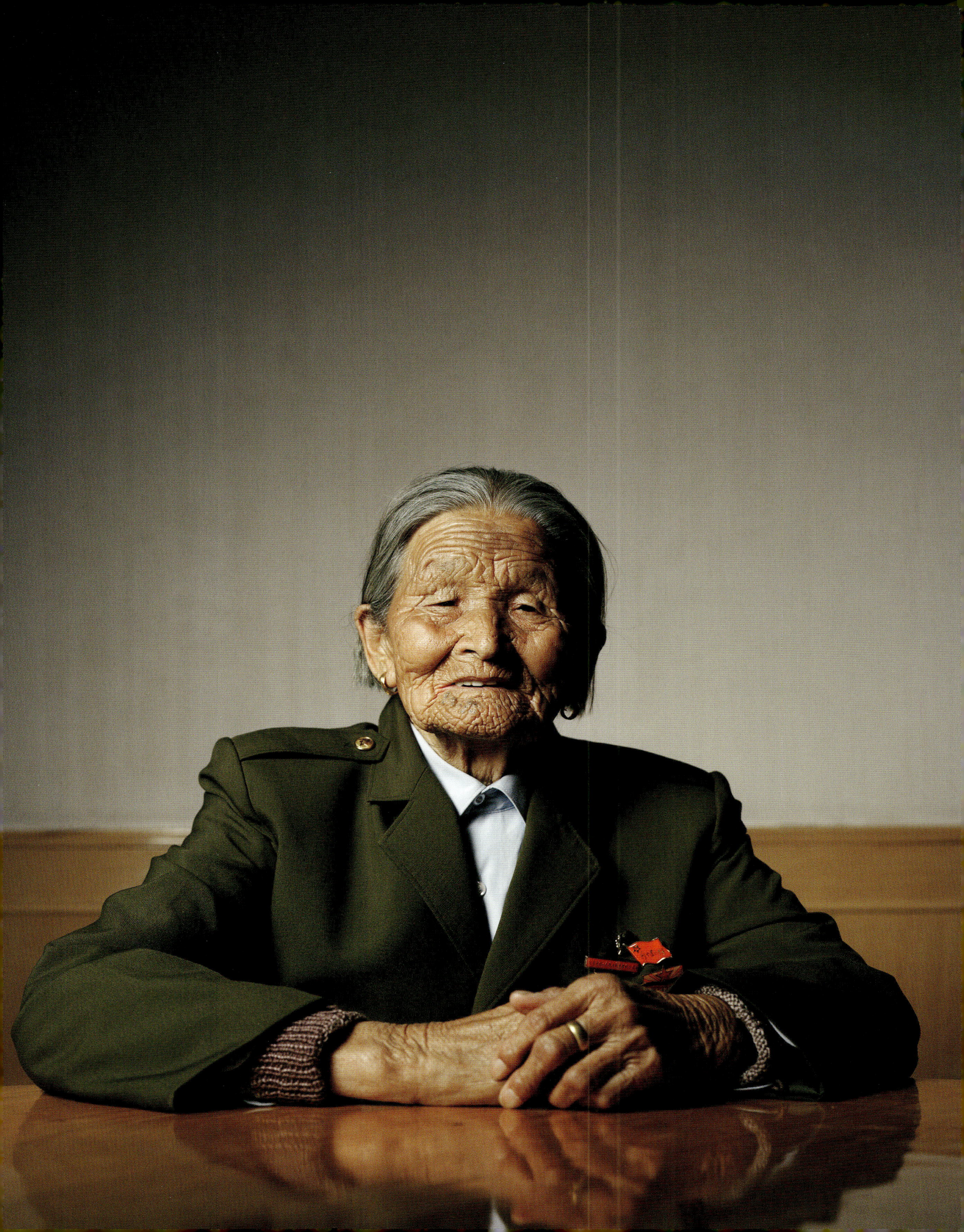

吴协恩

Wu Xie'en
Parteisekretär
Party Secretary
Huaxi, Jiangsu

Wu Xie'en ist Parteisekretär und Dorfvorsteher von Huaxi, dem reichsten Dorf Chinas. Er und seine Familie haben in dieser Modellstadt weitreichende Machtbefugnisse.

Wu Xie'en is the party secretary and village chief of Huaxi, the richest village of China. He and his family have far-reaching powers in this model town.

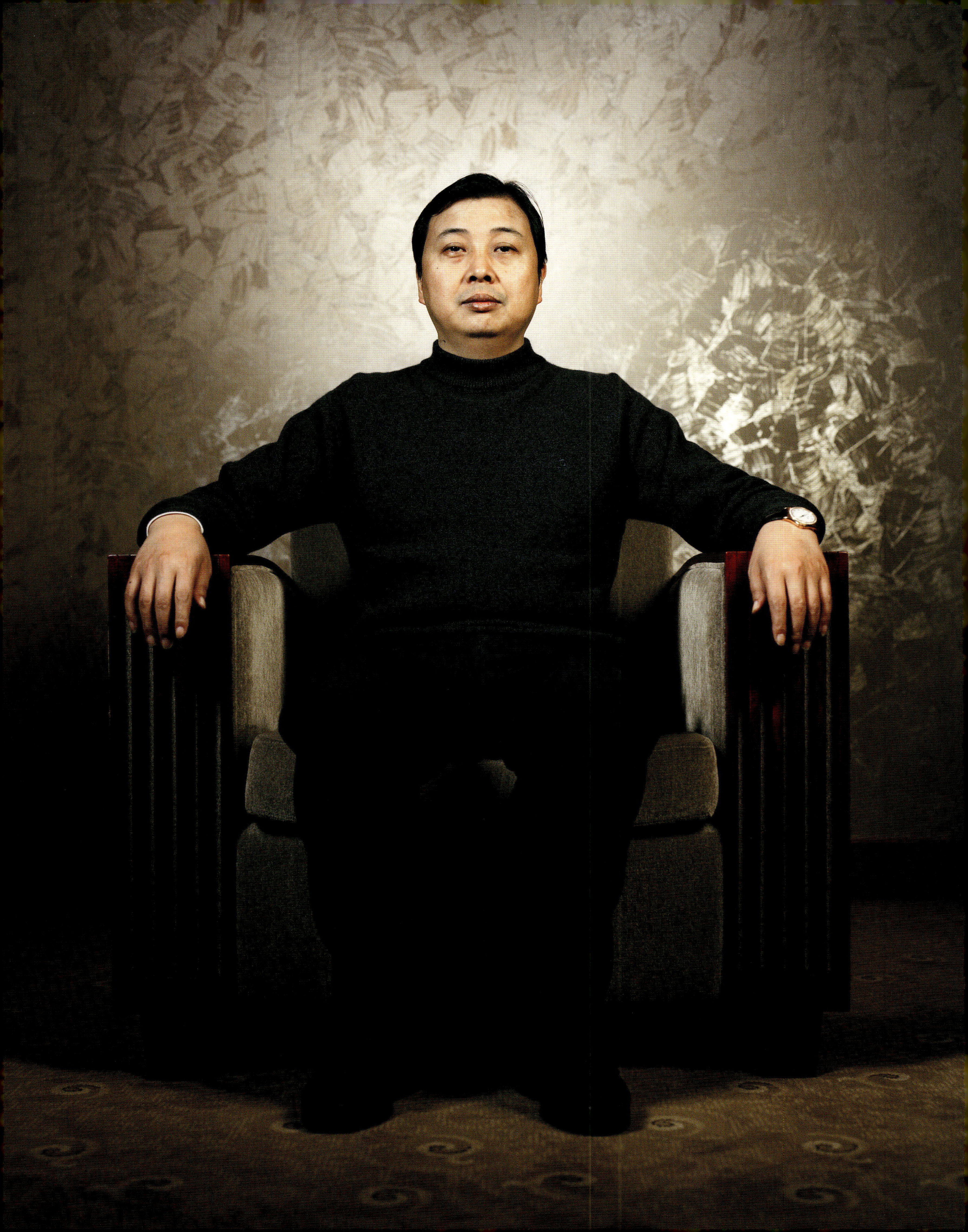

གི་ལོ་

Gilo (80)
Tibetisch-Buddhistische Nonne
Tibetan Buddhist nun
Duogongma, Qinghai

Gilo ist eine Nonne der tibetisch-buddhistischen Tradition. Sie lebt in der Nähe eines buddhistischen Tempels in einem abgelegenen Tal und verbringt die meiste Zeit mit Beten.

Gilo is a Tibetan Buddhist nun. She lives next to a Buddhist temple in a remote valley and spends most of her day in prayer.

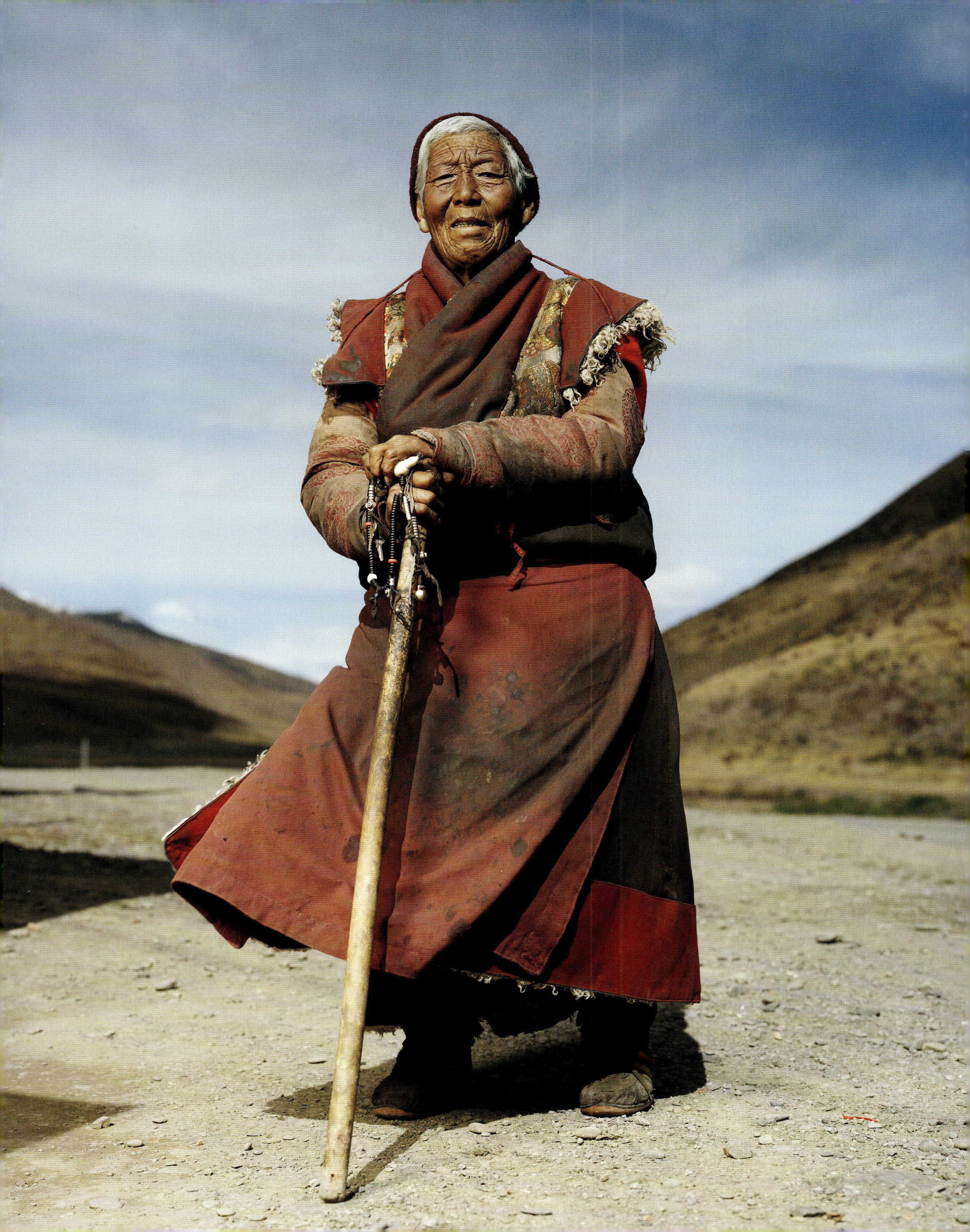

王偉

Wang Wei* (16)
LKW-Mechaniker
Truck mechanic
Xinmin, Liaoning

Der Teenager Wang Wei verdient sich seinen Lebensunterhalt als LKW-Mechaniker, ein Job, den unzählige Chinesen ausüben. Jeden Tag befahren hunderttausende, oft überalterte Lastwagen Chinas Straßen.

The teenager Wang Wei makes a living by working long hours as a truck mechanic, a very common job in China. Hundreds of thousands of often antiquated trucks navigate China's roads every day.

* Name geändert / changed name

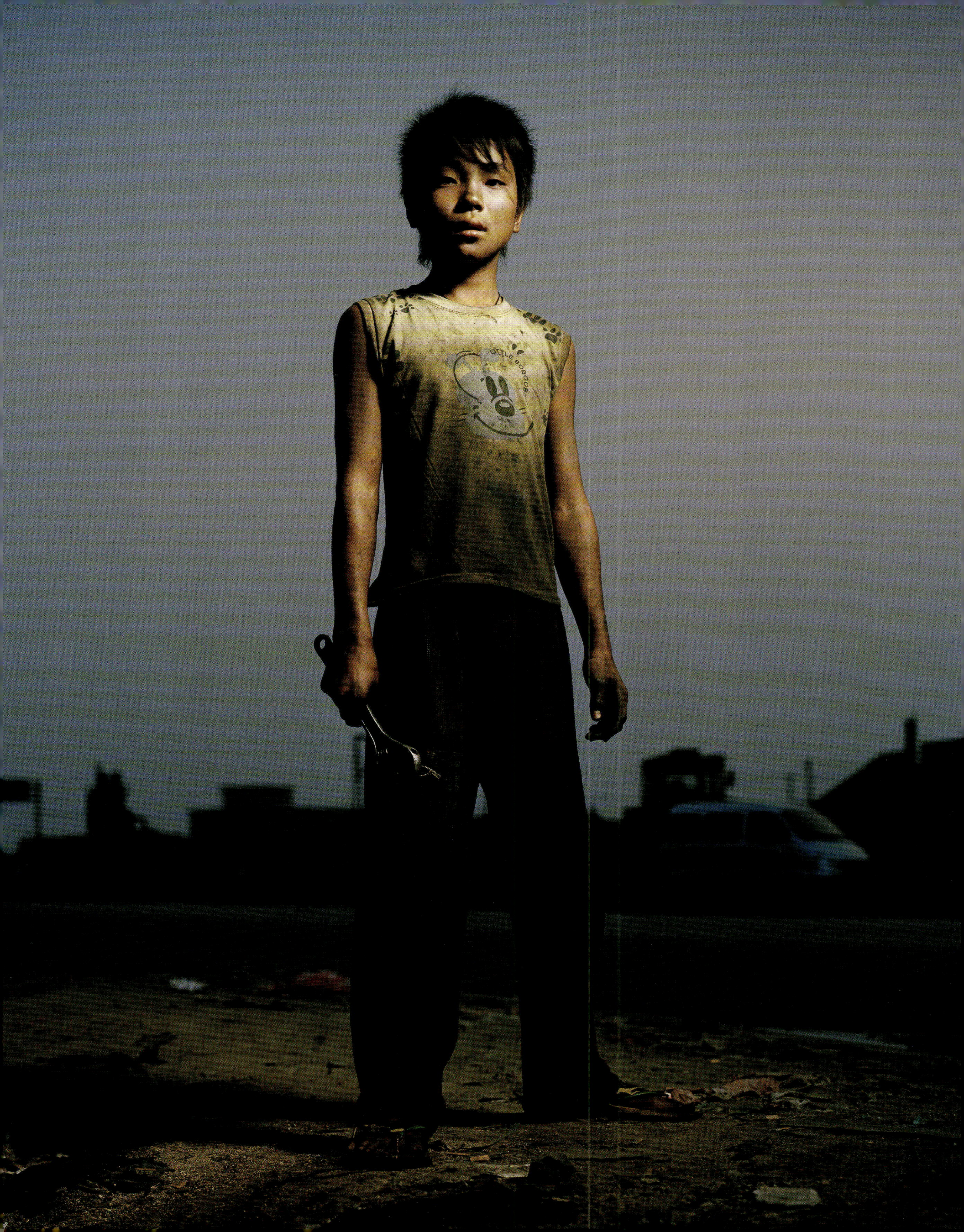

张文珠

Zhang Wenzhu (18)
Verkäuferin
Sales person in fashion shop
Anxi, Fujian

Zhang Wenzhu verkauft Trendklamotten in einer kleinen Modeboutique in der Stadt Anxi in der Provinz Fujian. Sie gehört zur wachsenden Gruppe der jungen Chinesen, die sich von den alten Traditionen abwendet und in westlichen Vorbildern Halt sucht.

Zhang Wenzhu sells trendy clothes in a small fashion shop in the town of Anxi in Fujian Province. She is part of a growing number of young Chinese who are abandoning old traditions and beginning to turn to Western role models.

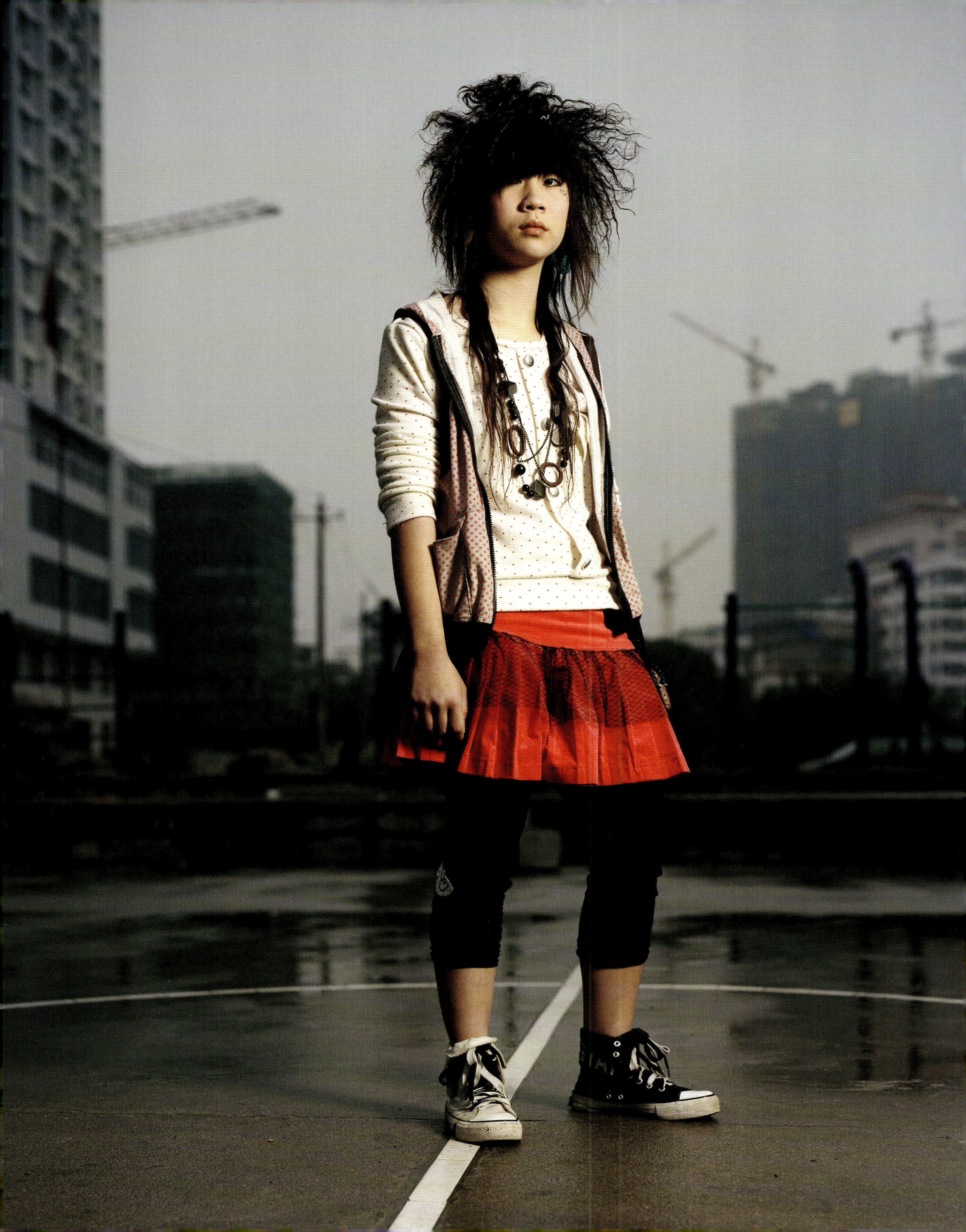

苏增林

Shu Zhengli (43)
Bergarbeiter
Coalminer
Ningwu, Shanxi

Shu Zhengli ist einer der unzähligen Bergarbeiter Chinas. Er arbeitet in einer relativ kleinen Kohlegrube in einer abgelegenen Gebirgsregion der Provinz Shanxi. Sein Job ist einer der gefährlichsten in ganz China. Über 5.000 Kumpel sterben jedes Jahr in chinesischen Kohlebergwerken. Shanxi ist mit Abstand die Provinz mit den meisten Gruben in China.

Su Zhengli is one of China's countless coalminers. He works in a medium-size mine in a remote mountain area of the Shanxi Province. He has a very dangerous job; more than 5,000 people die in Chinese coal mines every year. Shanxi is by far the province with the most mines.

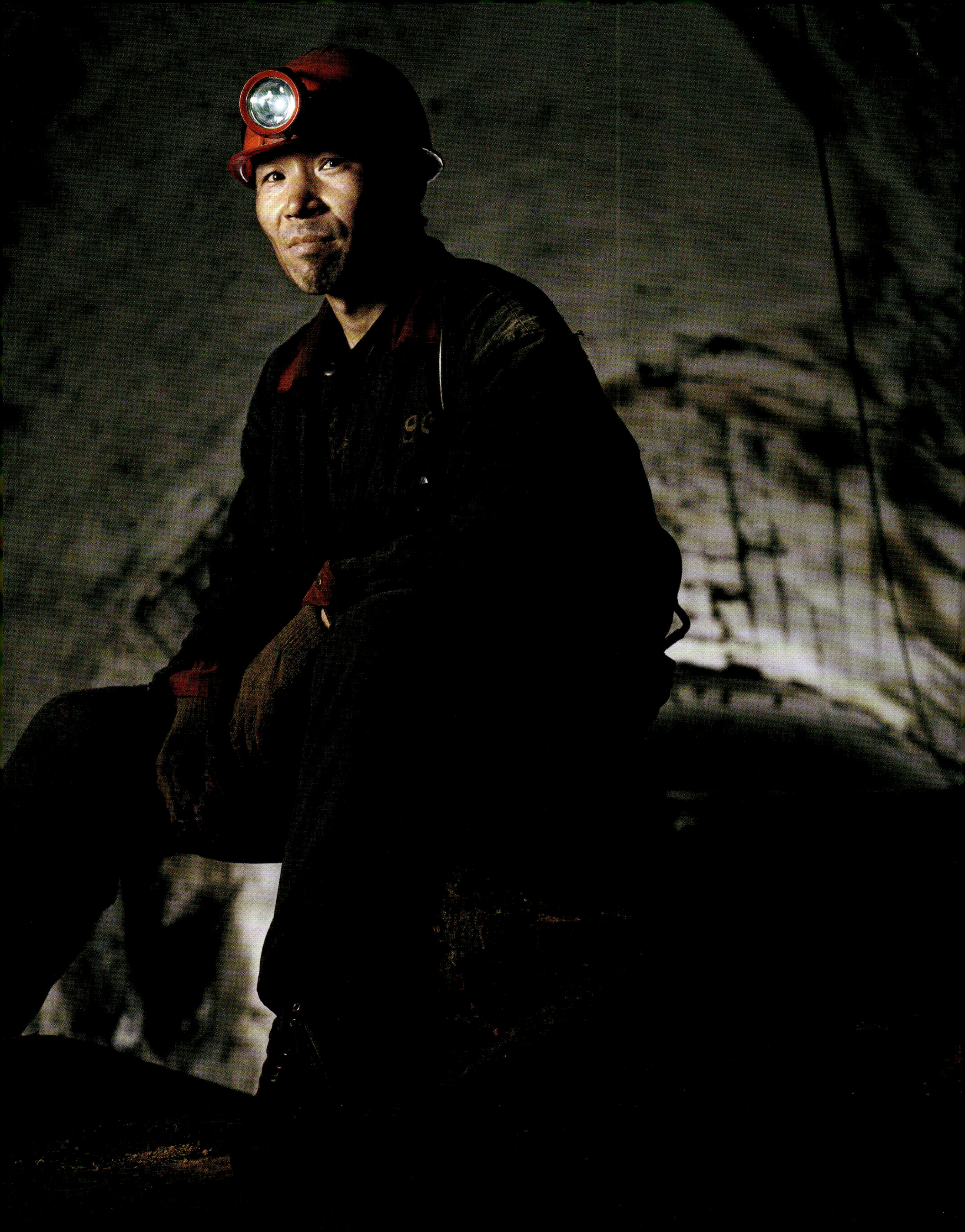

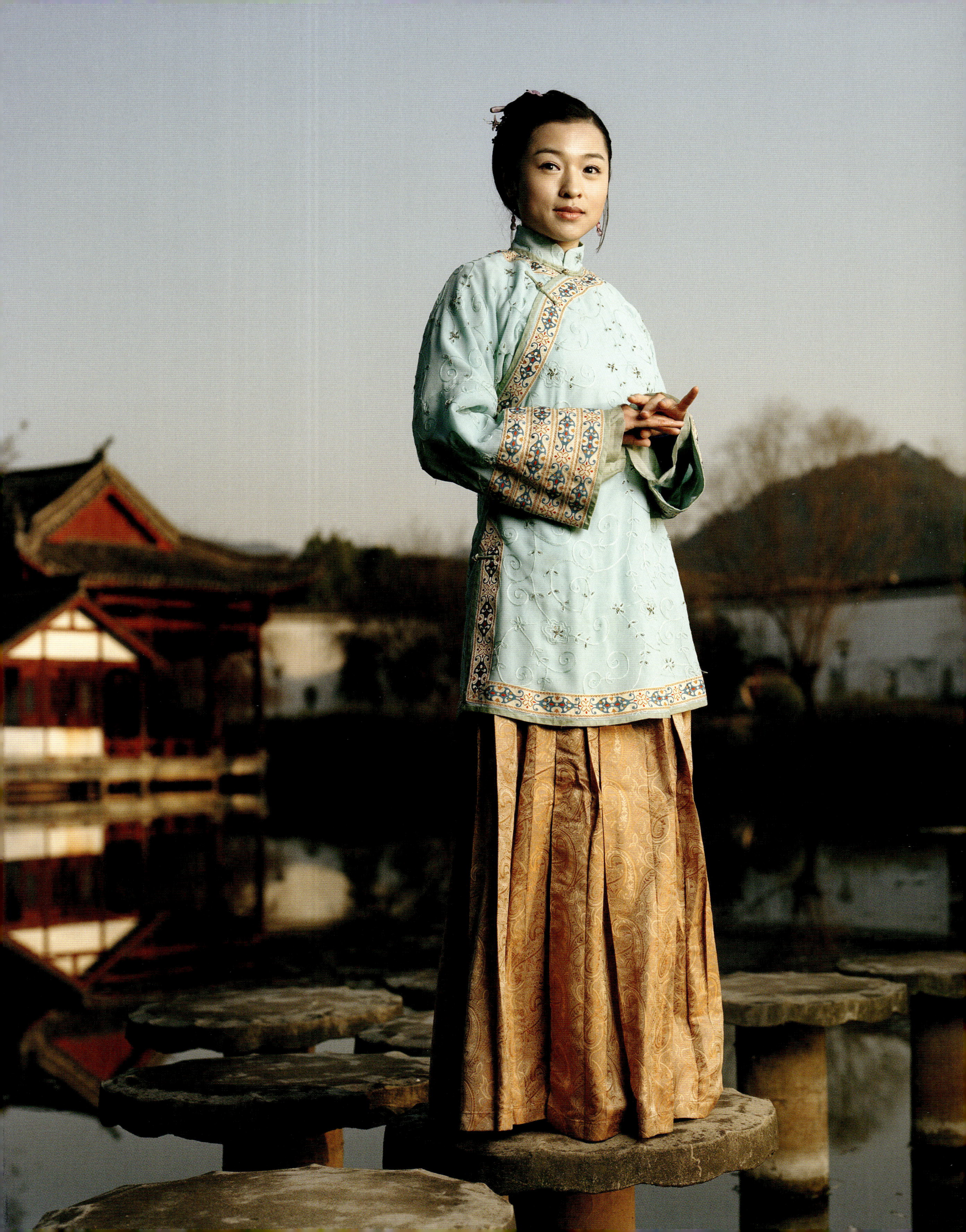

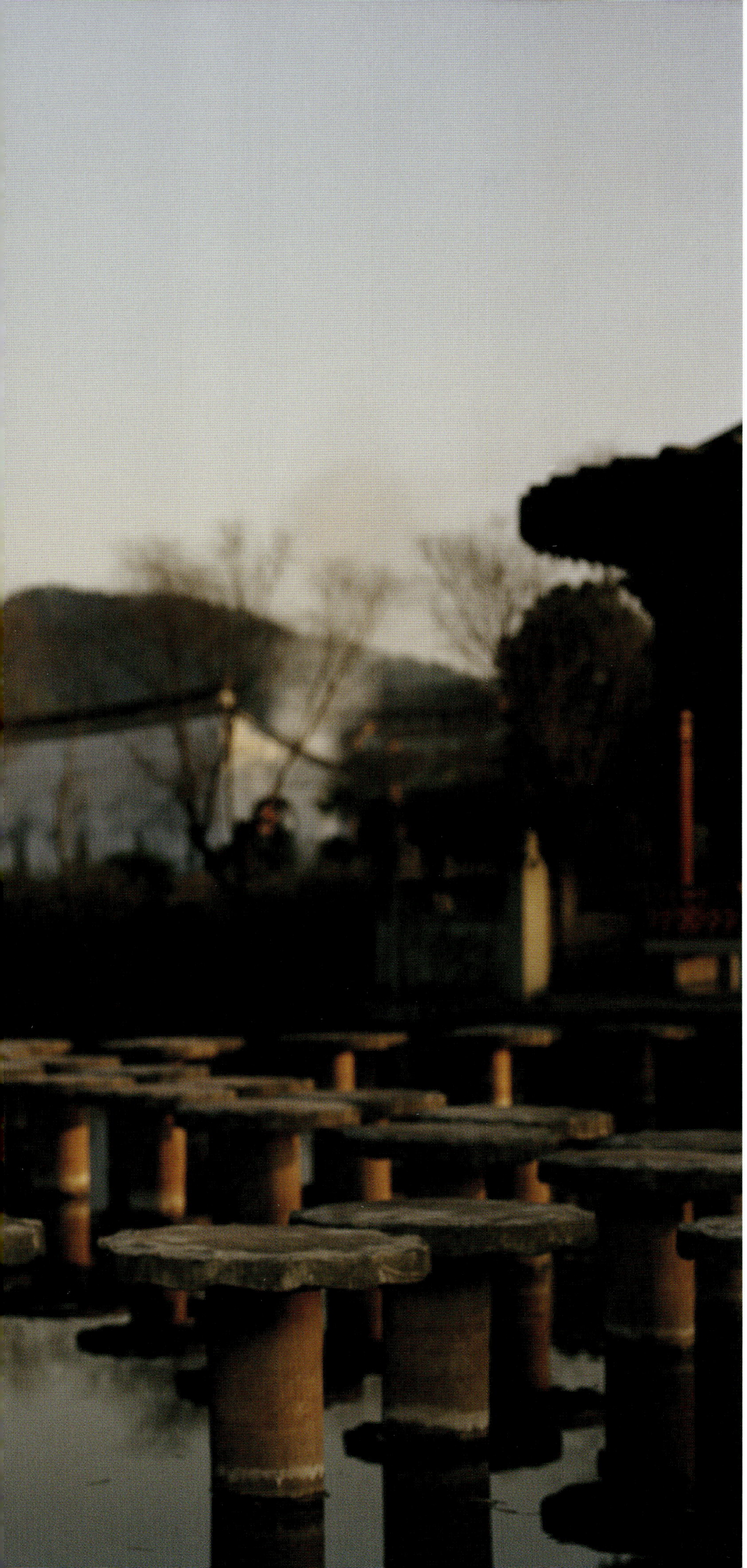

魏小军

Wei Xiaojun (26)
Schauspielerin
Actress
Hengdian World Studios
Hengdian, Zhejiang

Schauspielerin Wei Xiaojun spielt derzeit eine Nebenrolle in einer chinesischen Seifenoper, die in den Hengdian Studios produziert wird. Hengdian, Chinas Hollywood, verfügt über eine ganze Reihe verschiedener Kulissen, wie z. B. über einen Nachbau der gesamten Verbotenen Stadt.

Actress Wei Xiaojun is playing a supporting role for a Chinese soap opera that is being produced at Hengdian Studios. Hengdian, China's Hollywood, offers a vast variety of locations for film productions – for example a reconstruction of the entire Forbidden City.

孙学江

Sun Xuejiang (52)
Bauer
Farmer
Dujigou, Ningxia

Sun Xuejiang ist ein armer Bauer aus der Provinz Ningxia, der weder lesen noch schreiben kann. Da er keinen Traktor besitzt, bewältigt er die gesamte Arbeit mit einer Eselskarre. Vor allem im Norden Chinas ist dies kein ungewöhnlicher Anblick.

Sun Xuejiang is a poor, illiterate farmer in Ningxia Province. Since he does not own a tractor, he does all his work with a donkey cart; a very common sight, particularly in Northern China.

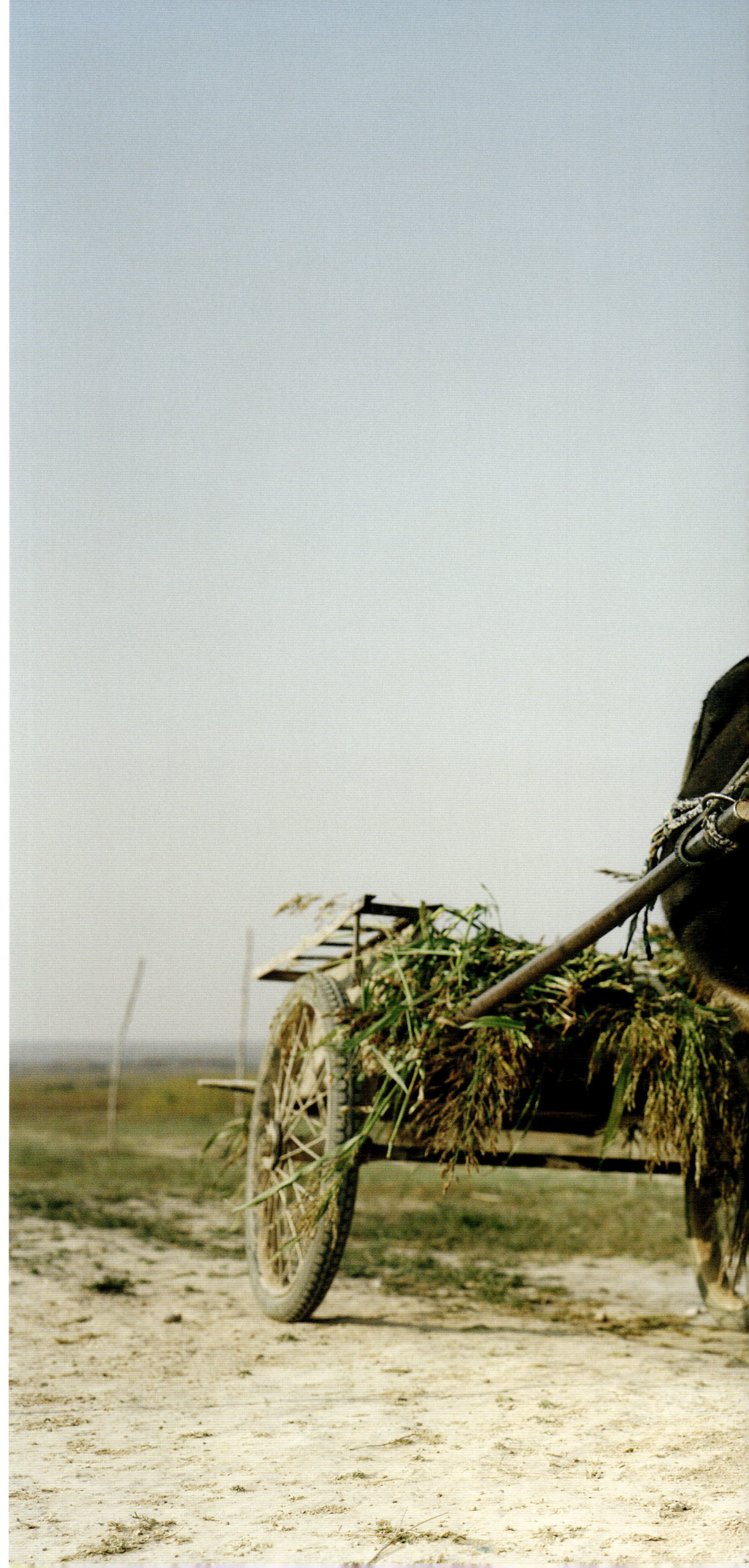

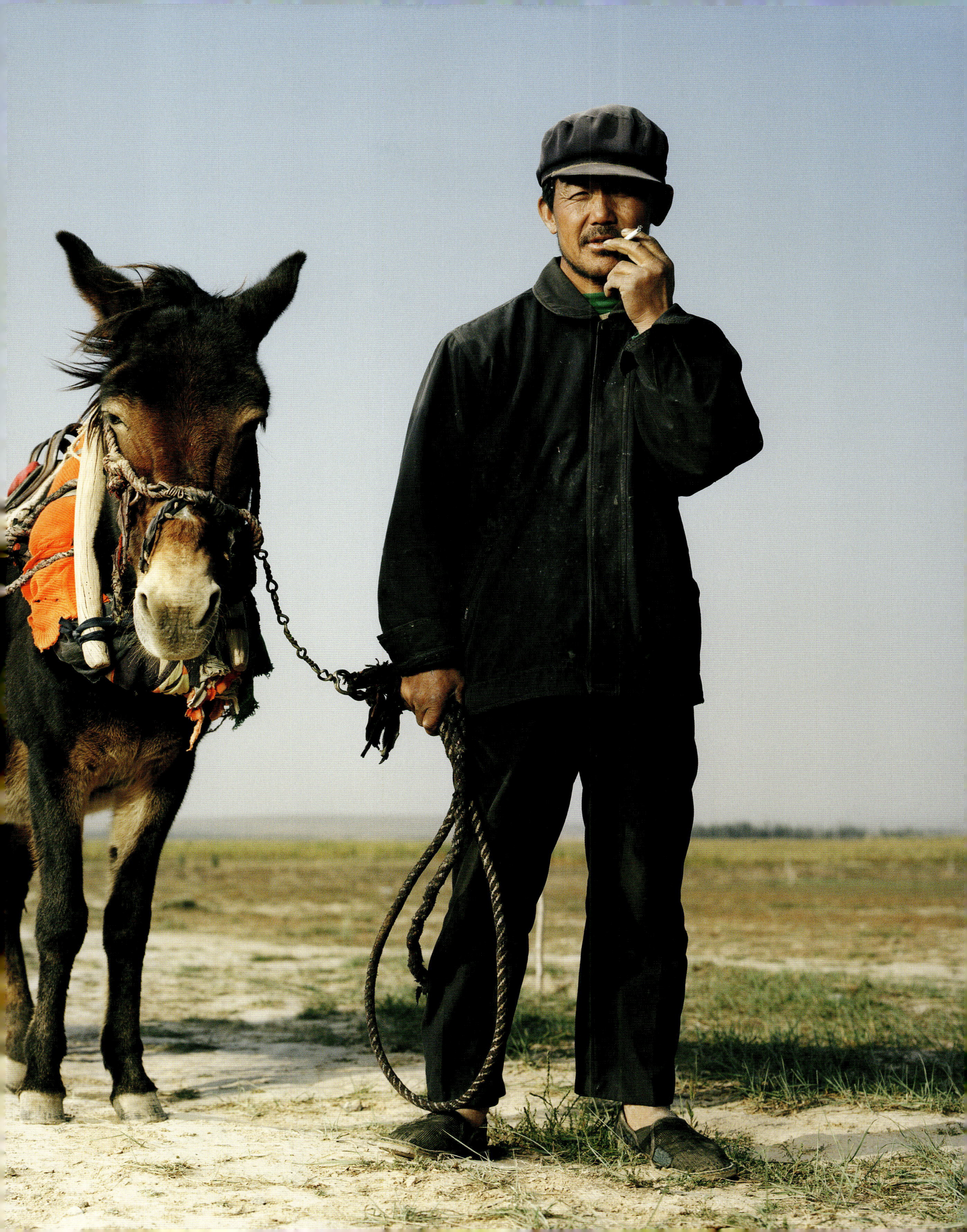

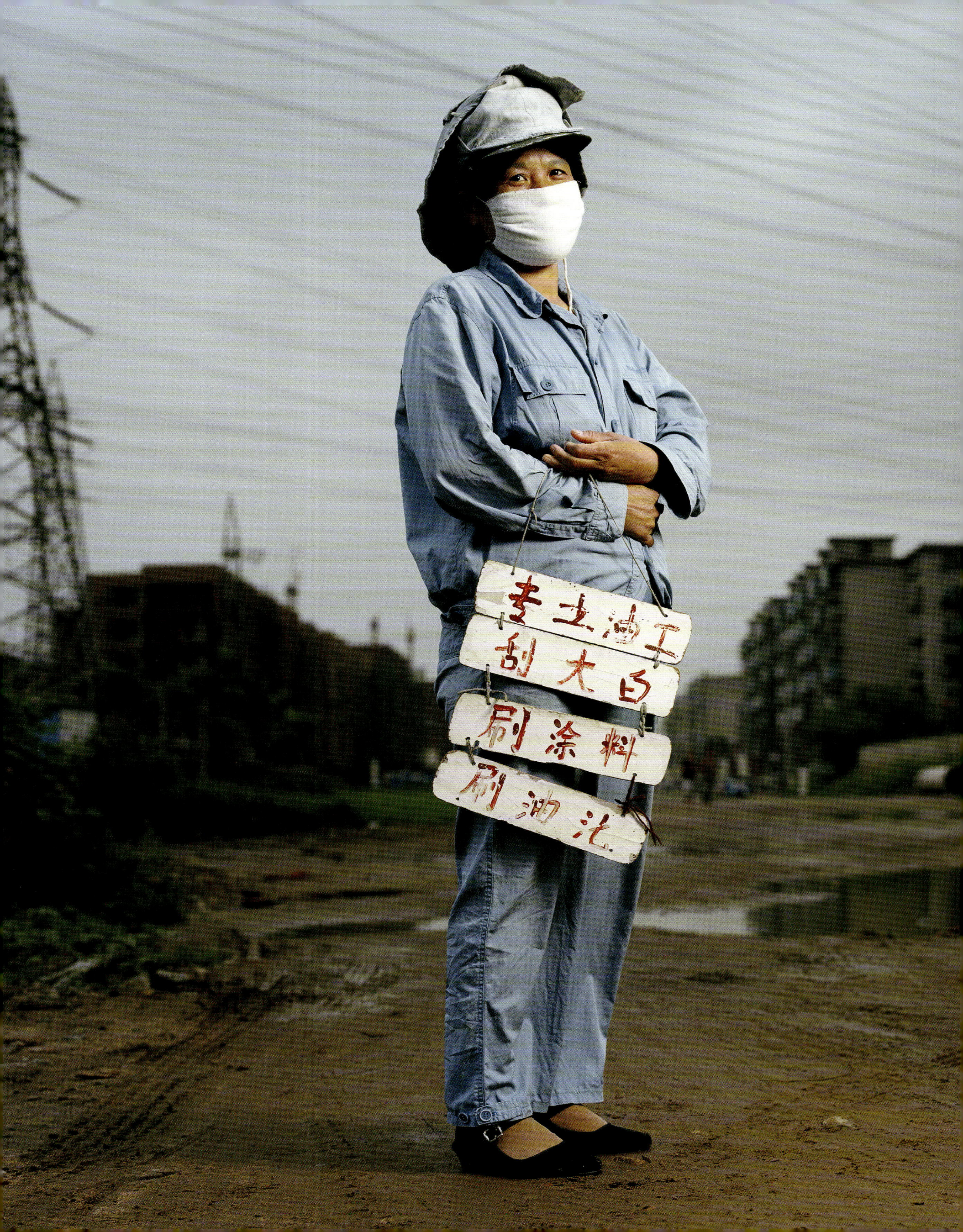
专业油工
刮大白
刷涂料
刷油漆

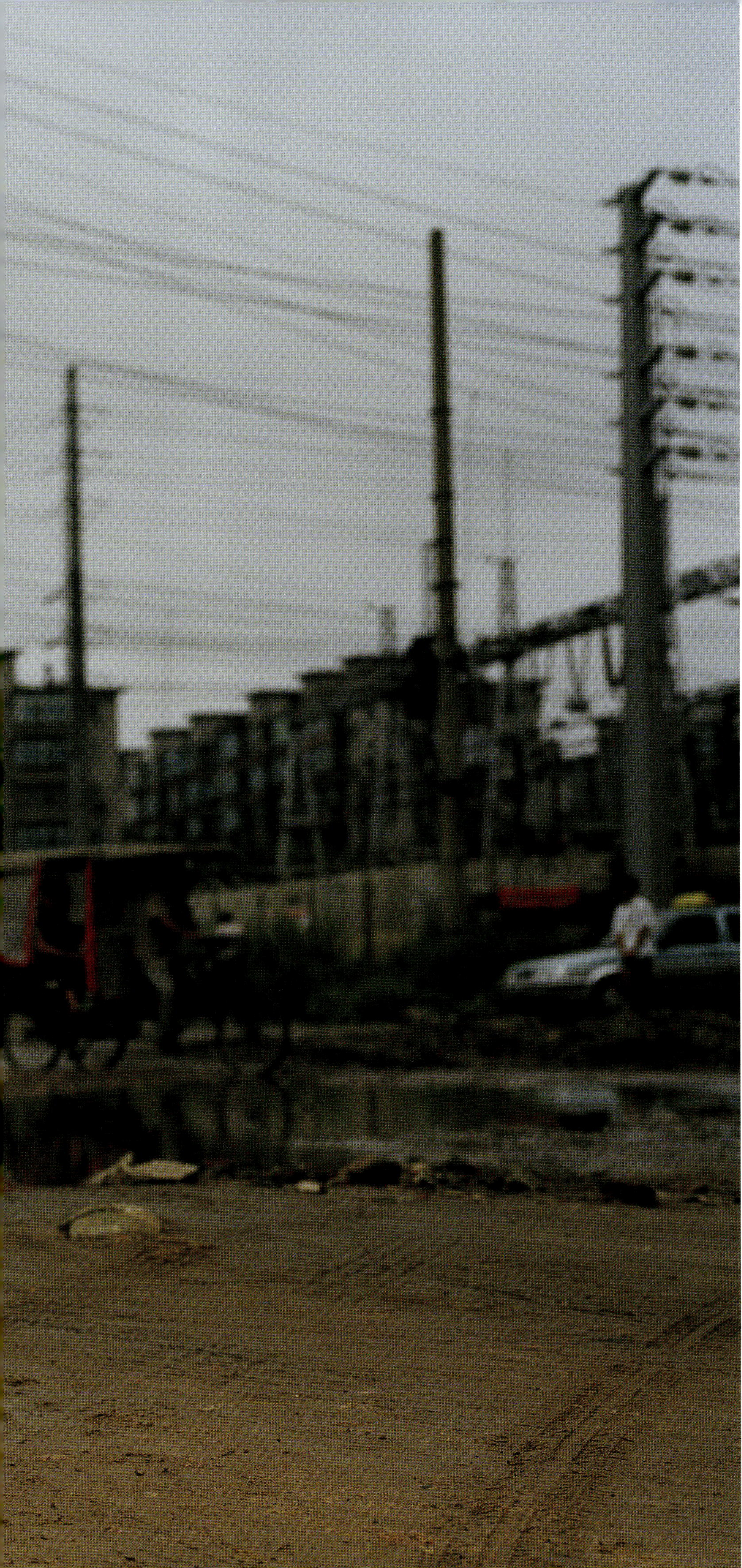

陈会清

Chen Huiqing (50)
Tagelöhnerin
Day laborer
Fushun, Liaoning

Als Tagelöhnerin steht Chen Huiqing jeden Tag an der Straße, in der Hoffnung auf einen Job. Das Schild, das sie in Händen hält, preist sie als Malerin an. Zwei- oder dreimal pro Woche nimmt jemand sie mit und gibt ihr für ein paar Stunden Arbeit.

As a day laborer, Chen Huiqing stands every day at the corner of a street and hopes to be picked up for a job. Her signs advertise her skills as a painter. She gets picked up two or three times a week and can work for a few hours.

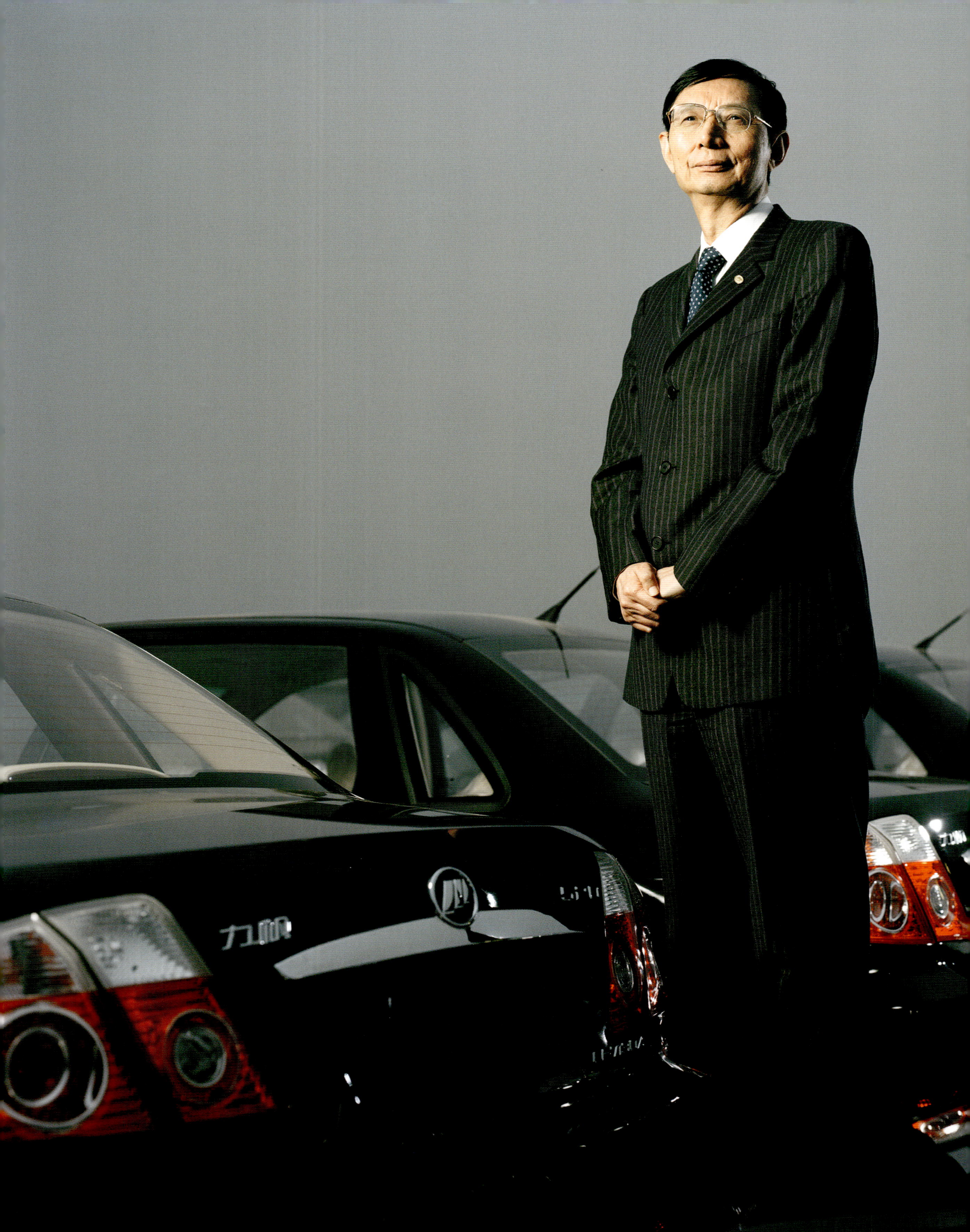
力帆

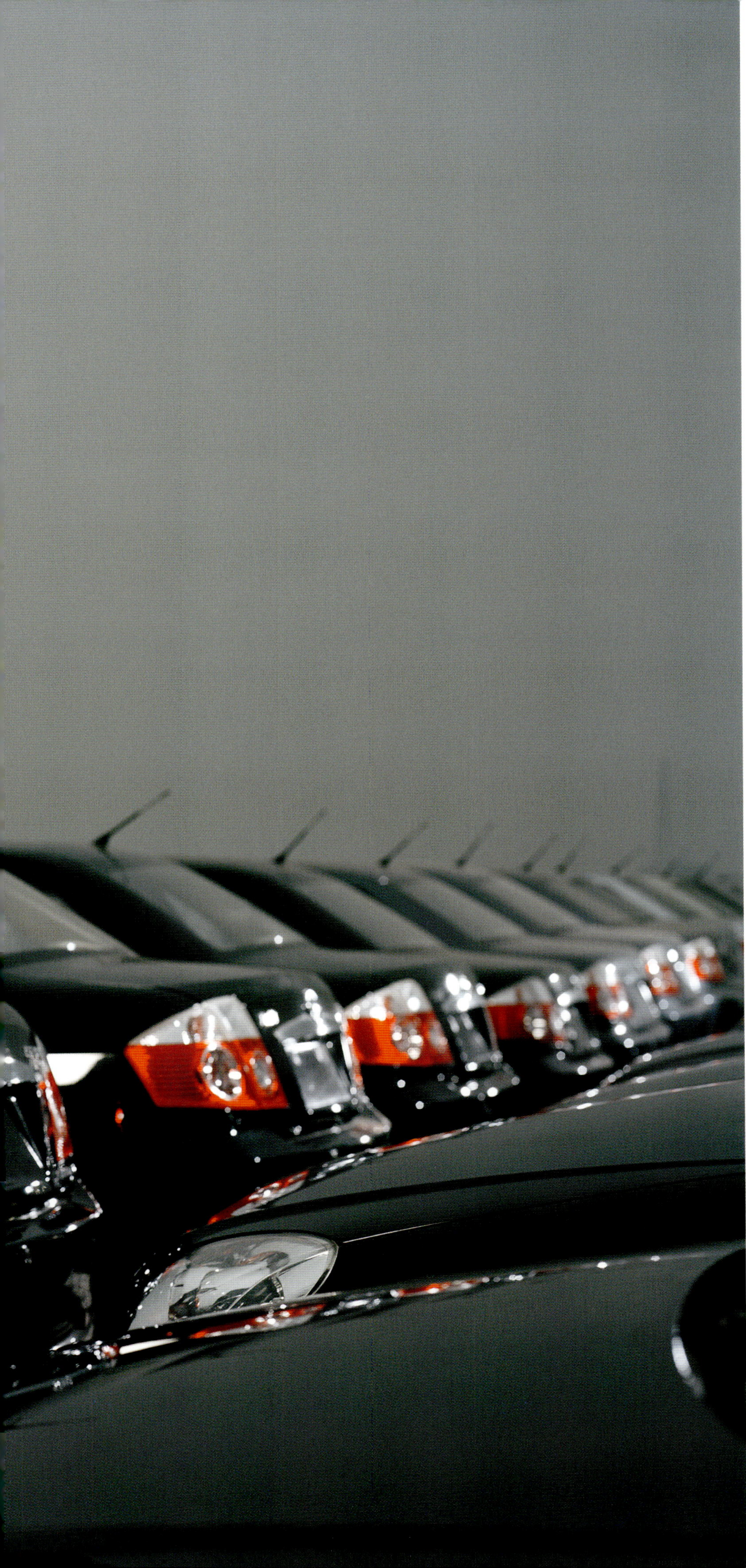

尹明善

Yin Mingshan (70)
Präsident und Gründer des Auto- und Motorrad-herstellers Lifan Holdings
President and founder of Lifan Holdings, Car and Bike Factory
Chongqing

Yin Mingshan ist Gründer und Inhaber der Lifan Gruppe, einem Auto- und Motorradhersteller in Chongqing. Seine erschwinglichen Fahrzeuge werden hauptsächlich für den chinesischen Markt produziert. Dank seines sehr erfolgreichen Unternehmens ist Yin Mingshan einer der reichsten Männer Chinas.

Yin Mingshan is the founder and owner of the Linfan Group, an automobile and motorcycle producer in Chongqing. Their affordable vehicles are produced mainly for the Chinese market. His company is highly successful and has made Yin Mingshan one of the richest men in China.

王维

Wang Wei (57)
Ehemaliger Parteisekretär
Former Party Secretary
Boshan, Shandong

Wang Wei war früher Parteisekretär einer Keramikfabrik mit ungefähr tausend Angestellten. Wie so viele andere ging auch seine Fabrik aufgrund der wirtschaftlichen Veränderungen der letzten Jahre bankrott. Der gesamte Maschinenpark verfiel, und sämtliche Mitarbeiter verloren ihre Arbeitsplätze.

Wang Wei used to be the party secretary of a ceramics factory with around 1,000 employees. As did so many others, his factory went bankrupt during the economic changes, all the machinery was destroyed and all workers lost their jobs.

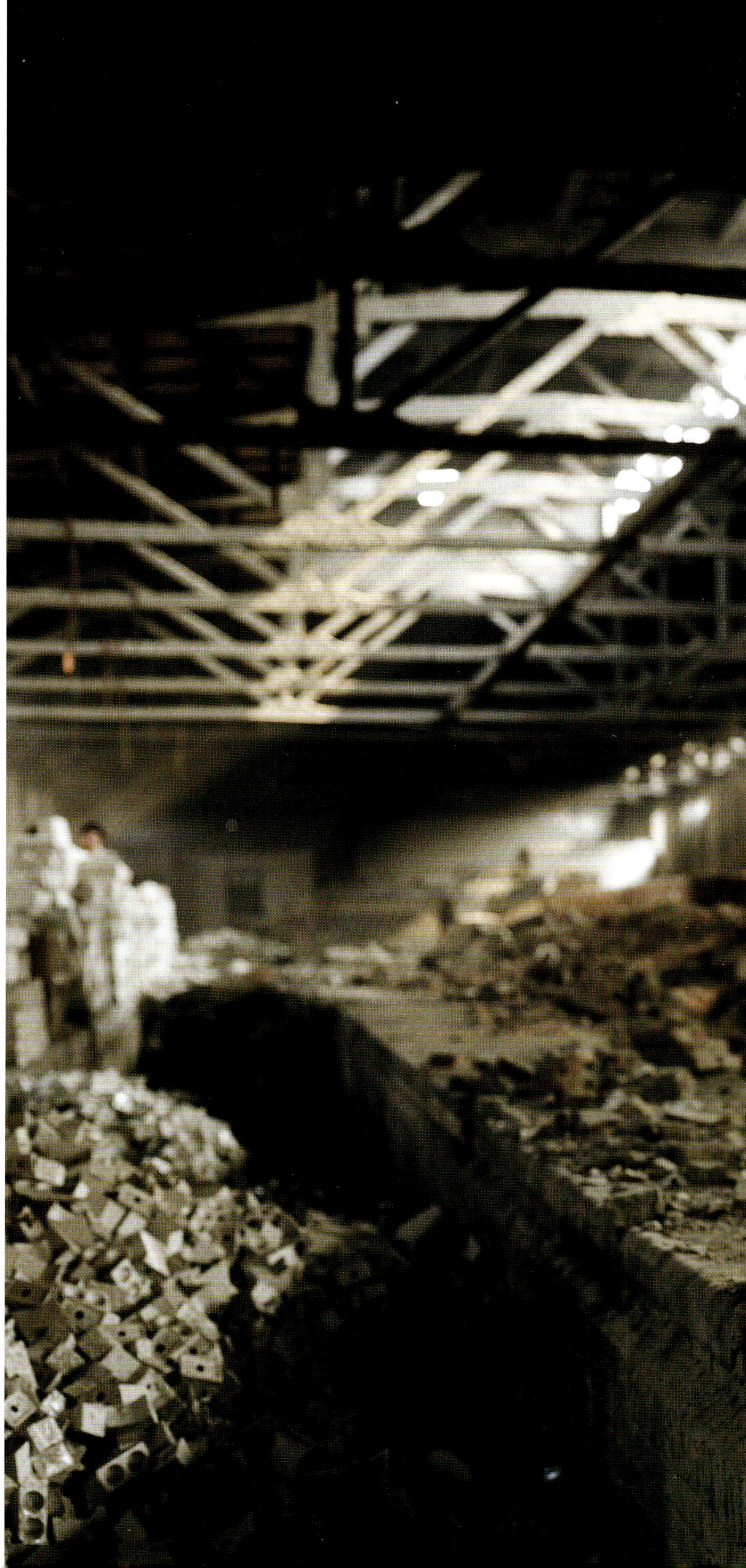

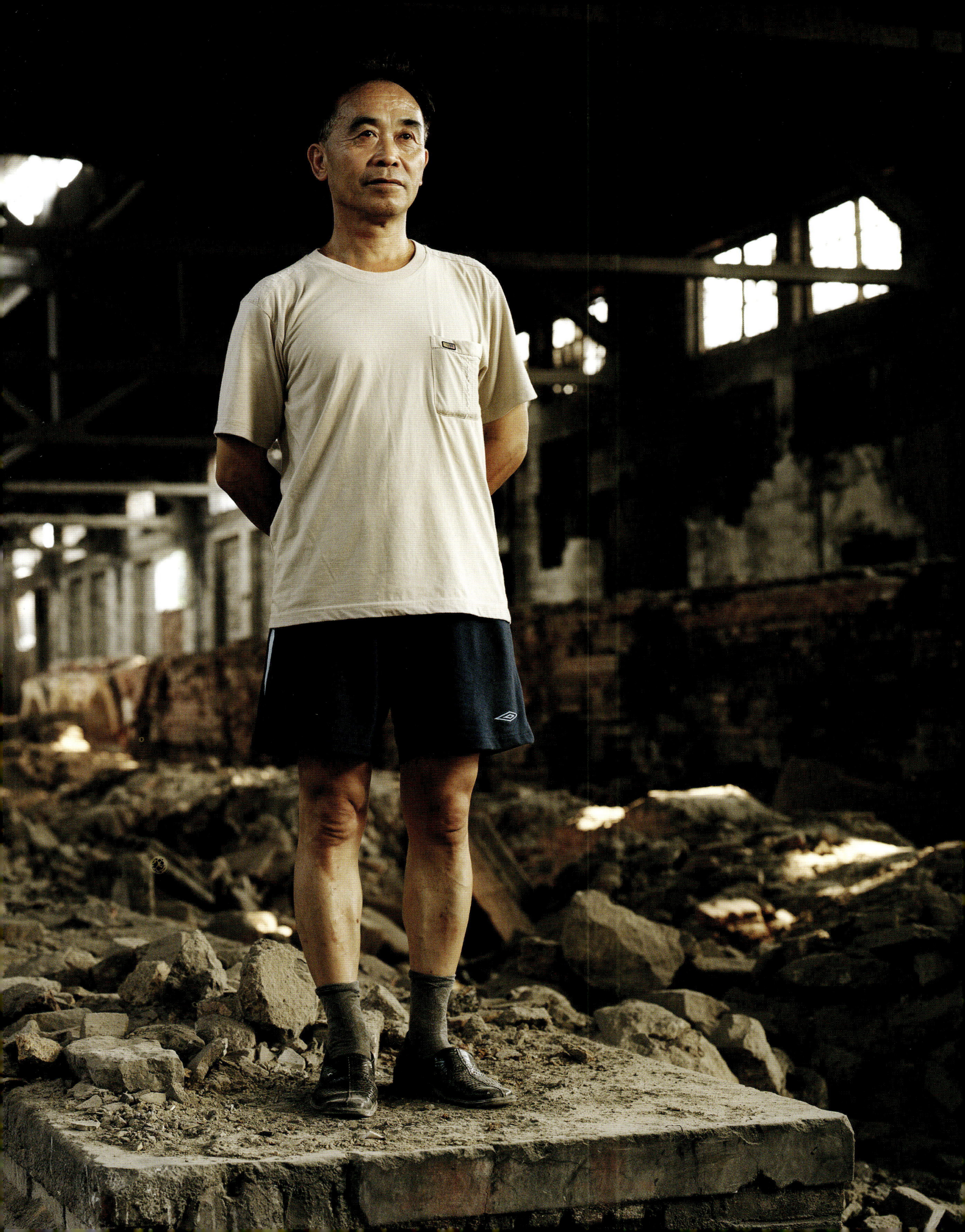

包克顺

Bao Keshun (53)
Bettler
Beggar
Shenzhen, Guangdong

Bao Keshun war früher Bauer in der Provinz Henan. Jetzt bettelt er sich seinen Lebensunterhalt in Shenzhen, der reichen Millionenstadt an der Grenze zu Hongkong, zusammen. Um mehr Aufmerksamkeit auf sich zu ziehen, stellt er einen einbeinigen Affen zur Schau.

Bao Keshun used to be a farmer in Henan Province. Now he makes a living as a beggar in Shenzhen, the rich multimillion person city on the Hong Kong border. In order to draw more attention, he parades a monkey that is missing one leg.

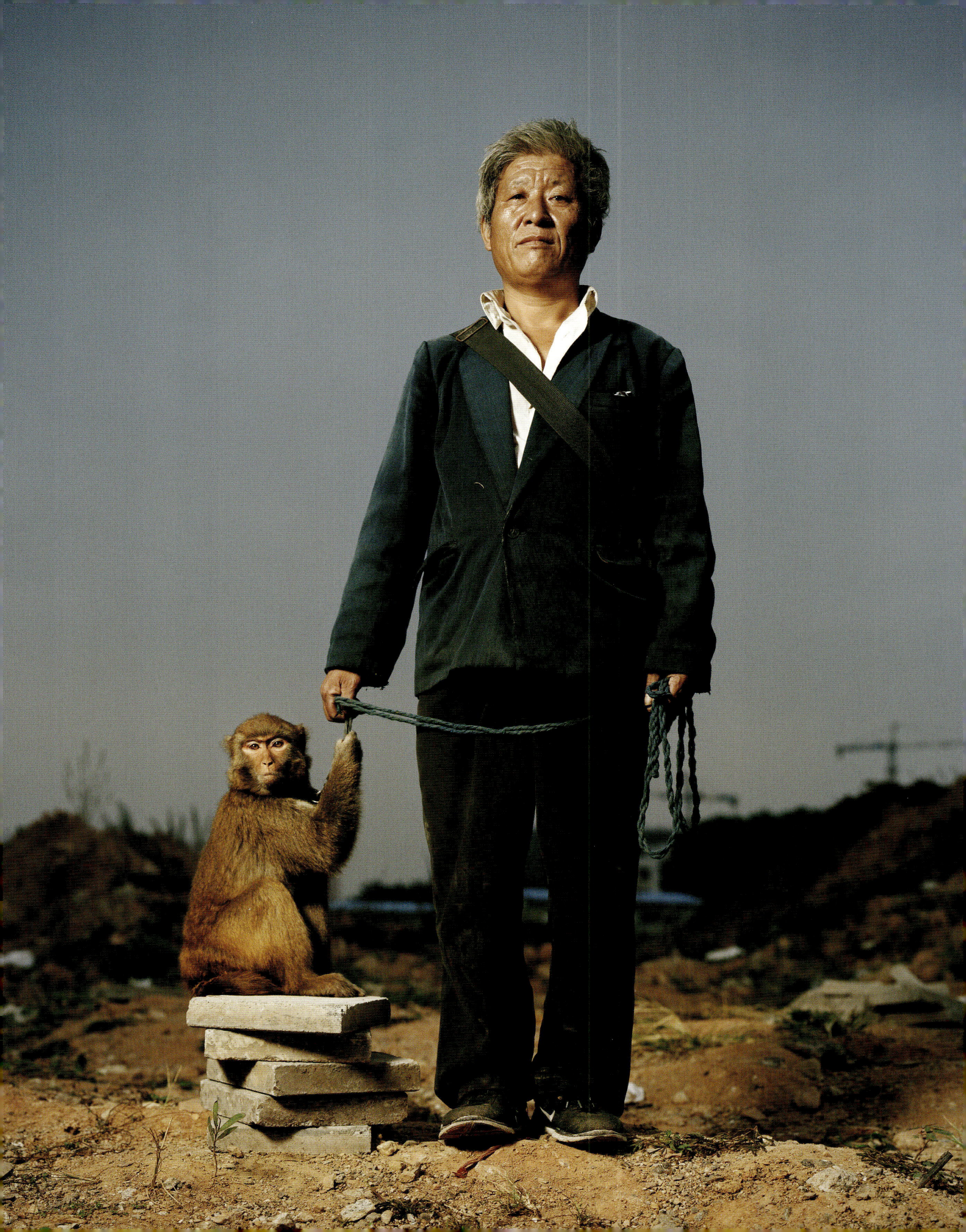

高涵

Gao Han (12)
Schüler einer Akrobatikschule
Student at an acrobat school
Wuqiao, Hebei

Alle Hoffnungen seiner Familie liegen auf Gao Han. Er trainiert jeden Tag von früh bis spät in einem Akrobatikinternat, zusammen mit fünf weiteren Hoffnungsträgern im Alter zwischen drei und zwölf Jahren. Wuqiao liegt ungefähr 200 Kilometer südlich von Peking und ist Chinas Zirkusstadt. Die meisten chinesischen Zirkuskünstler durchlaufen dort ihre harte Ausbildung.

All hopes of his family lay on Gao Han. Together with five other students aged 3 to 12, he trains for long hours every day at the acrobat school. Wuqiao, located about 200 km south of Beijing, is China's circus town, a small community in which most Chinese circus artists are trained.

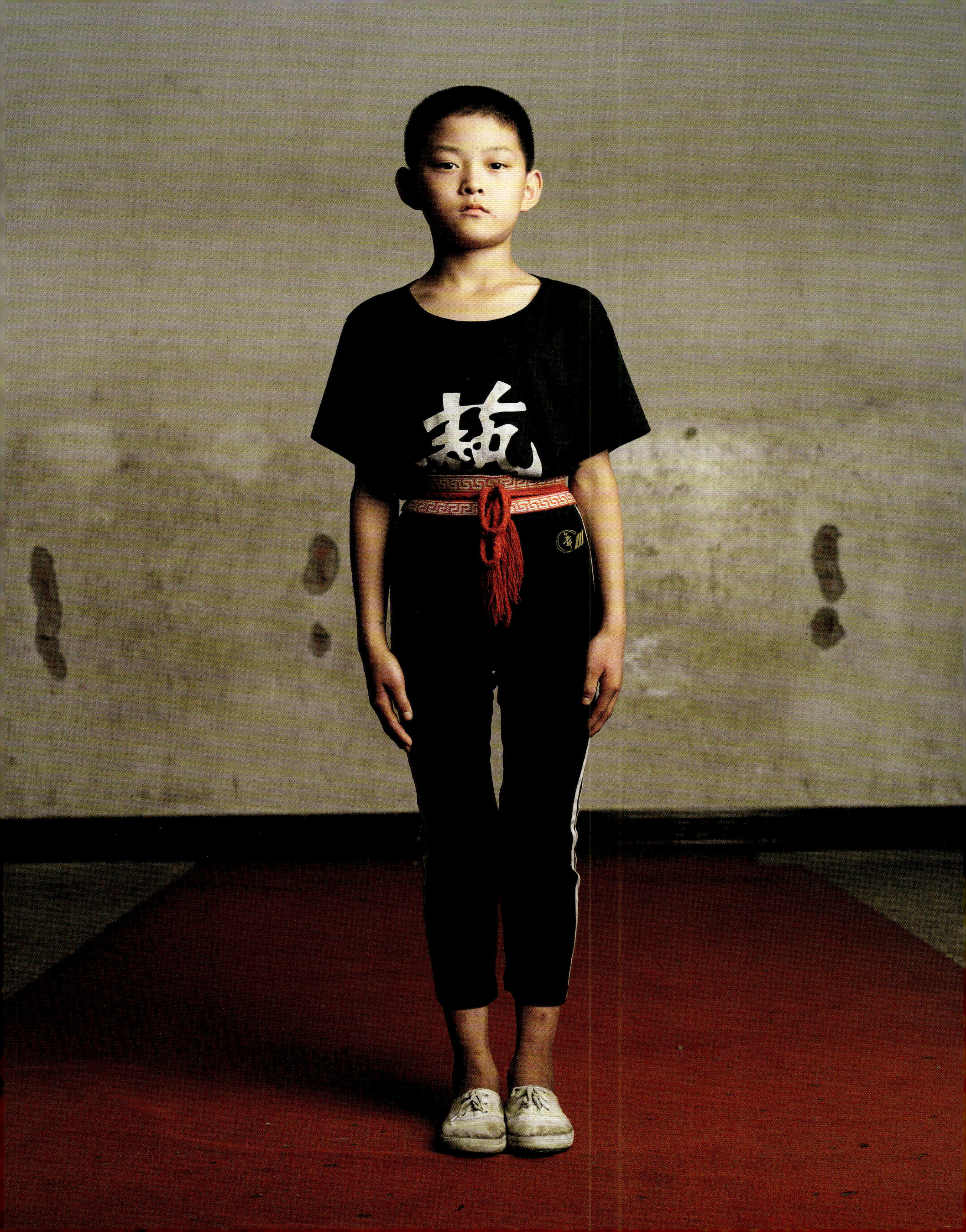

孙莉萍 黄坤华 黄景轩

Sun Liping (28), Huang Kunhua (27) und / and
Huang Jingxuan (4)
Ein-Kind-Familie
One-child family
Huaxi, Jiangsu

Sun Liping, Huang Kunhua und ihr Sohn Huang Jingxuan leben in Huaxi, dem reichsten Dorf Chinas. Huaxi befindet sich ca. 150 Kilometer nordöstlich von Shanghai und ist Chinas Modelldorf. Die Einwohner bekommen Auto und Haus gestellt und werden hauptsächlich mit Anteilen der Firmen entlohnt, für die sie arbeiten. Bei einem Wegzug aus dem Ort verlieren sie jedoch alle ihre Privilegien.

Sun Liping, Huang Kunhua and their son Huang Jingxuan live in Huaxi, China's richest village. Huaxi, located about 150 km northeast of Shanghai, is China's model town. The inhabitants receive a free car, a free house and are paid mainly in stocks of the companies they work for. Should they decide to leave town, they lose all their privileges.

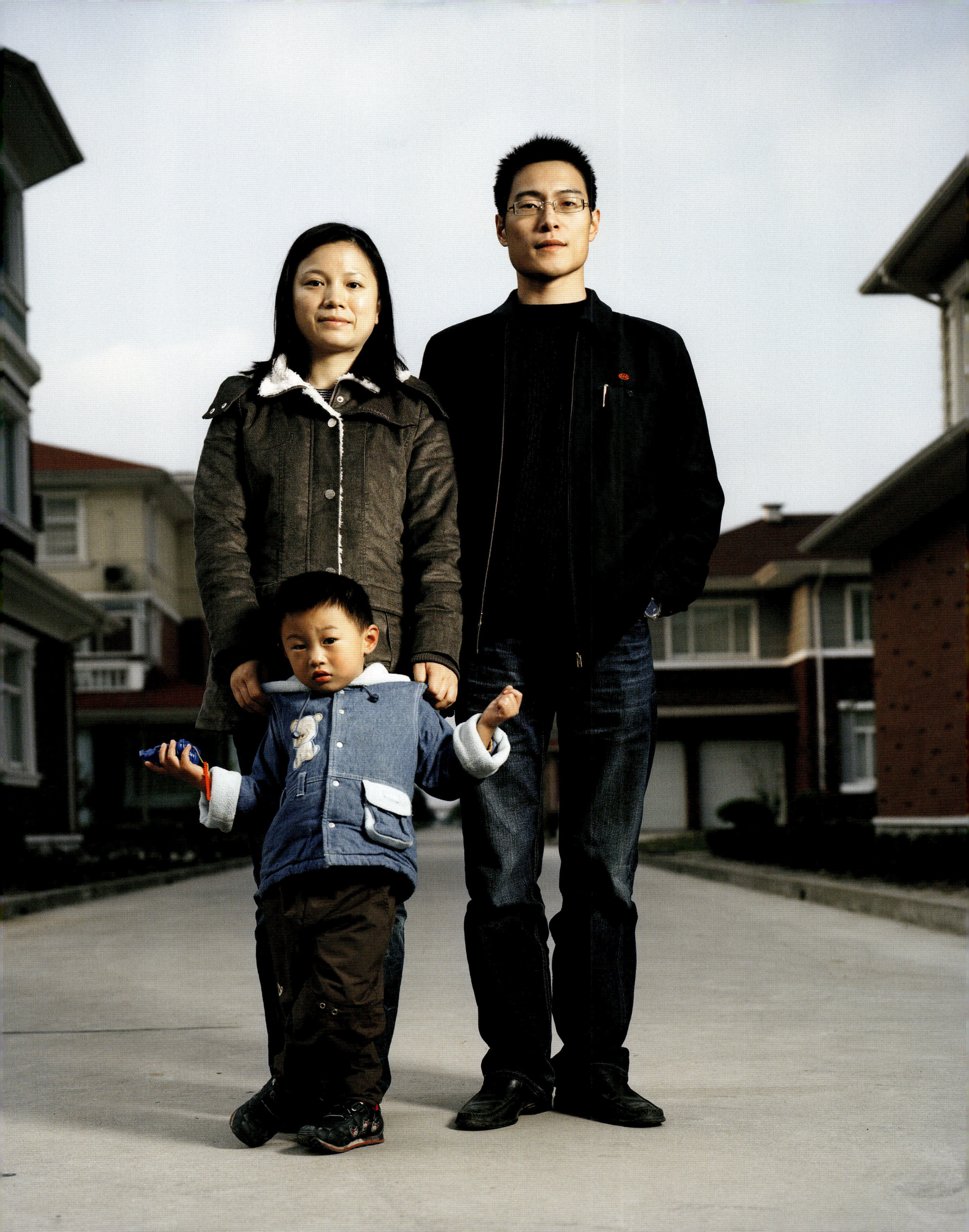

方展光

Jason Fong (34)
Leiter der Abteilung Vermögensmanagement, UBS
Director of Wealth Management, UBS Shanghai
Shanghai

Jason Fong ist Leiter des Bereichs Vermögensmanagement in der UBS-Niederlassung Shanghai. China ist ein interessanter neuer Markt für internationale Banken, da die Anzahl reicher Chinesen schnell wächst.

Jason Fong is Director of the Wealth Management Department of the UBS Shanghai office. China is an interesting new market for international banks, since the number of rich Chinese is growing rapidly.

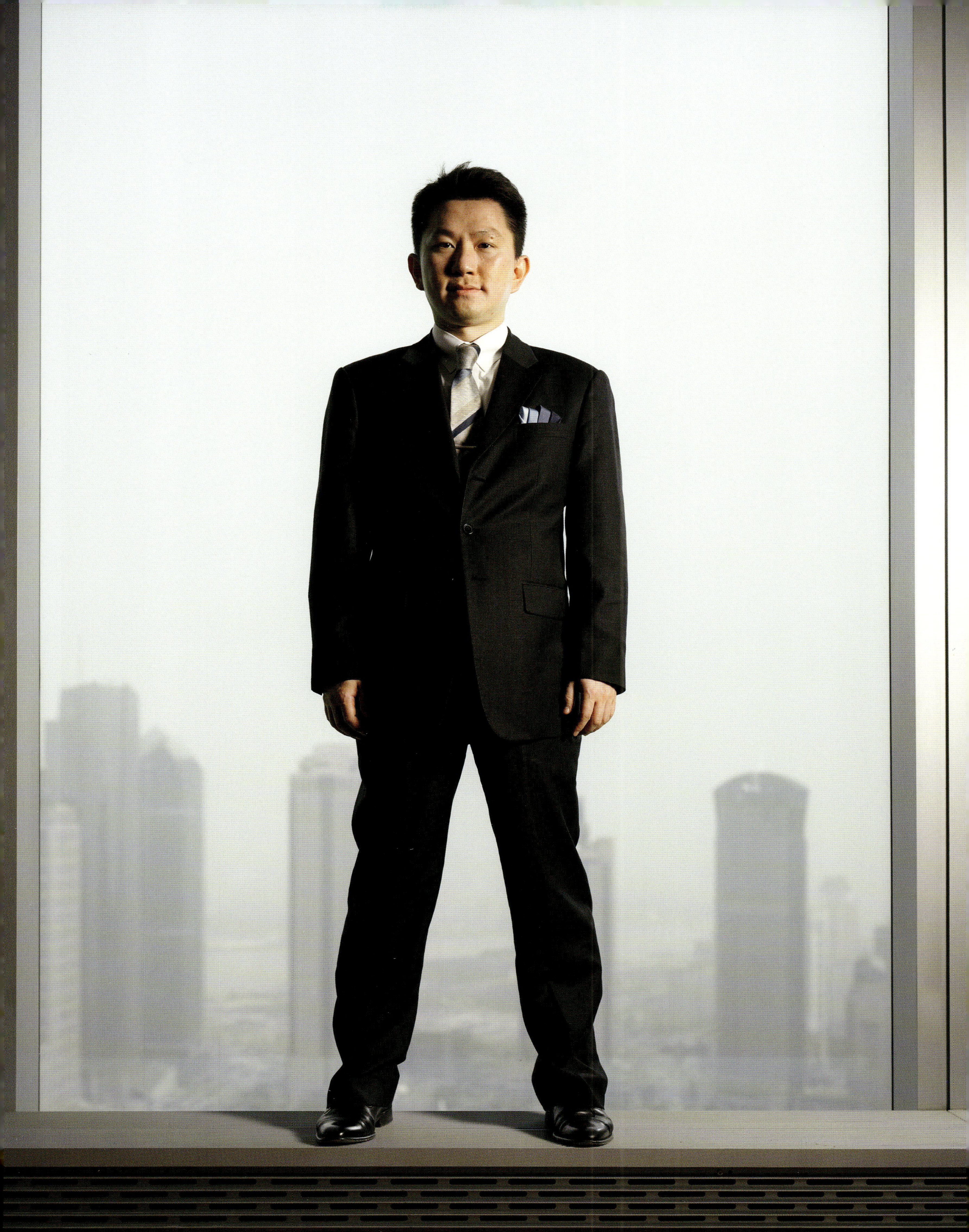

罗重阳

Luo Chongyang (10)
Baumwollpflückerin
Cotton picker
Hami, Xinjiang

Jedes Jahr während der Erntezeit werden Schulkinder auf die Felder der Provinz Xinjiang geschickt, um bei der Baumwollernte zu helfen. Luo Chongyang träumt davon, eines Tages Lehrerin zu werden.

Each year during harvest time, school children are sent to the fields of Xinjiang to help harvest the cotton. Chongyang's dream is to become a teacher one day.

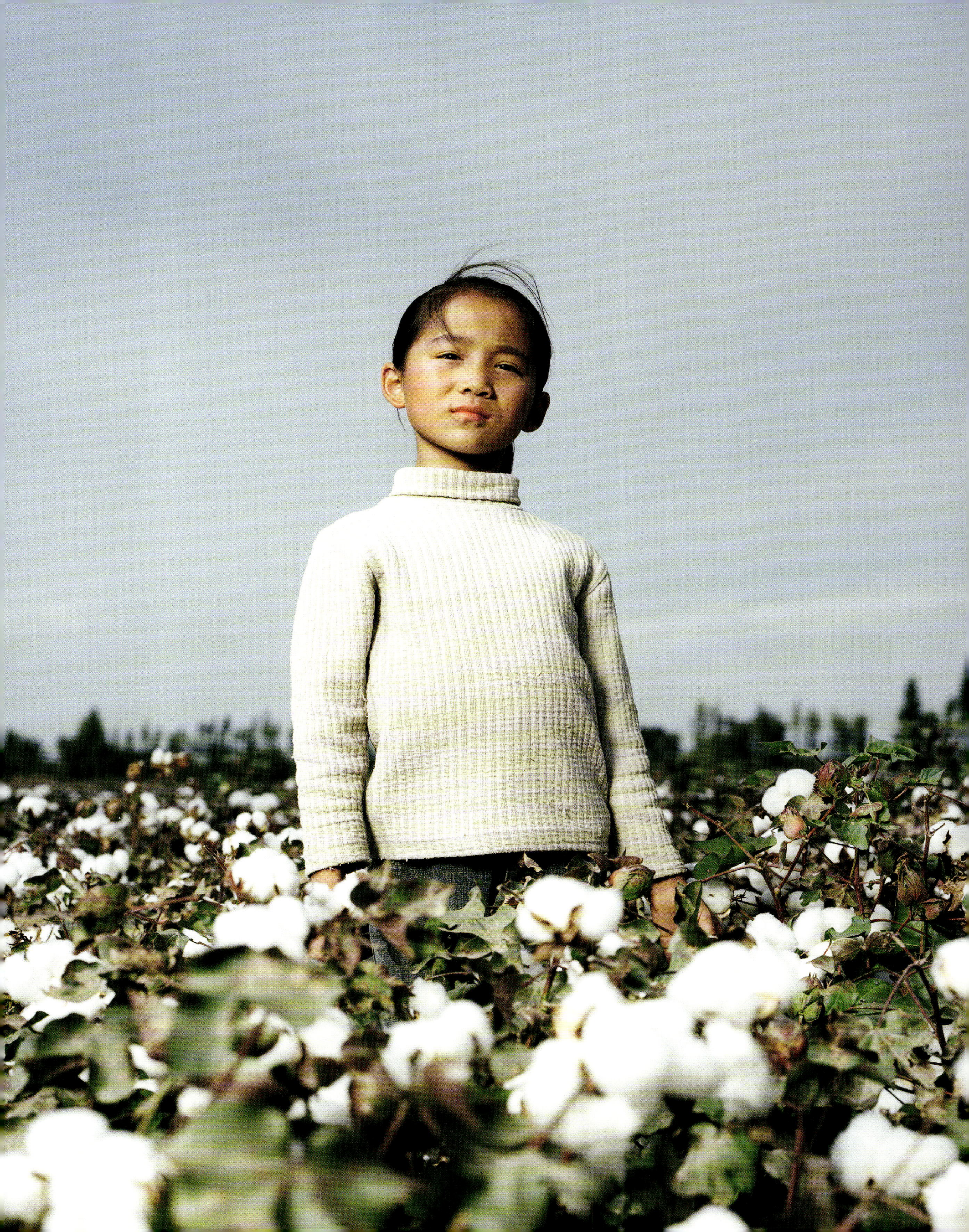

张志强

Zhang Zhiqiang (41)
Architekt für klassische chinesische Architektur
Chinese classical architect
Changzhi, Shanxi

Zhang Zhiqiang hat sich als Architekt für klassische chinesische Architektur darauf spezialisiert, antike Tempel und Denkmäler wieder zu errichten. Er hat sein Handwerk von einem Altmeister der chinesischen Architektur erlernt.

As a classical Chinese architect, Zhang Zhiqiang is specialized in reconstructing antique temples and monuments. He learned the craft from his old master.

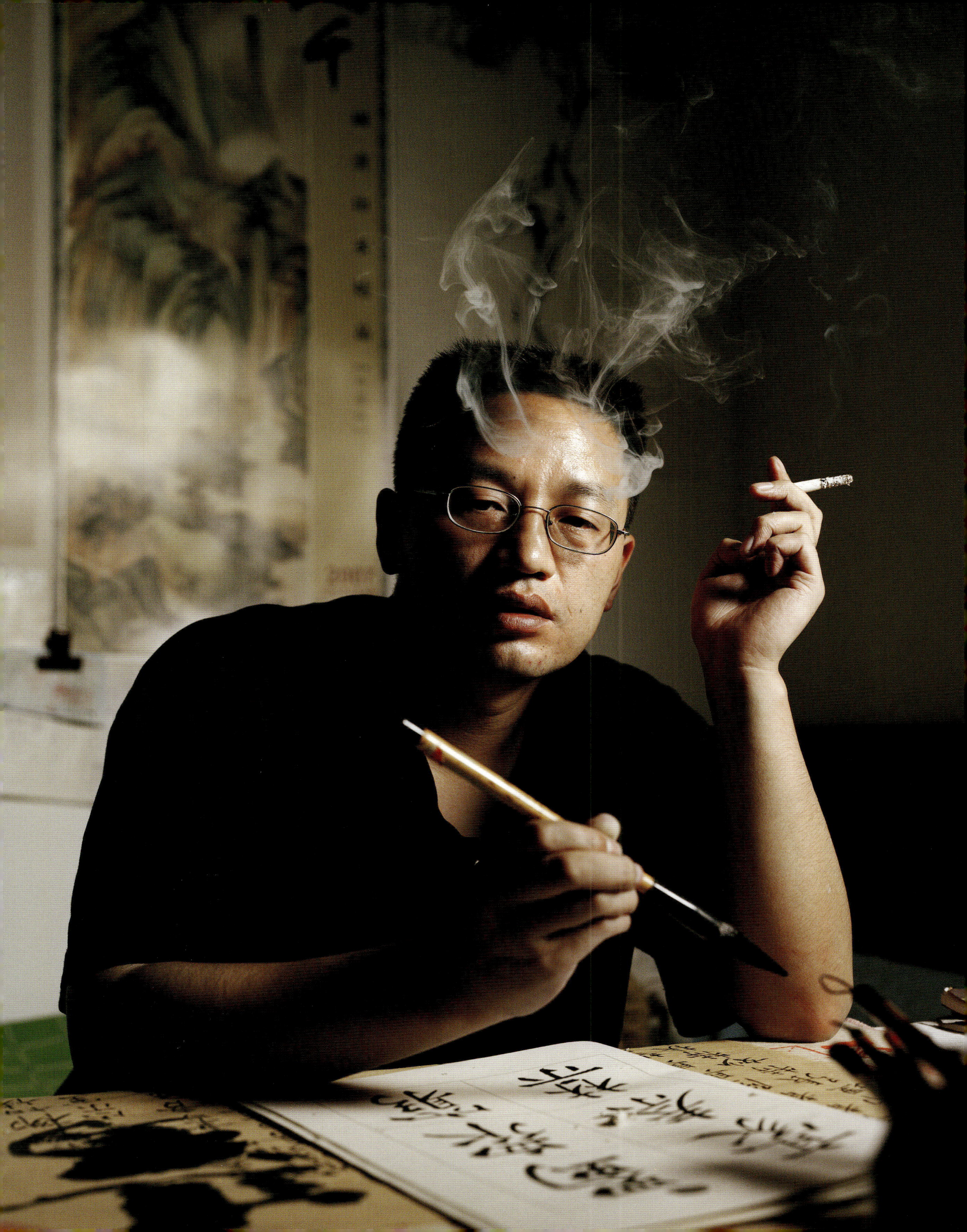

白兆芳 白清元

Bai Zhaofang (64) und / and Bai Qingyuan (39)
Besitzer eines Ersatzteilladens
Spare parts shop owners
Jinzhou, Liaoning

Bai Zhaofang und sein Sohn Bai Qingyuan haben einen kleinen Laden für Ersatzteile. Die ganze Familie arbeitete früher in einer großen Fabrik, die stillgelegt wurde. Die wirtschaftlichen Umstürze der letzten 20 Jahre haben Chinas Nordosten besonders hart getroffen, da in dieser Region viele der großen, staatlich geführten Fabriken standen. Als die Regierung ihre Politik zugunsten privatwirtschaftlicher Unternehmen änderte, mussten viele dieser Betriebe ihre Tore schließen.

Bai Zhaofang and his son Bai Qingyuan run a small shop for mechanical parts. The whole family used to work in a large factory, which was shut down. China's Northeast, where many big, state-run factories were located, was hard hit by the economic changes of the last 20 years. When the government changed policies away from a purely state-run economy, many of them had to close their gates.

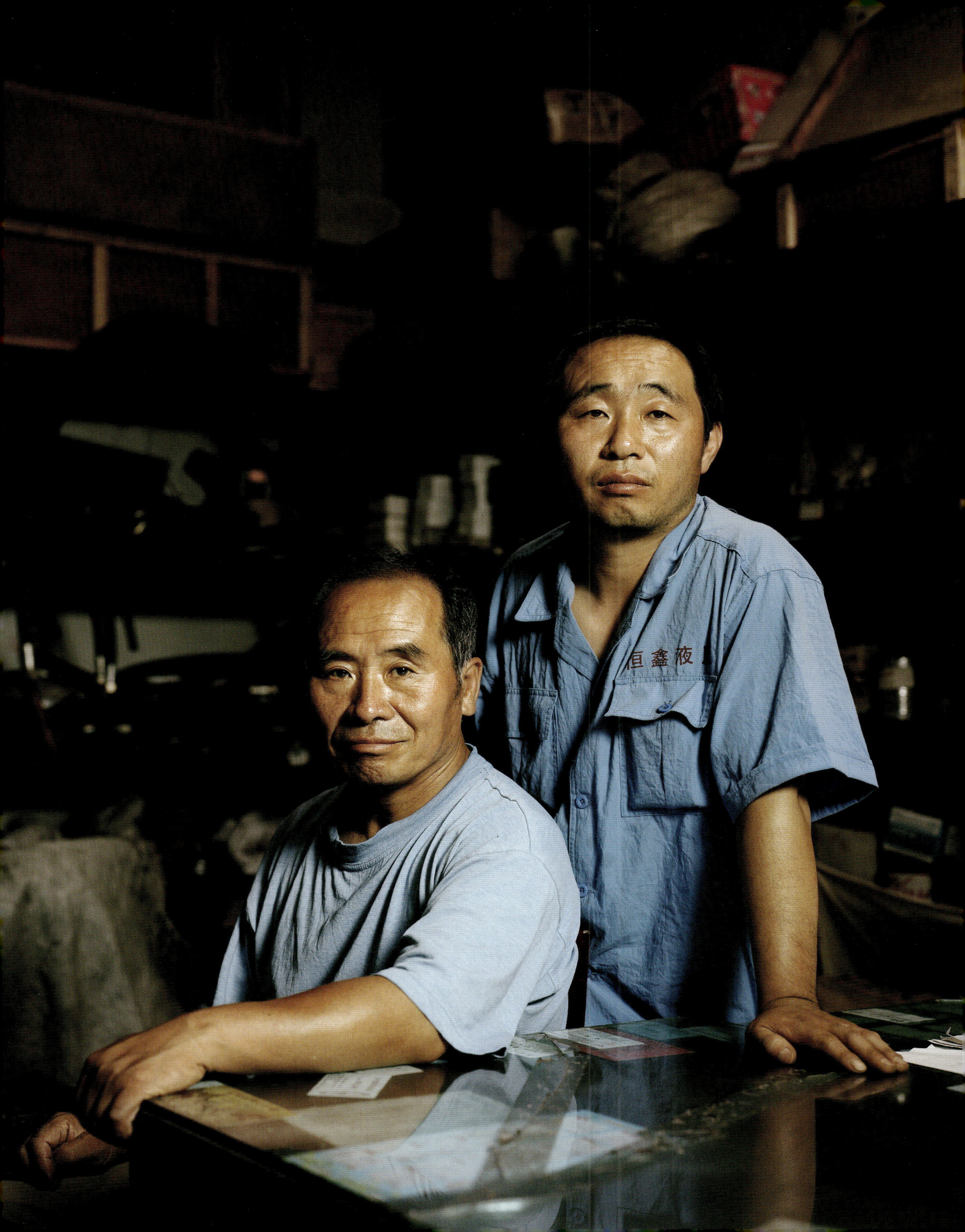
恒鑫液

陈丽琴

Chen Liqin (22)
Arbeiterin auf einer Chilifarm
Worker at a chili drying farm
Bulongji, Gansu

Die Familie von Chen Liqin besitzt eine Chilifarm inmitten der Wüste in der Provinz Gansu. Die getrockneten Chilis sind hauptsächlich für die Kosmetikindustrie bestimmt. Die leuchtend roten Pigmente finden sich in Puderdosen und Lippenstiften auf der ganzen Welt wieder. Zwei furchtlose und gefährliche Hunde schützen die kostbaren Chilis bei Dunkelheit vor möglichen Dieben.

Chen Liqin's family owns a chili farm in a desert area of Gansu Province. The dried chilies are mainly used for cosmetics. The bright red pigments are found in powders and lipsticks around the world. At night, two fearless and dangerous dogs guard the precious chilies against potential thieves.

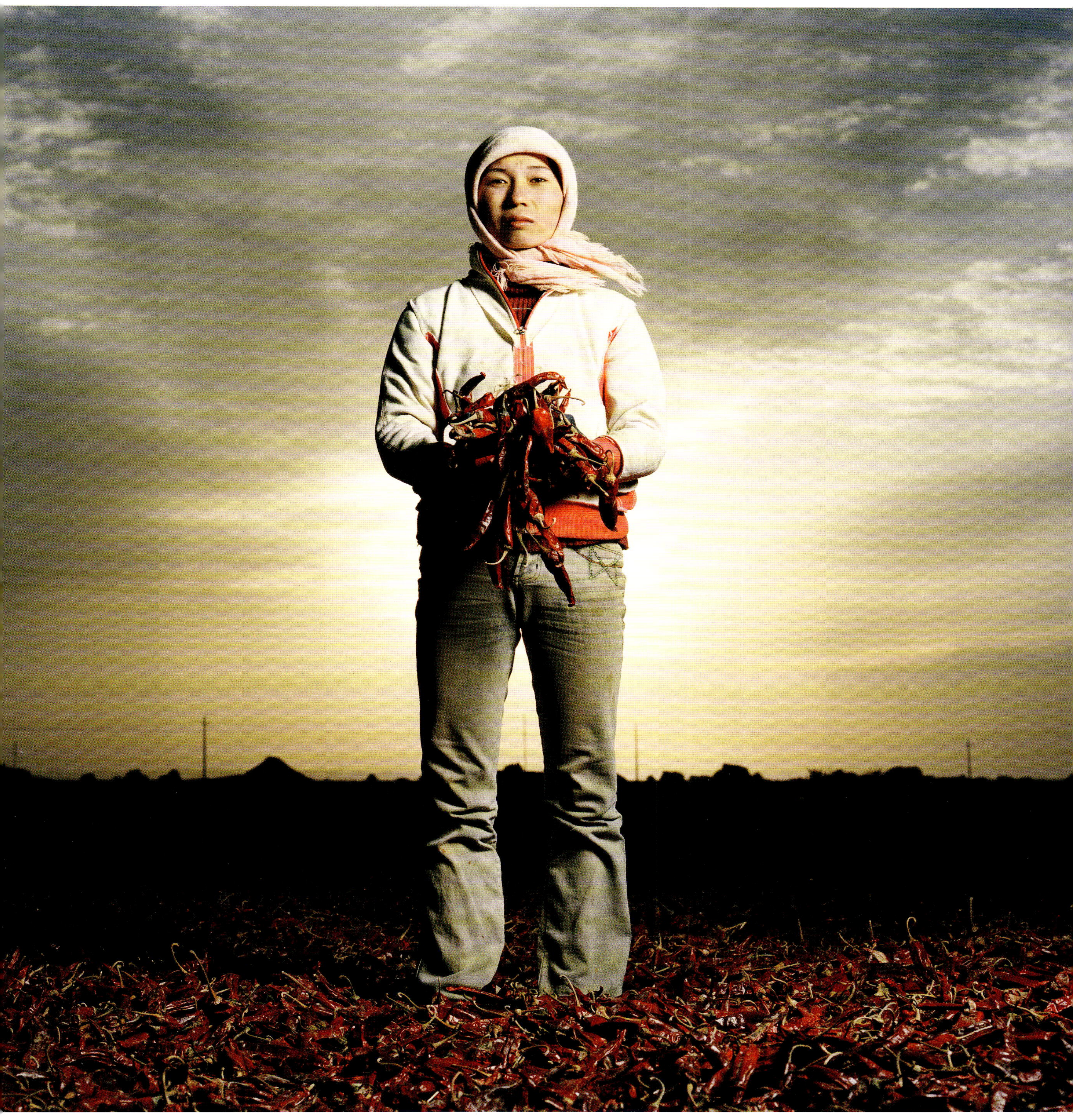

马春

Ma Chun (27)
Mitarbeiter des Bahnsicherheitsdienstes
Railway security patrol
Dubancheng, Xinjiang

Als Sicherheitsbeamter der Bahn prüft Ma Chun die endlosen Schienenkilometer in der Provinz Xinjiang. Der offiziellen Begründung nach tut er dies, um zu verhindern, dass sich Schafe auf die Schienen verirren und so Züge gefährden.

Ma Chun walks the endless tracks in Xinjiang Province as a railway security guard; officially to prevent sheep from crossing the tracks and endangering trains.

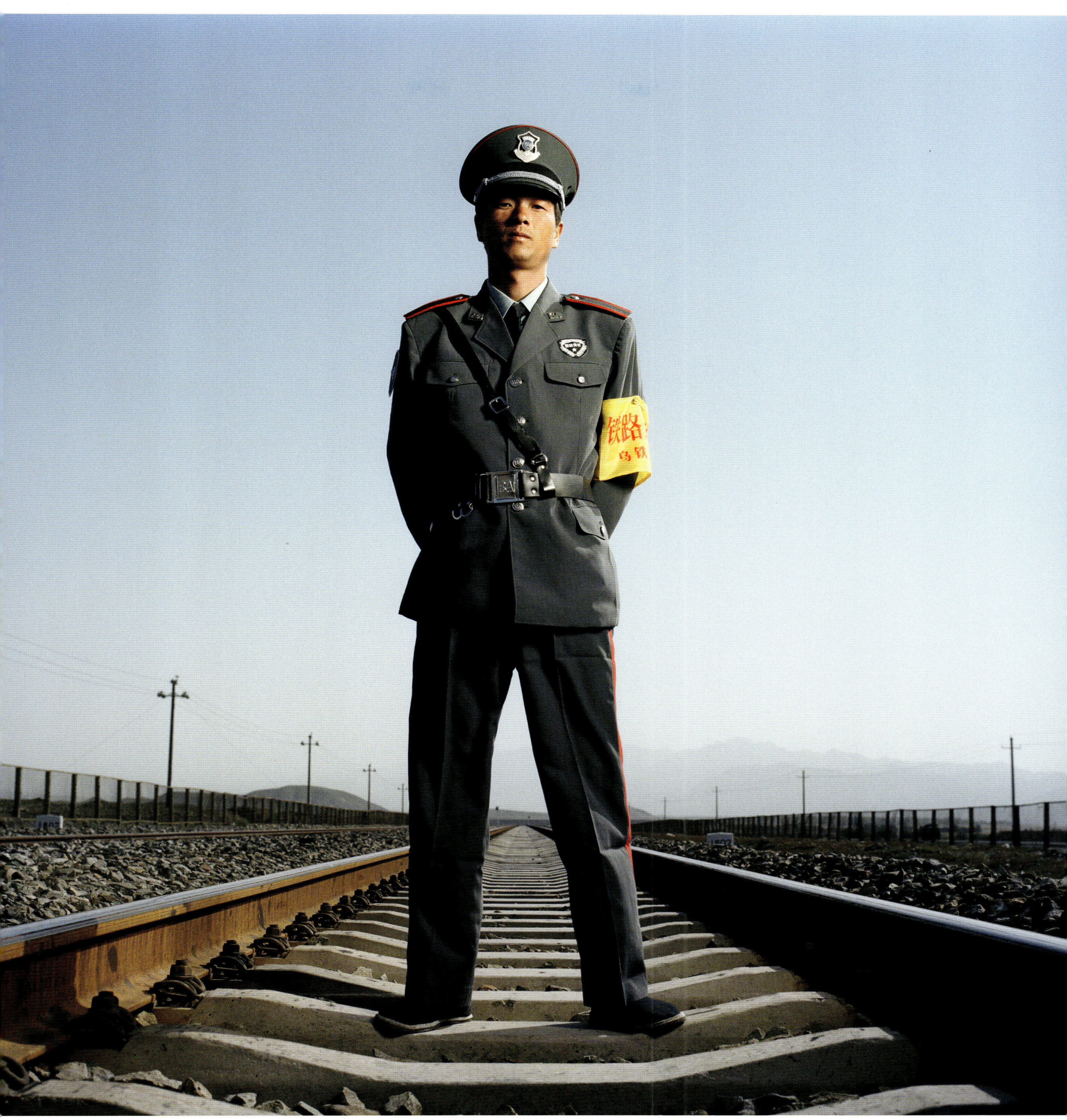
铁路
乌铁

代怀全

Dai Huaiquan (62)
Friseur
Barber
Mengdingshan, Sichuan

Dai Huaiquans Friseurladen befindet sich in einer Garage und ist Treffpunkt für das ganze Dorf. Ein Haarschnitt kostet dort 2 Yuan, was ungefähr 20 Cent entspricht.

Dai Huaiquan's barber shop is set up in a garage. It is the meeting point for the entire village, where a haircut costs 2 Yuan, which is about 20 cents.

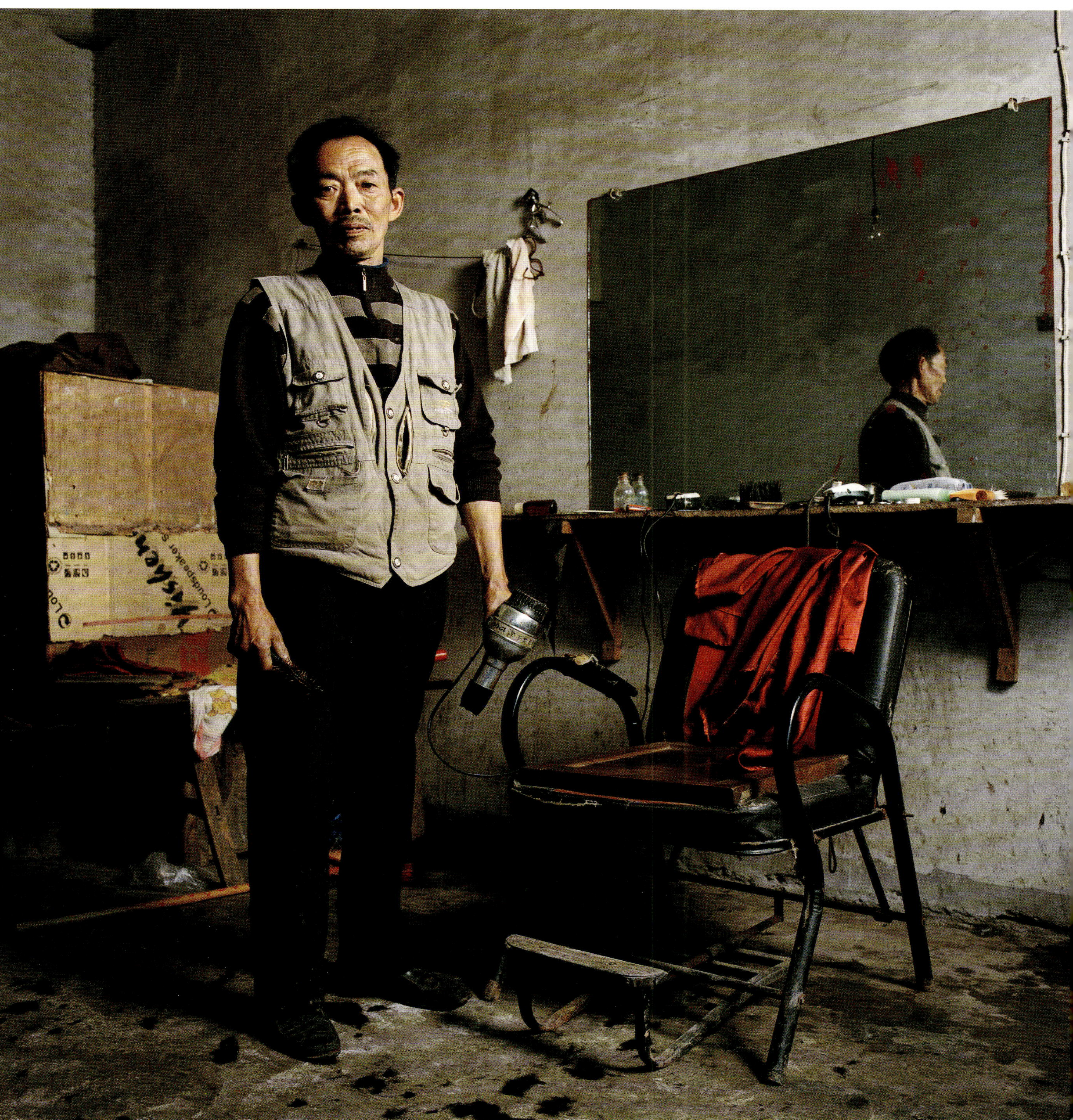
Loudspeaker

李慧

Li Hui (37)
Qualitätskontrolleurin für Baumwolle
Cotton quality control worker
Yuli, Xinjiang

In einem großen Baumwollbetrieb in der Provinz Xinjiang durchwühlt Li Hui Berge schneeweißer Baumwolle und sortiert alles aus, was der Qualität abträglich sein könnte. Die Baumwollindustrie ist eine der wichtigsten Industrien in Xinjiang.

In a big cotton mill in Xinjiang Province, Li Hui rakes through mountains of snow-white cotton and picks out any object that could diminish its quality. Cotton is one of the most important industries in Xinjiang.

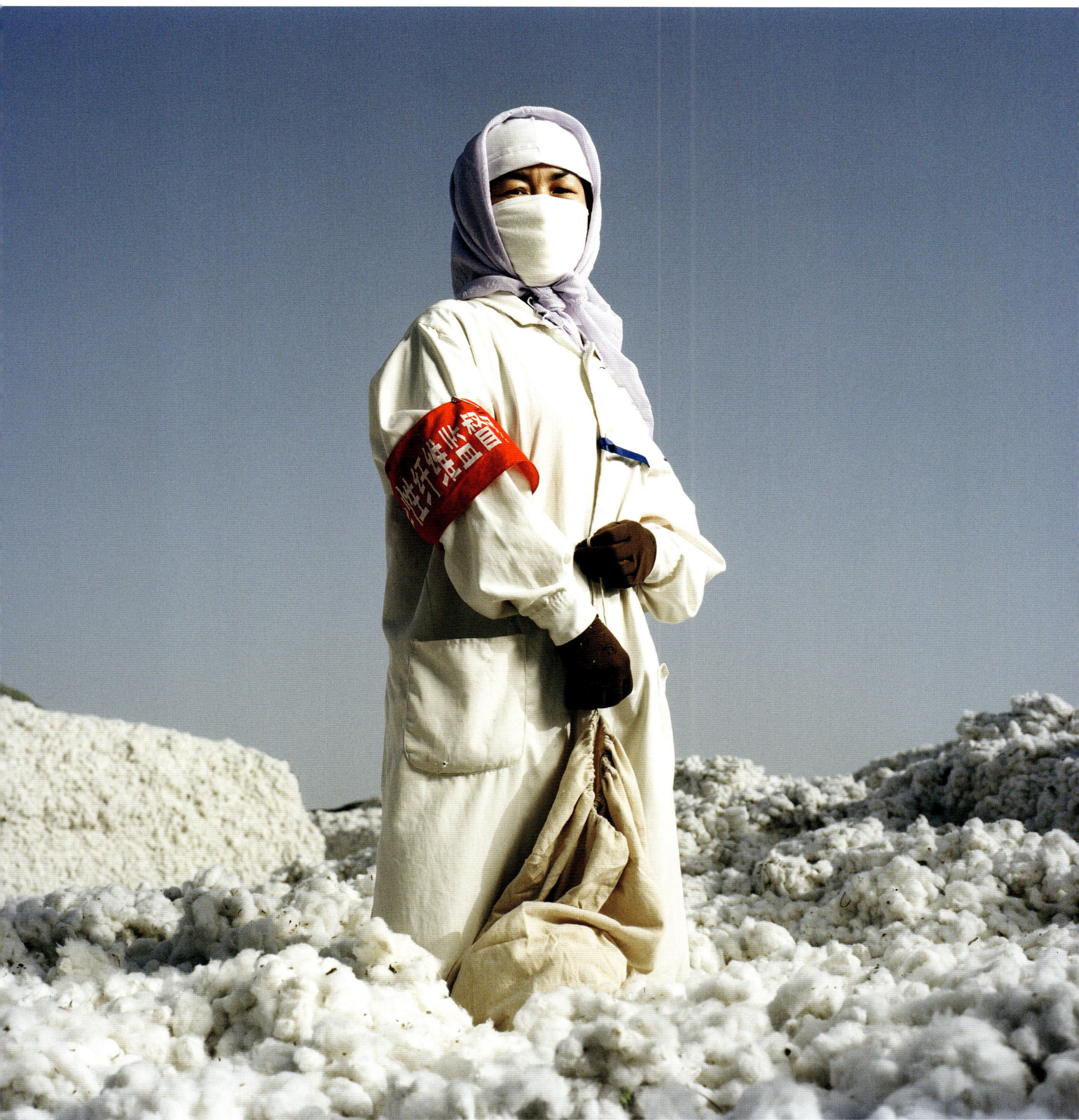

郭素池

Guo Shuchi (40)
Fischerin
Fisherwoman
Wudixian, Shandong

Guo Shuchi führt ein karges Leben als Frau eines Fischers in der Deltaregion des Gelben Flusses. Das Paar nutzt den niedrigen Gezeitenstand, um das gemeinsame Boot zu reparieren.

Guo Shuchi leads a tough life as the wife of a fisherman in the Yellow River Delta region. The couple takes advantage of the low tide to repair their boat.

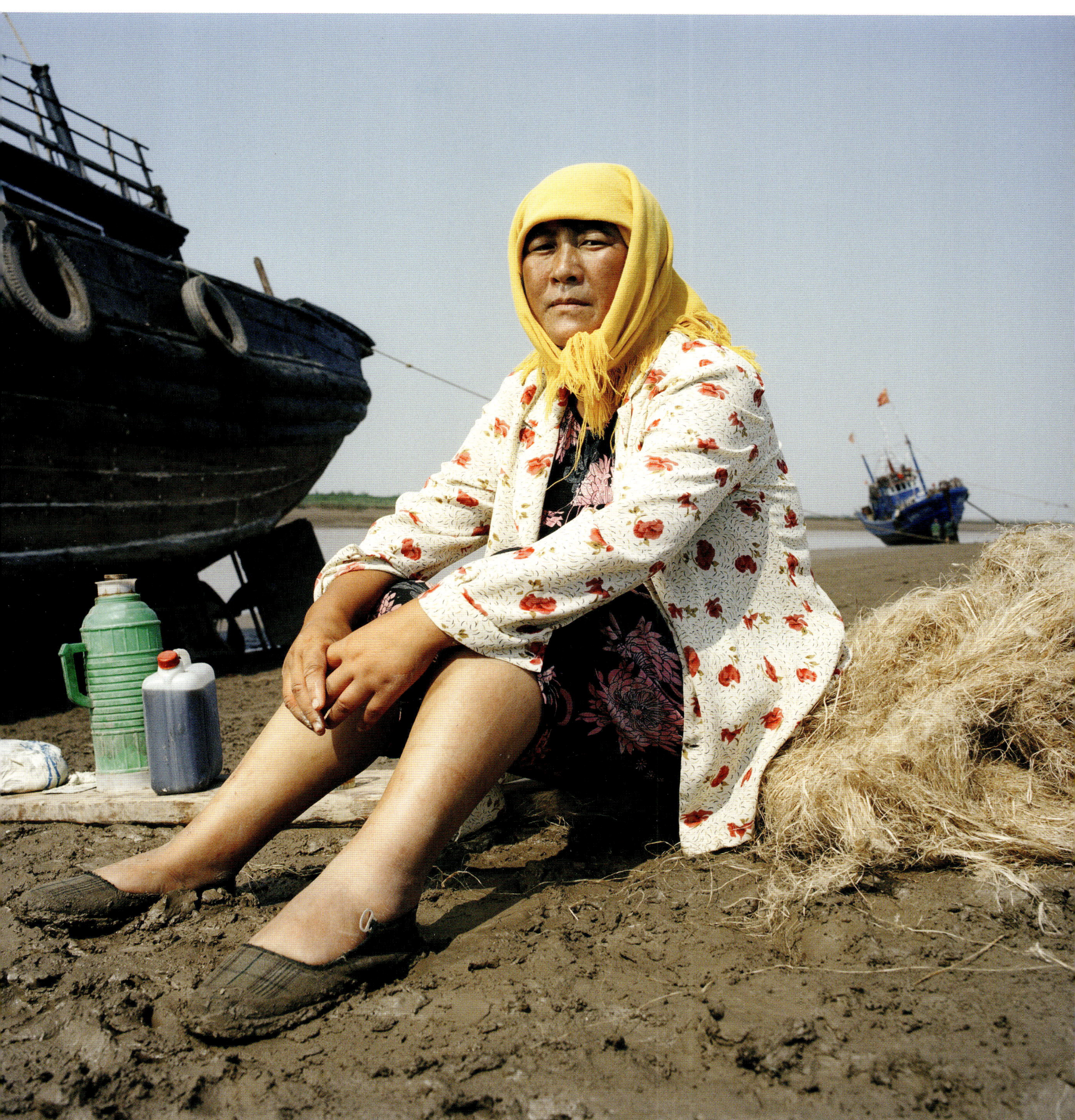

卢山杉

Lu Shanshan (24)
„DJ Samanda“
Peking / Beijing

Arena ist ein brandneuer Club in einem der vielen Einkaufszentren in Pekings Chaoyang-Viertel. DJ Samanda hält die jungen und trendigen Städter bei Laune, die jedes Wochenende auf der Jagd nach einer Party sind.

Arena is a brand new club in a mall located in Beijing's Chaoyang district. DJ Samanda entertains the new young, trendy urbanites who look for fun on weekends.

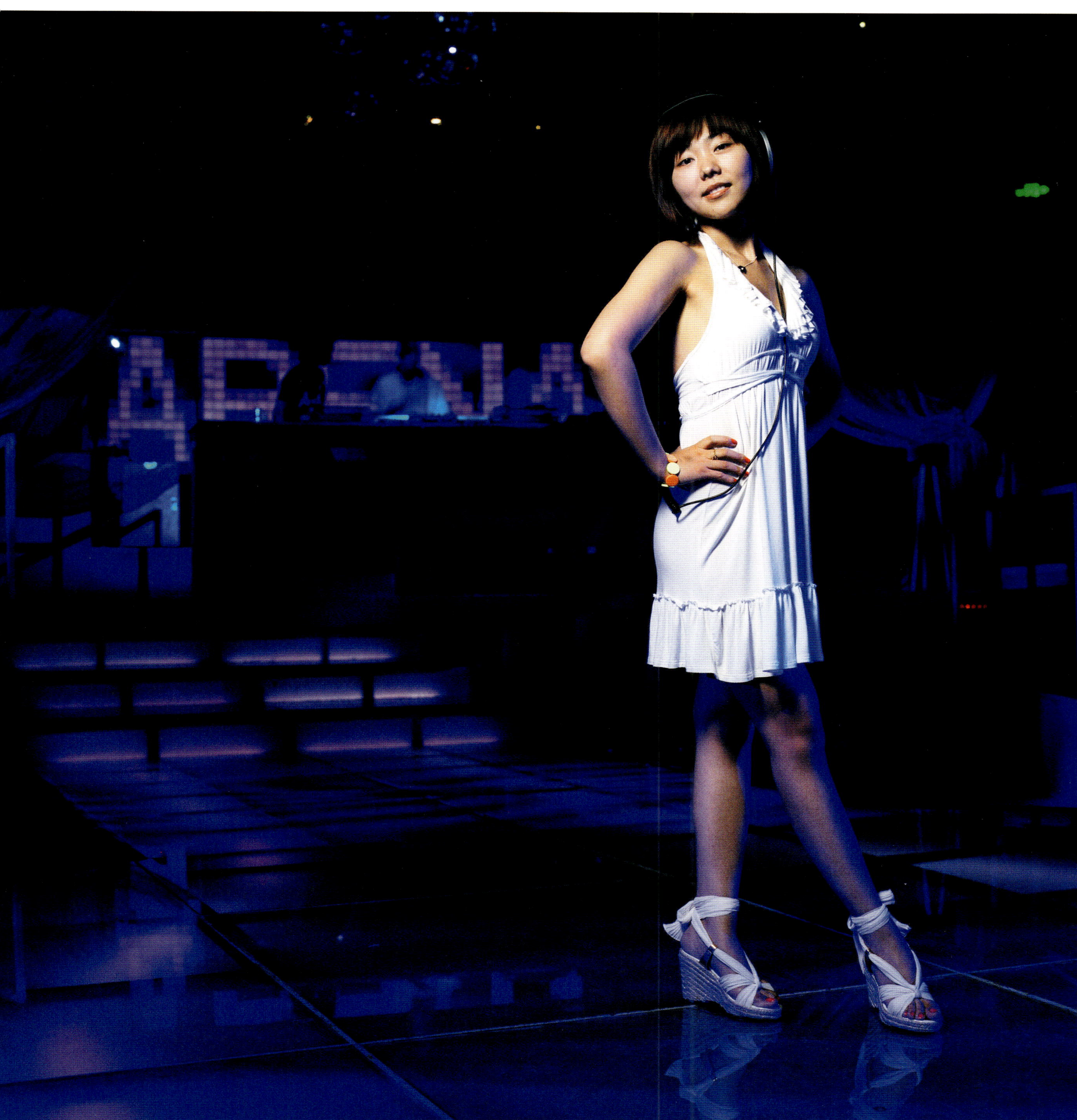

王利民

Wang Limin (34)
Arbeiter auf einem Ölfeld
Oilfield worker
Honggang, Heilongjiang

Wang Limin arbeitet auf dem Ölfeld Daqing, dem größten Bohrfeld Chinas. Überall stehen Fördertürme und Ölpumpen. Sogar in den Städten findet man Ölförderpumpen, mitten in Gebäudekomplexen oder sogar direkt neben Spielplätzen.

Wang Limin works in the Daqing oil field, the largest one in China. Rigs and oil pumps are everywhere, even in tcwns, amid housing complexes or adjacent to playgrounds

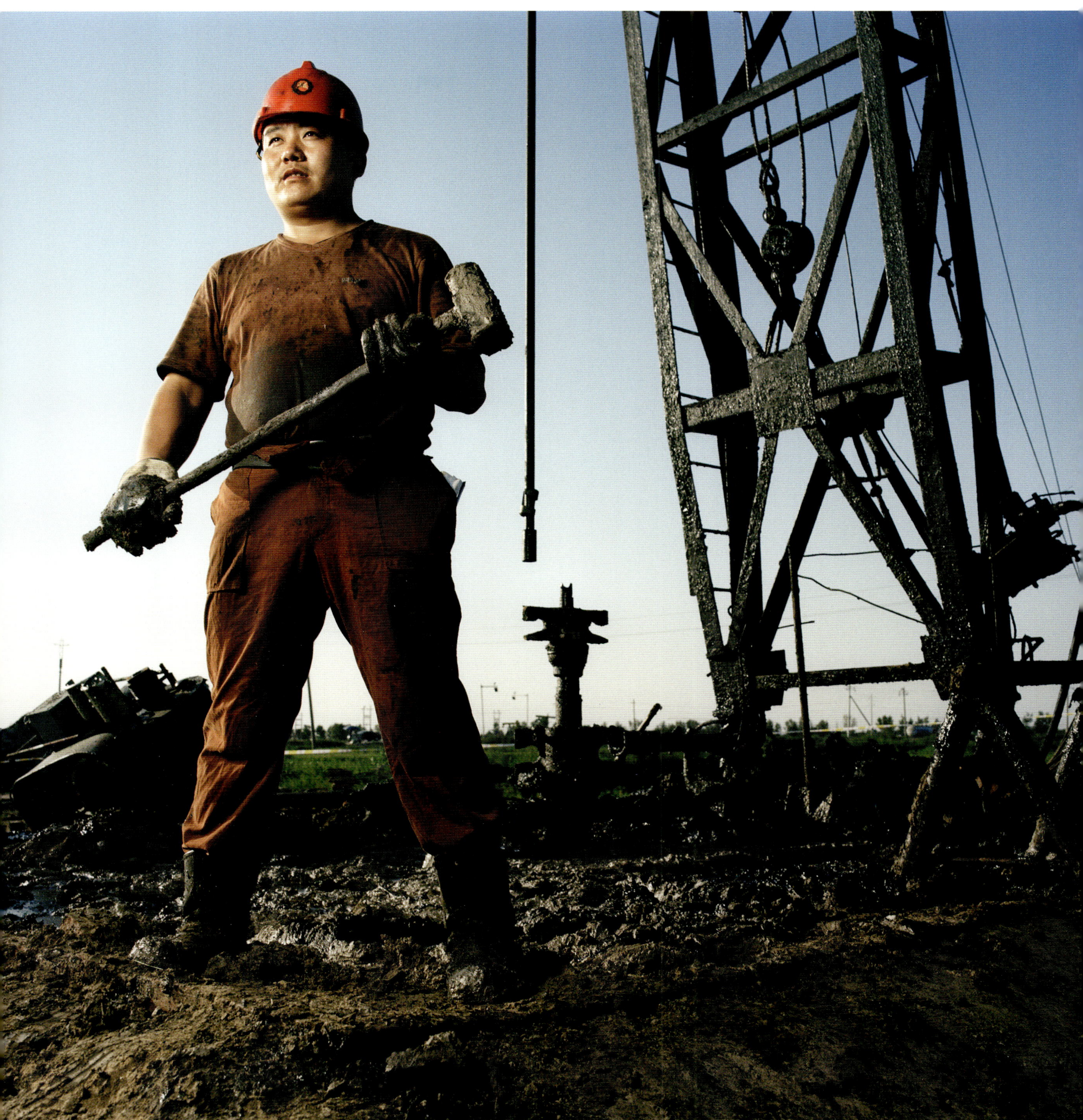

ག་ཚང་

Gazang (24)
Tibetisch-buddhistischer Mönch
Tibetan Buddhist monk
Heimahe, Qinghai

Als er 12 Jahre alt war, beschloss Gazang Mönch zu werden. Seine fromme Familie ist äußerst stolz darauf, dass eines ihrer Mitglieder in einem tibetischen Kloster aufgenommen wurde. Normalerweise studiert Gazang am Ta' er shi Tempel in Xining. Zweimal im Jahr reist er in seine Heimat Heimahe, ein traditionelles tibetisches Dorf, um seine Familie zu besuchen.

Gazang chose to become a Tibetan monk when he was 12 years old. His devout family is very proud that a family member was accepted by a Tibetan monastery. Normally Gazang studies at the Ta'er shi Temple in Xining. He travels to his hometown Heimahe, a traditional Tibetan village, to visit his family twice a year.

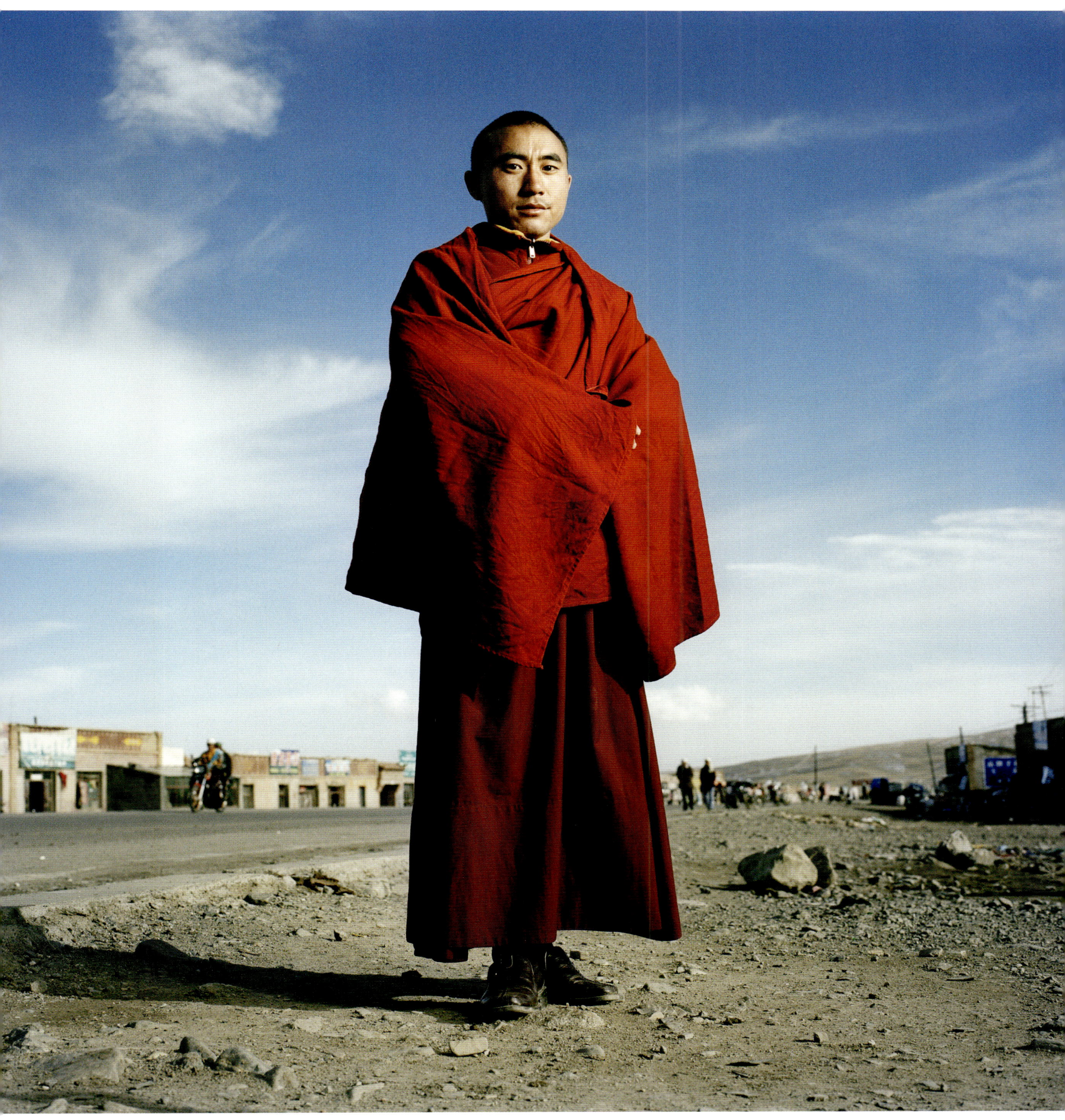

陈骏

Chen Jun / Kirk Chen (35)
Geschäftsführer des Nine Dragons Admirals Yachtclub
General Manager of Nine Dragons Admirals Yacht Club
Pinghu, Zhejiang

Kirk Chens Familie gehört das luxuriöse Nine Dragons Estate, einer der exklusivsten Country Clubs von Shanghai. Auf dem Anwesen befinden sich ein Golf- und ein Poloclub sowie ein beachtlicher Yachthafen. Kirk Chen ist Geschäftsführer des Yachtclubs und verantwortlich für den Yachthafen. Er führt gerne seinen Lamborghini vor, den er am liebsten auf der Clubterrasse direkt am Wasser parkt.

The luxurious Nine Dragons Estate, one of Shanghai's most exclusive country clubs, belongs to Kirk Chen's family. The estate includes a golf course, a polo club and an extraordinary marina. He is the general manager of the Marina / Yacht Club. Kirk's favorite toy is his beloved Lamborghini, parked on the club terrace at the waterfront.

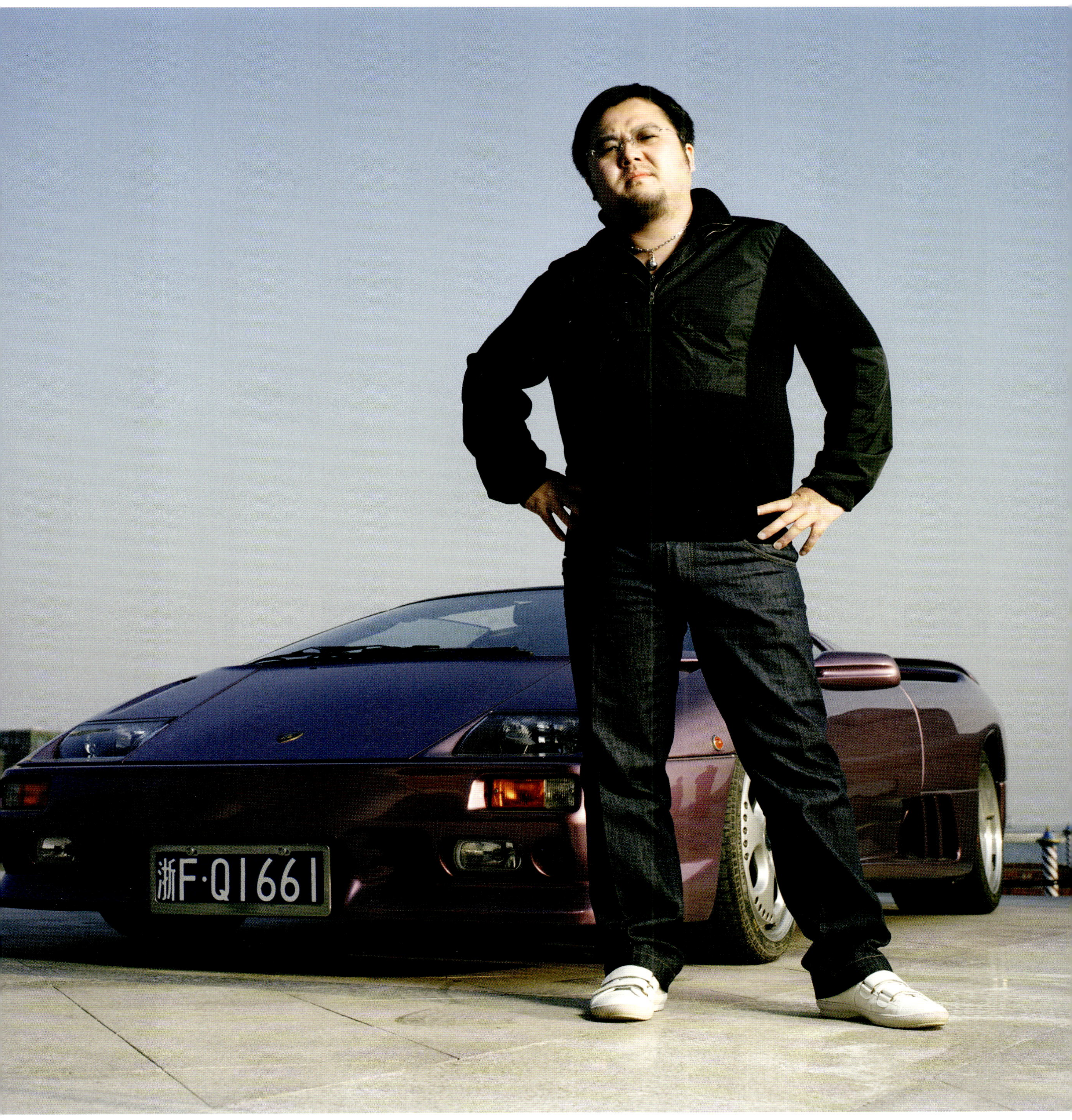
浙F·Q1661

张李

Zhang Li* (25)
Gastarbeiter / Sicherheitsbeamter
Migrant worker / Security guard
Peking / Beijing

So wie die meisten Arbeiter auf der Baustelle des Olympiastadions in Peking, ist auch Zhang Li ein Gastarbeiter, der jede Woche sechs Tage lang in 12-Stunden-Schichten arbeitet. Mit den 800 Yuan (ungefähr 80 Euro), die er im Monat verdient, muss er seine gesamte Familie in einer Kleinstadt in der Provinz Shanxi ernähren.

Most employees at the Olympic Stadium construction site in Beijing are migrant workers like Zhang Li. He works 12 hours shifts, six days a week. With the 800 Yuan (about 80 euro) he receives each month, he provides for his entire family back in a small town in Shanxi Province.

* Name geändert / changed name

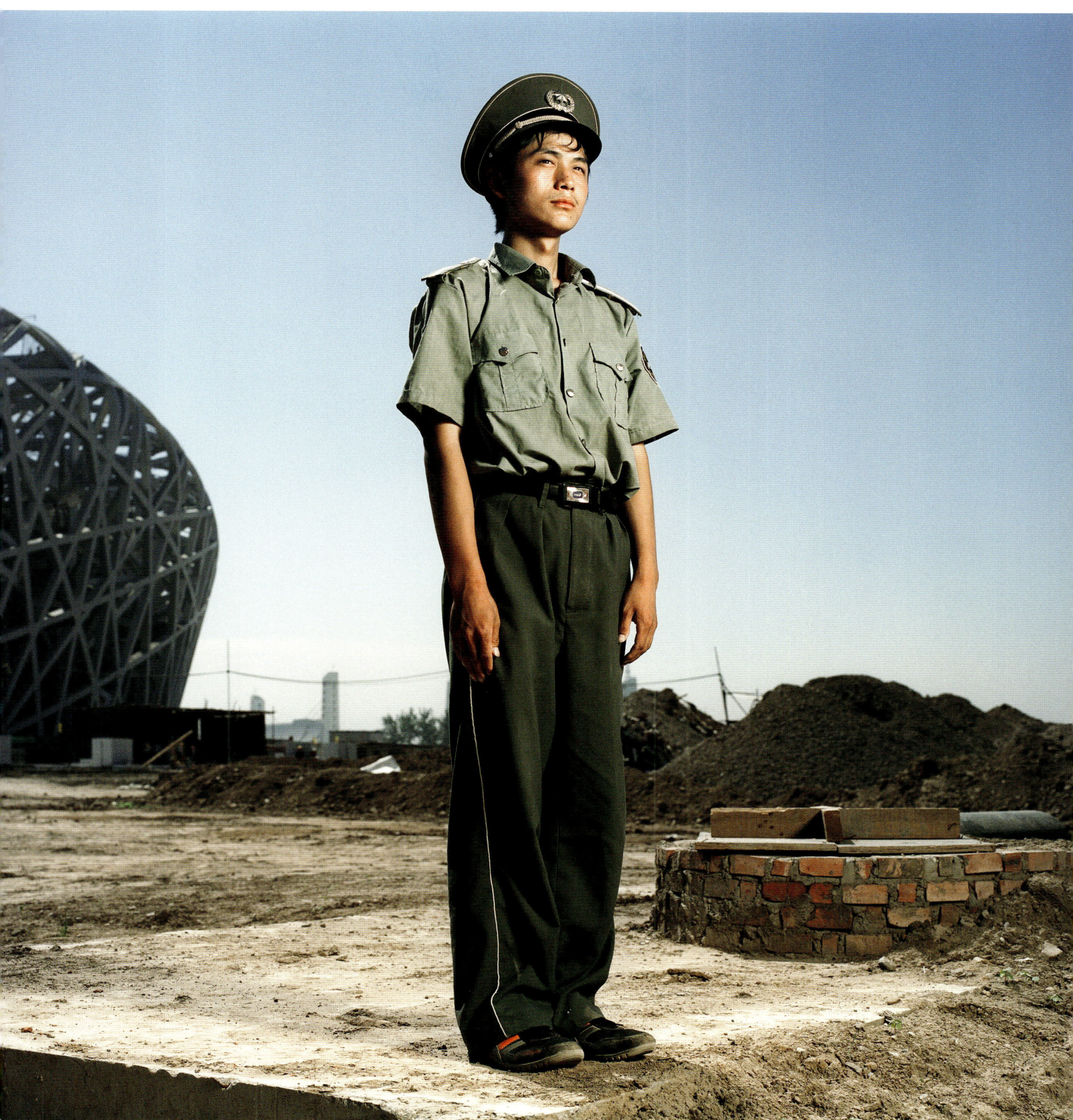

秦玲玲

Qin Lingling (5)
Zirkusakrobatin
Circus acrobat
Hukou, Shanxi

Qin Lingling ist der Star in einem Wanderzirkus. Ihre Mutter, die Zirkusdirektorin, hat mit ihrem Training bereits im Kleinkindalter begonnen. Sobald die zwei bunt bemalten Zirkuswagen in einer Stadt ankommen, beginnt sie ihre Vorstellung auf einer behelfsmäßigen Bühne, einem einfachen Holztisch.

Qin Lingling is the star of a travelling circus. Her mother, the head of the circus, started to train her at the earliest age. Upon the arrival of the two painted circus trucks at a town square, she starts to perform on her makeshift stage, a simple wooden table.

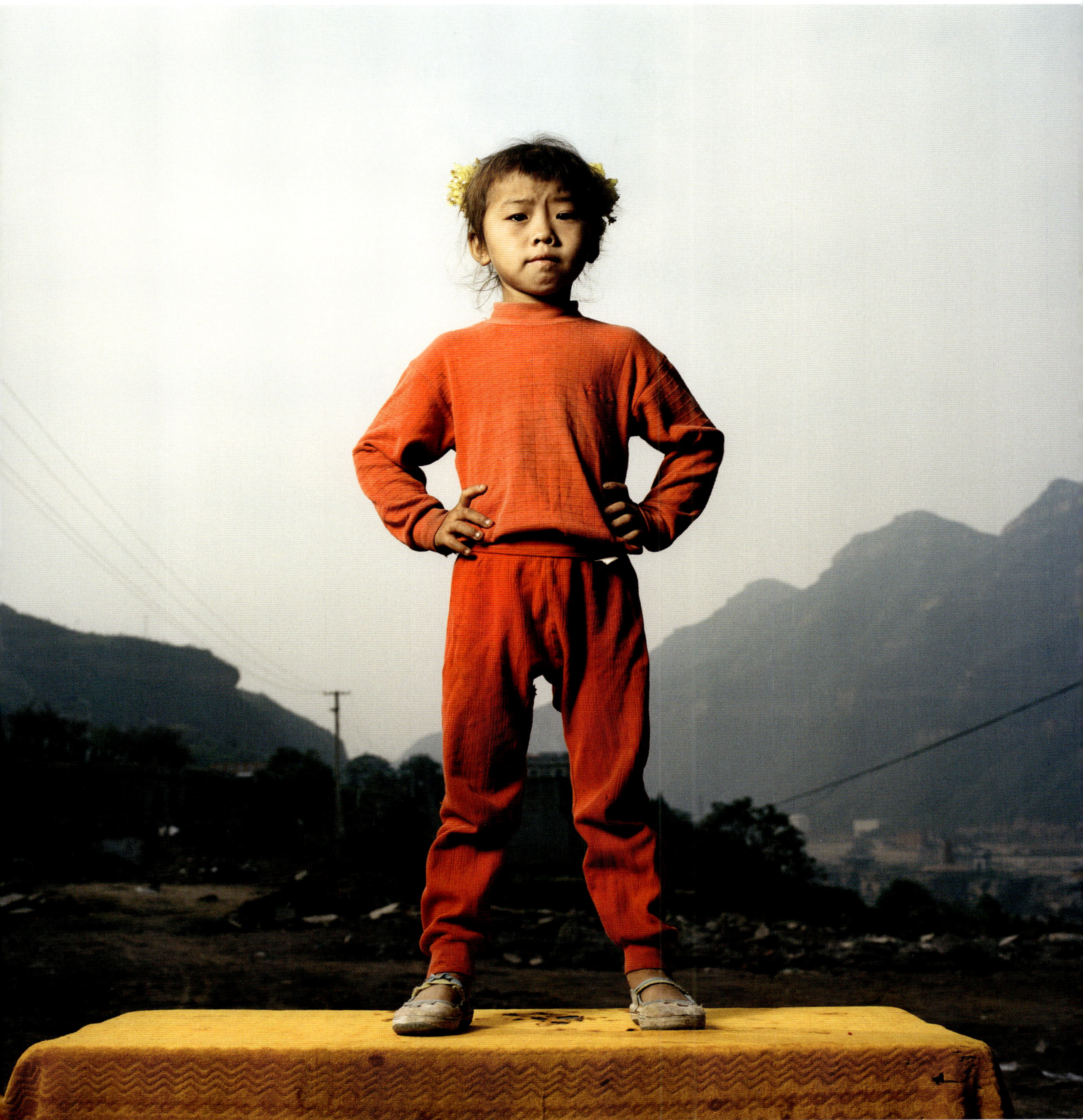

艾未未

Ai Weiwei (51)
Künstler / Aktivist
Artist / Activist
Peking / Beijing

Ai Weiwei ist nicht nur einer der berühmtesten zeitgenössischen Künstler Chinas, sondern auch ein couragierter Aktivist, der nicht davor zurückschreckt, mit der Regierung auf Konfrontationskurs zu gehen.

Ai Weiwei is not only one of the most famous Chinese contemporary artists, but also a courageous activist who does not shy away from confrontation with the government.

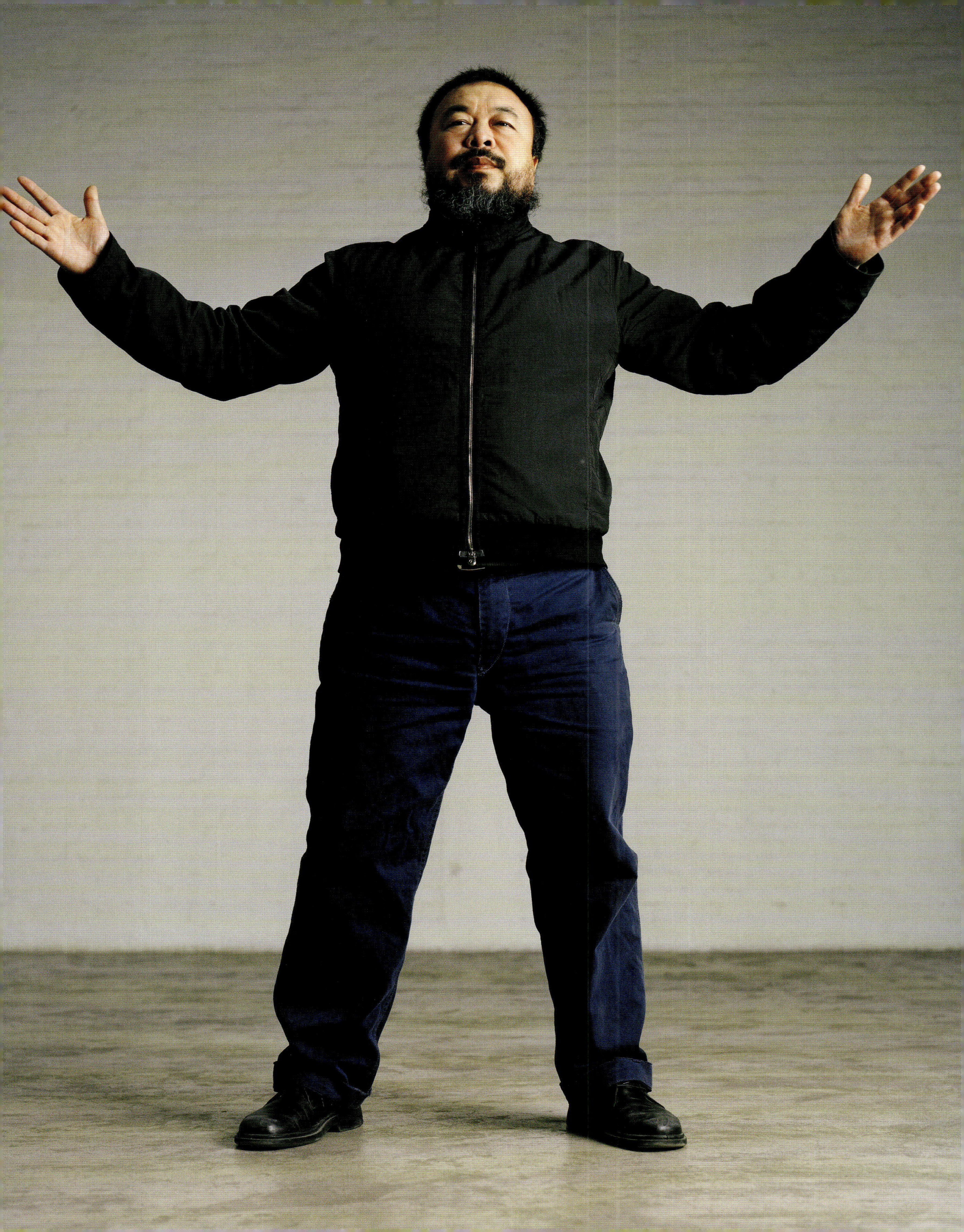

吴诗雅

Wu Shiya (8)
Schülerin
Student
Yong'an, Jilin

Wu Shiya ist ein Schulmädchen aus einem abgelegenen Dorf in der Provinz Jilin im Nordosten Chinas.

Wu Shiya is a school girl who lives in a remote village in Jilin Province, in Northeastern China.

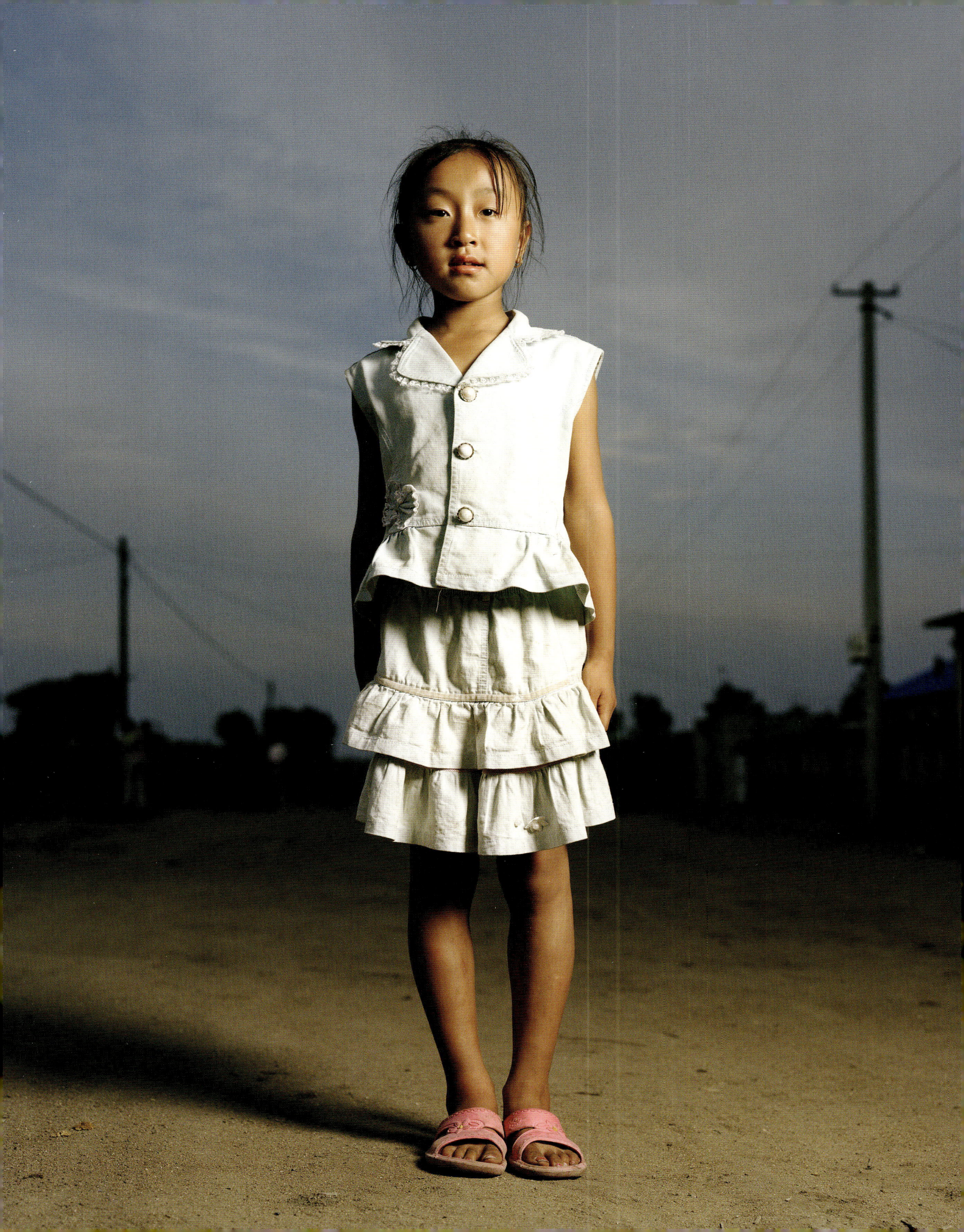

辛玉田

Xin Yutian (52)
Schauspieler
Actor
Yuan Ping, Shanxi

Der Schauspieler Xin Yutian spielt ausschließlich die Rolle von Chiang Kai-shek. Er ist einer von nur vier Schauspielern in ganz China, die auf diese Rolle spezialisiert sind. Außerdem betreibt er eine Restaurantkette, die hervorragende chinesische Dumplings anbietet.

The actor Xin Yutian exclusively plays the role of Chiang Kai-shek. He is one of only four actors in China specialized in this role. Besides acting, he runs a chain of dumpling restaurants.

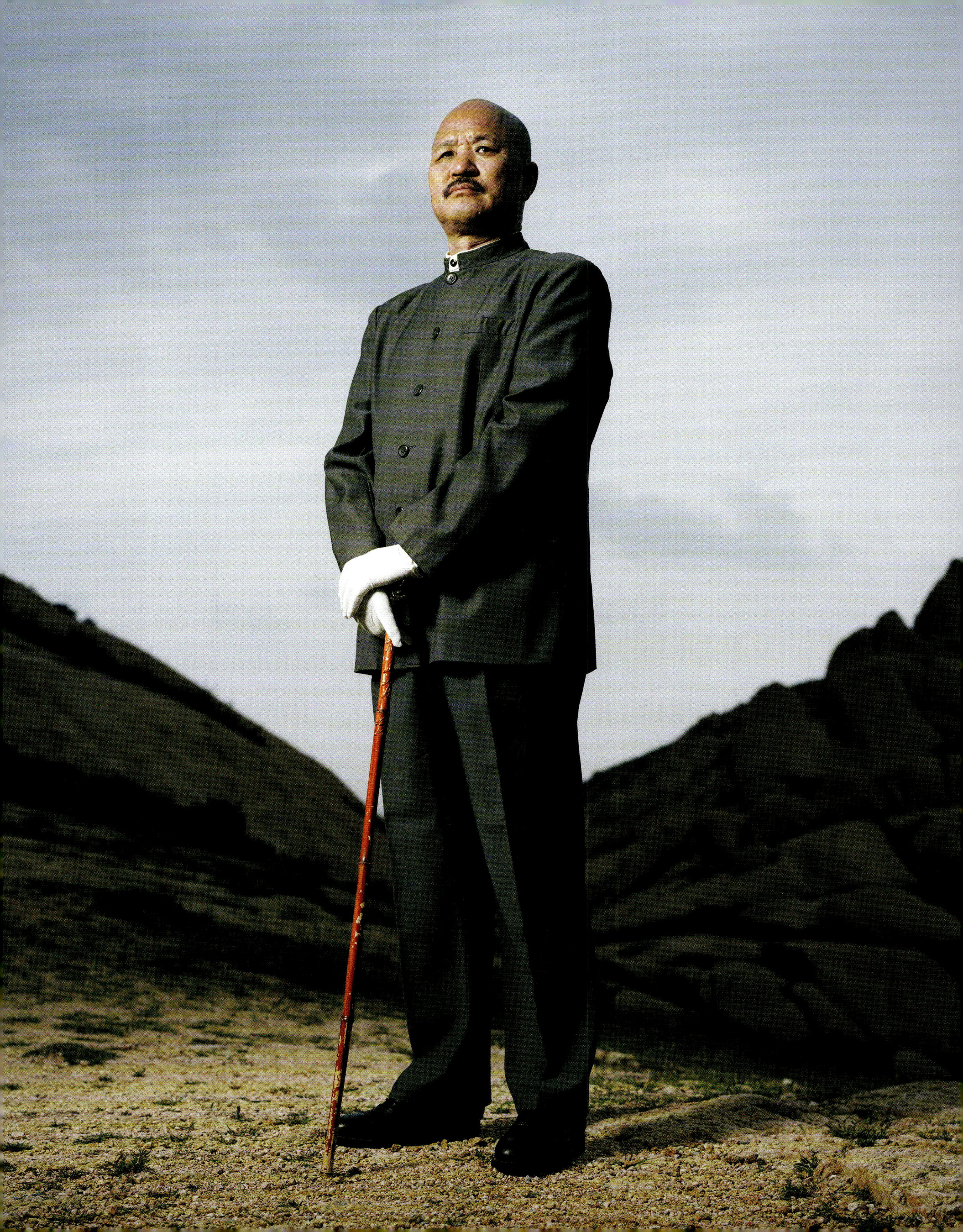

孙菲菲

Sun Feifei (26)
Schauspielerin
Actress
Hengdian World Studios
Hengdian, Zhejiang

Sun Feifei ist TV-Sternchen und Hauptdarstellerin einer historischen Fernsehserie, die in Chinas Hollywood, den Hengdian Filmstudios, produziert wird.

Sun Feifei is the star of a historical TV series that is being produced at Hengdian Film studios, China's Hollywood.

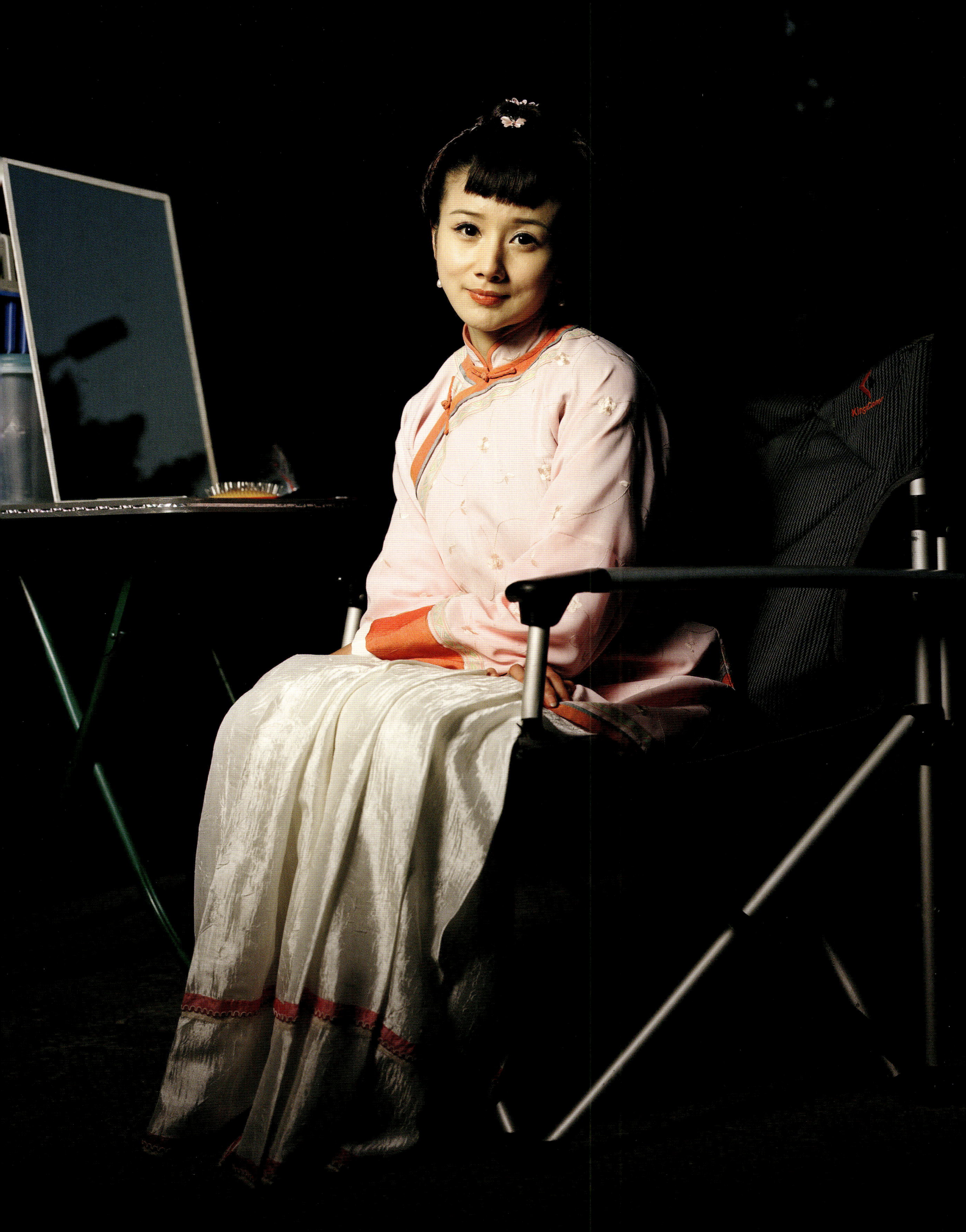

དཔའ་མོ་ རི་མོ་རྒྱ་

Pagmo (48) mit / with Rinmogya (5)
Tibetische Nomaden
Tibetan nomads
Qusina, Qinghai

Pagmo und ihre Enkelin Rinmogya leben mit ihrer Familie und Dutzenden Yaks ein sehr traditionelles Leben als Nomaden in der Provinz Qinghai im tibetischen Hochland.

Pagmo and her granddaughter Rinmogya live a very traditional life with their family and dozens of yaks in the highlands of the Qinghai Tibet Plateau.

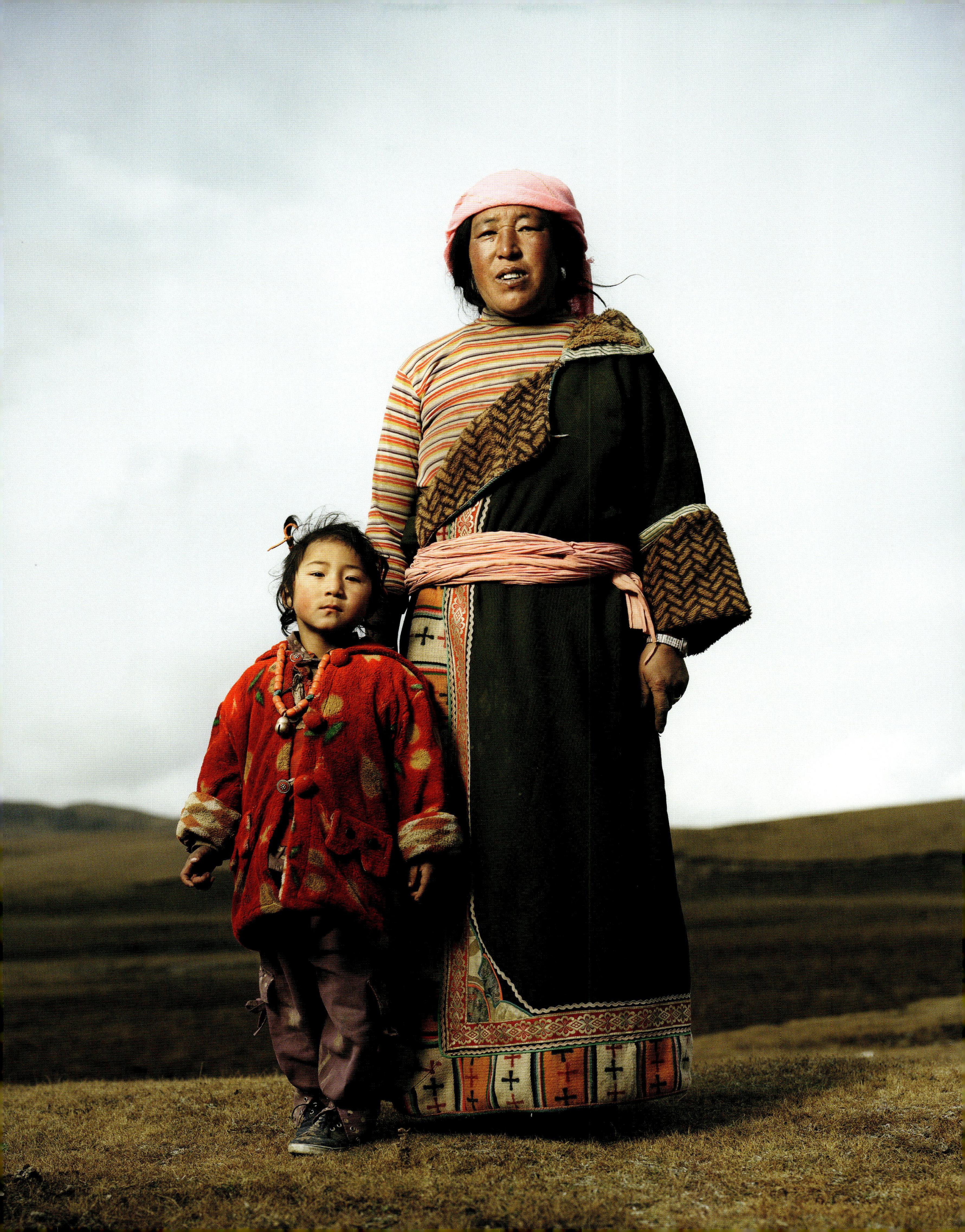

爱尔莎曼

Elsa Man (21)
Bankangestellte
Bank employee
Hongkong

Elsa Man ist ein typisches Hongkong-Girl. Sie arbeitet hart, macht Karriere und in der Freizeit liebt sie es, in den angesagtesten Läden einzukaufen.

Elsa Man is a typical Hong Kong girl. She works hard on her career and in her free time loves to go shopping in the hippest stores.

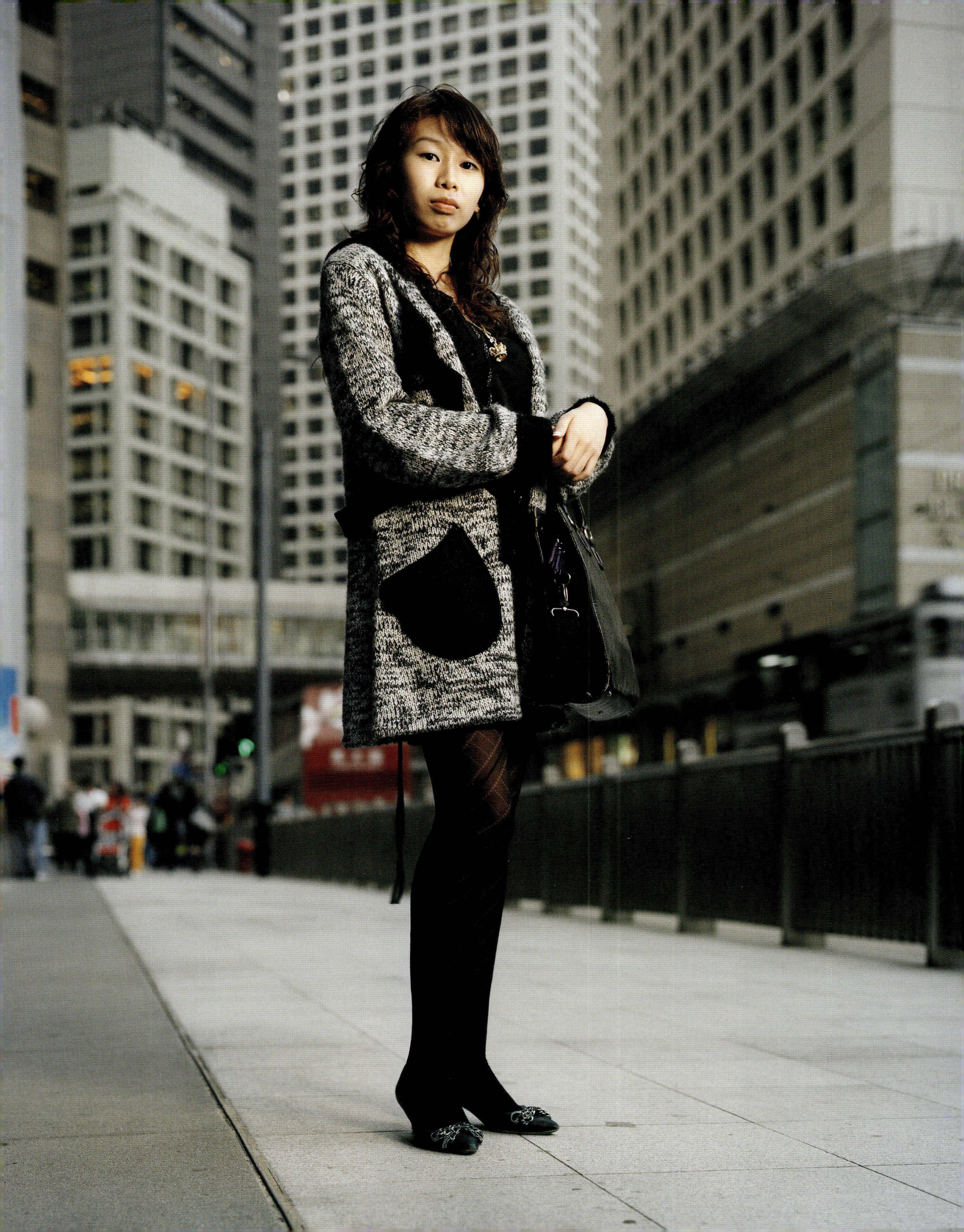

羽西

Yue-Sai Kan (58)
Produzentin und TV-Moderatorin
Producer and TV host
Shanghai

Yue-Sai Kan ist eine echte Berühmtheit in China. Das People Magazine nannte sie einmal die berühmteste lebende Chinesin. Sie hat vier Bücher geschrieben und 1989 die erste große Kosmetikproduktlinie in China etabliert. Mittlerweile hat sie ihr Kosmetikgeschäft an L'Oreal verkauft, hält aber immer noch eine Mehrheitsbeteiligung und ist weiterhin das öffentliche Gesicht der Linie.

Yue-Sai Kan is a famous celebrity in China. People Magazine once called her the most famous Chinese woman alive. She has written four books and in 1989 launched the first major cosmetic line in China. Her cosmetic line has since been sold to L'Oreal, but she has kept a controlling interest and remains its public face.

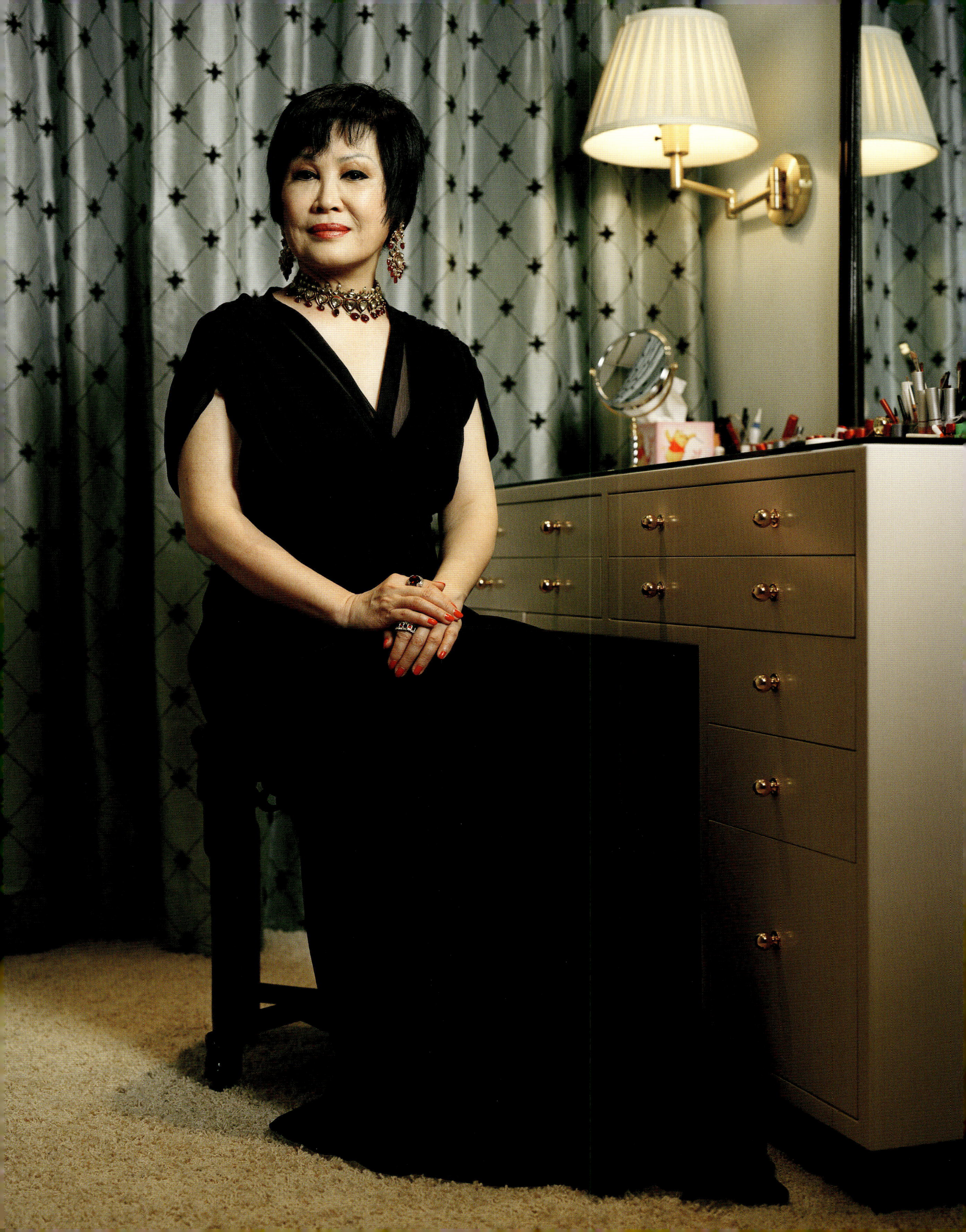

محمتقربان

Mehmet Kurban (30)
Metzger
Butcher
Yingsu, Xinjiang

Mehmet Kurban ist der Metzger in einem kleinen uigurischen Dorf, das mitten in der riesigen Taklamakan-Wüste in der Provinz Xinjiang liegt.

Mehmet Kurban is the butcher of a tiny Uyghur village in the vast Taklamakan Desert in Xinjiang Province.

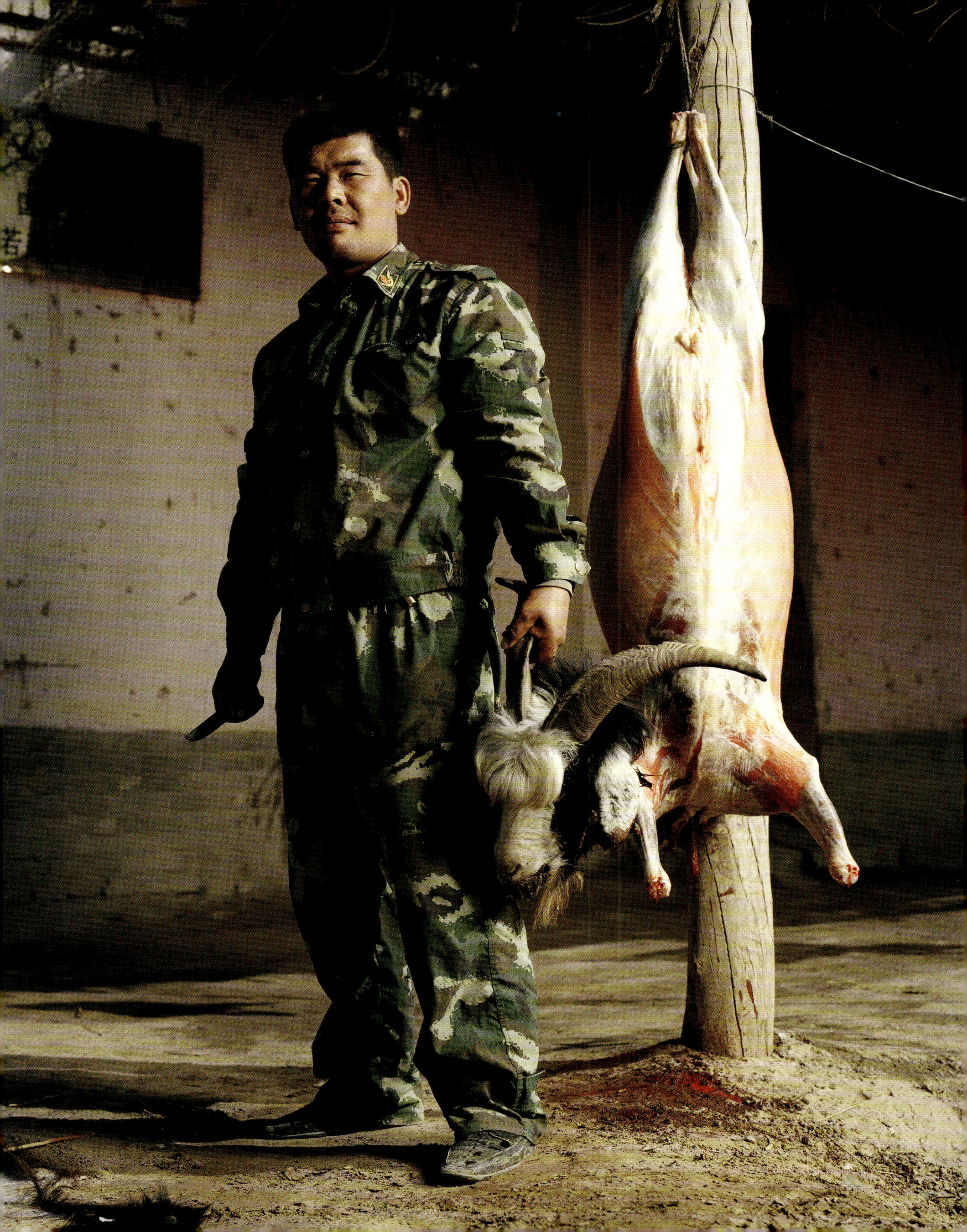

贾妞

Jia Niu* (33)
Abfallsammlerin
Scavenger
Linghou, Guangdong

Abfall am Straßenrand aufzusammeln und nach Verwertbarem zu suchen, wird in China als einer der niedrigsten Jobs betrachtet. Trotzdem muss sich Jia Niu wie viele andere ihren Lebensunterhalt auf diese Weise verdienen.

Picking up trash along the highway is one of the lowest regarded jobs in China. Nevertheless, Jia Niu, like so many, is forced to do it to make a living.

* Name geändert / changed name

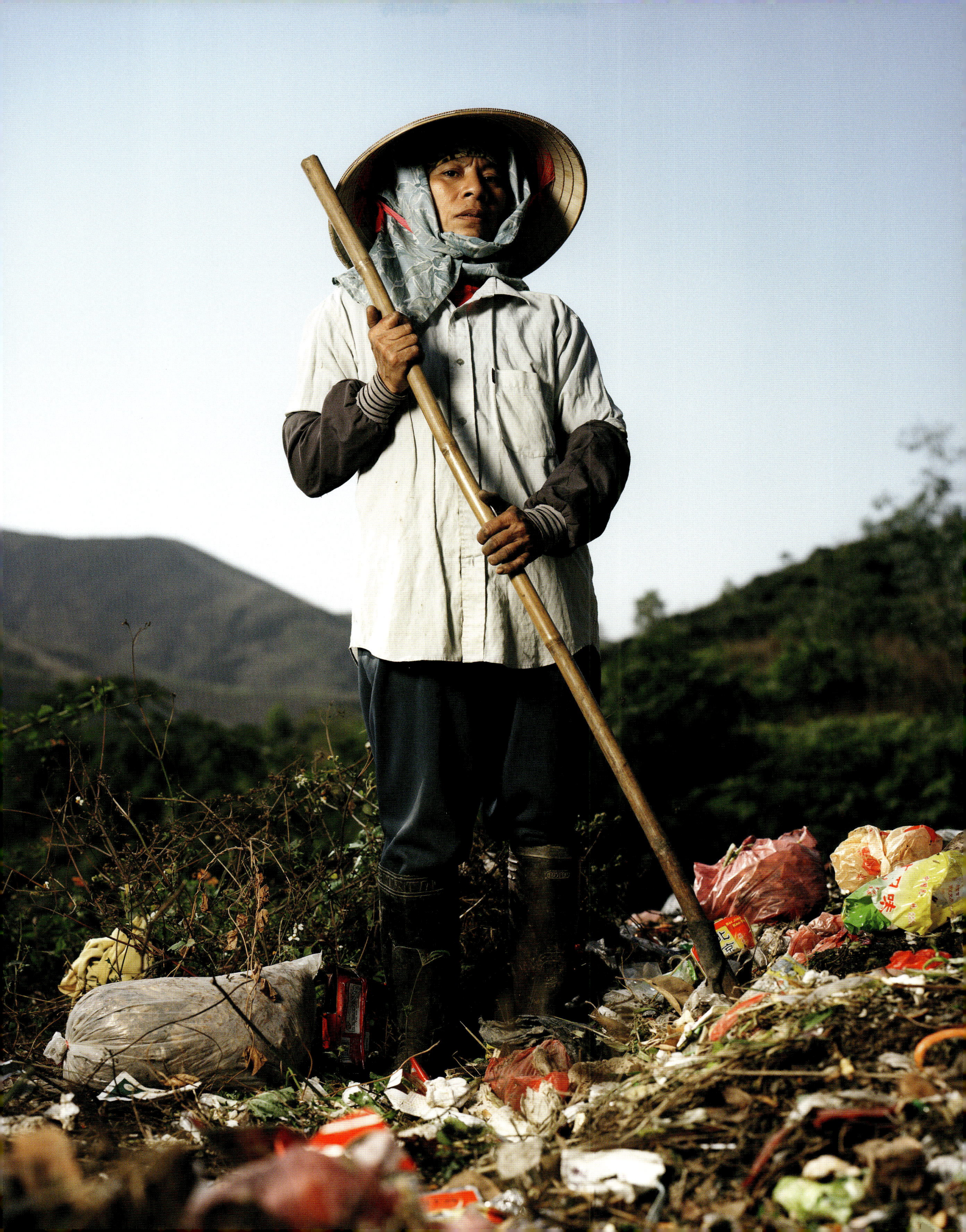

陈显民

Chen Xianmin (55)
Bauer
Pig farmer
Beitou, Sichuan

Der Schweinezüchter Chen Xianmin lebt in einem unzugänglichen Gebirgstal in der südwestlichen Provinz Sichuan. Das Gras, das er entlang einer kurvigen Gebirgsstraße sammelt, ist für seine Schweine bestimmt.

Chen Xianmin lives in a steep mountain valley in Southwestern Sichuan Province. The grass he collects alongside a wild mountain road is destined to feed his pigs.

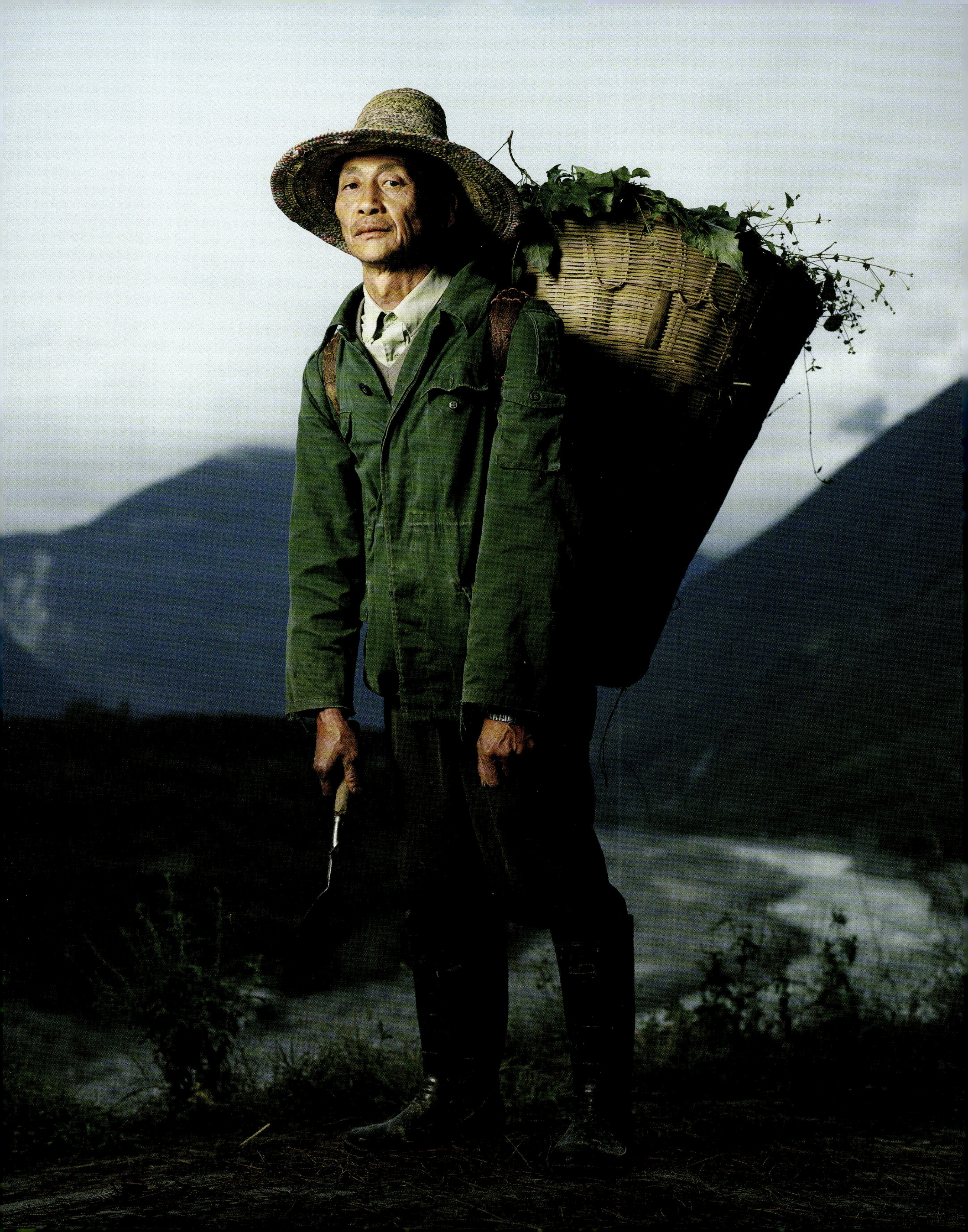

夏兰

Xia Lan* (20)
Prostituierte
Prostitute
Shenzhen, Guangdong

Xia Lan stammt ursprünglich aus der ländlich geprägten Provinz Guangxi. Sie verließ ihr Dorf, um sich in Shenzhen ihren Lebensunterhalt als Prostituierte zu verdienen. Bevor die Region vor 25 Jahren in eine Sonderwirtschaftszone umgewandelt und ein Eldorado für Geschäftsleute wurde, war die 8,9-Millionen-Einwohner-Stadt am Rande von Hongkong ein kleines Fischerdorf. Es gibt vermutlich keine andere Stadt in China, in der mehr Prostituierte arbeiten, als in Shenzhen, wo Zehntausende ihre Körper für ein paar Groschen verkaufen. Xia Lan arbeitet gemeinsam mit vier anderen jungen Mädchen in einem 30-Quadratmeter-Apartment im 20. Stock eines unscheinbaren Hochhauses.

Originally from the rural Guangxi province, Xia Lan left her village to make a living as a prostitute in Shenzhen. This city, with a present population of 8.9 million on the Hong Kong border, was just a small fishing village 25 years ago before it was turned into a special economic zone and became a business Eldorado. There is probably no city in China with more prostitutes than Shenzhen where tens of thousands of them sell their bodies for a few Yuan. Together with four other young girls, Xia Lan works in a 30-square-meter apartment on the 20th floor of a non-descript block.

* Name geändert / changed name

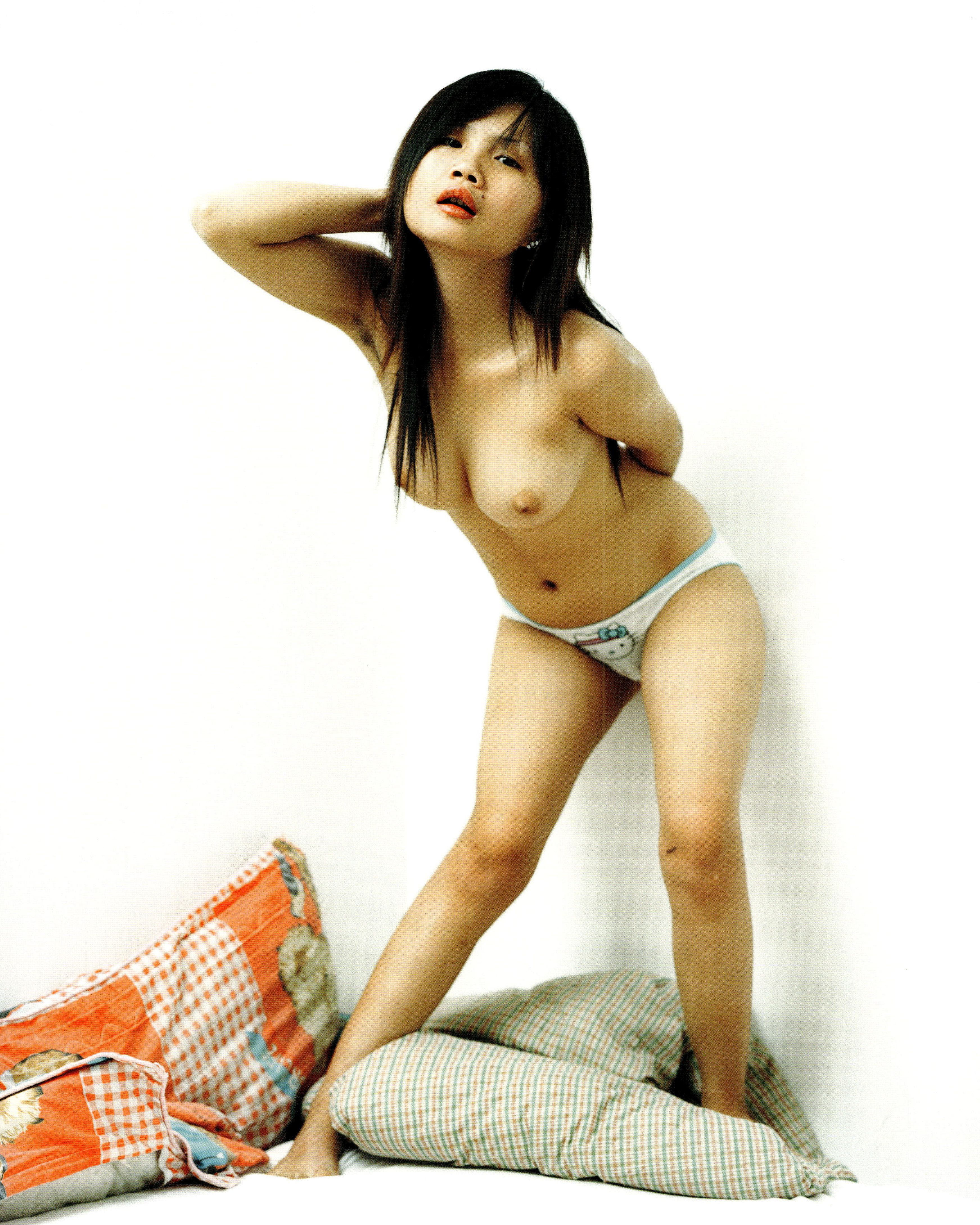

释永信

Shi Yongxin (42)
Buddhistischer Abt
Buddhist Abbot
Shaolin-Tempel, Henan

Shi Yongxin ist nicht nur Abt des weltberühmten Shaolin-Klosters, sondern auch Abgeordneter des Nationalen Volkskongresses.

Shi Yongxin is not only the abbot of the world famous Shaolin monastery, but also a deputy of the National People's Congress.

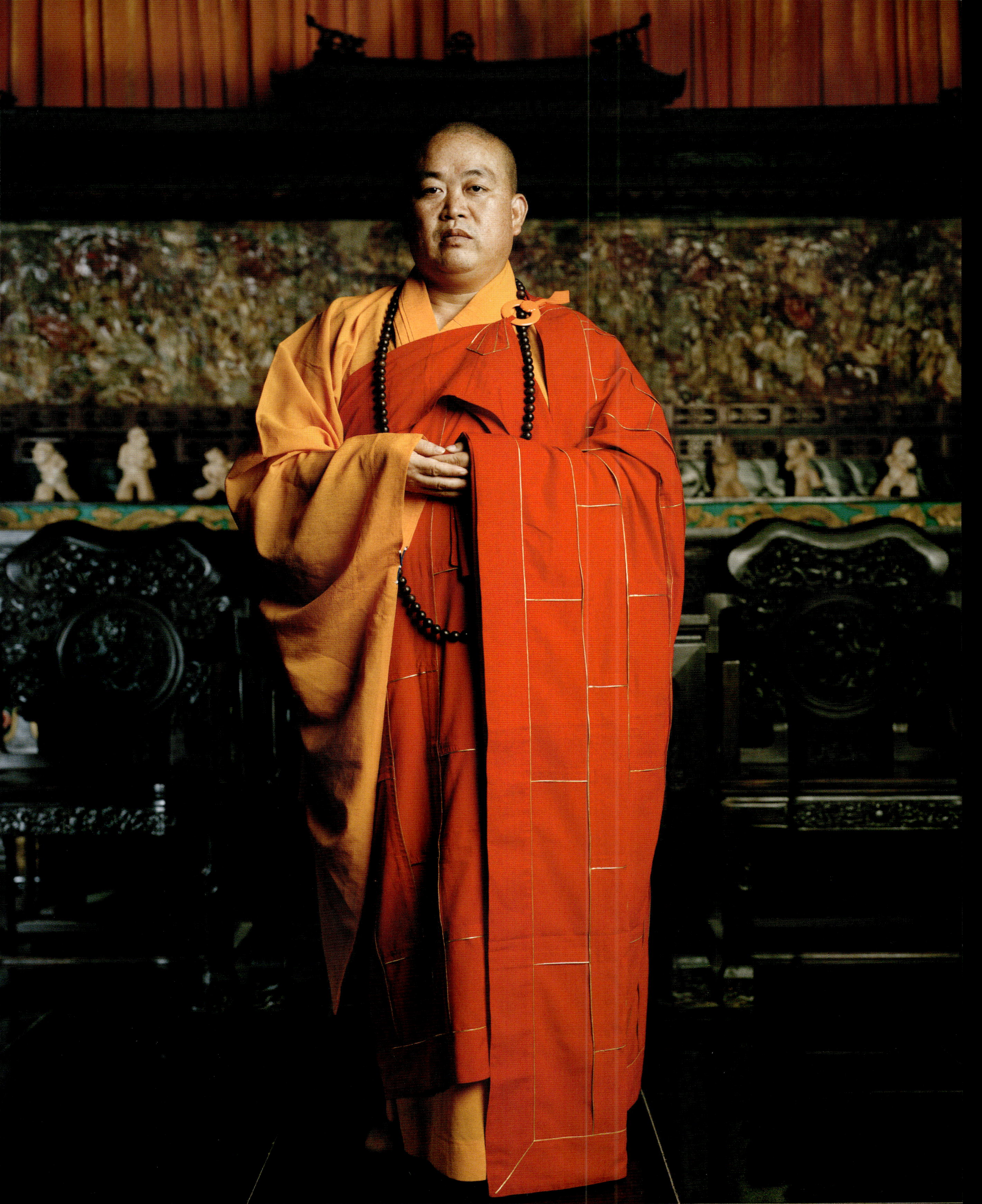

陈可梅

Chen Kemei (37)
Recycling-Arbeiterin
Recycling worker
Yunyang, Chongqing

Die Stadt Yunyang hatte einmal 40.000 Einwohner, die allesamt wegen des Drei-Schluchten-Damms umgesiedelt werden mussten. Jetzt versinkt sie im sich allmählich füllenden Jangtse-Reservoir. Das Metall, das Chen Kemei aufbereitet, stammt aus Gebäuden, die abgerissen wurden, bevor sie in den Fluten versanken.

Yunyang used to have 40,000 inhabitants, all of whom had to be relocated due to construction of the Three Gorges Dam. Now it is vanishing in the rising Yangtze River Reservoir. The metal Chen Kemei recycles was taken from buildings that were torn down before they were flooded.

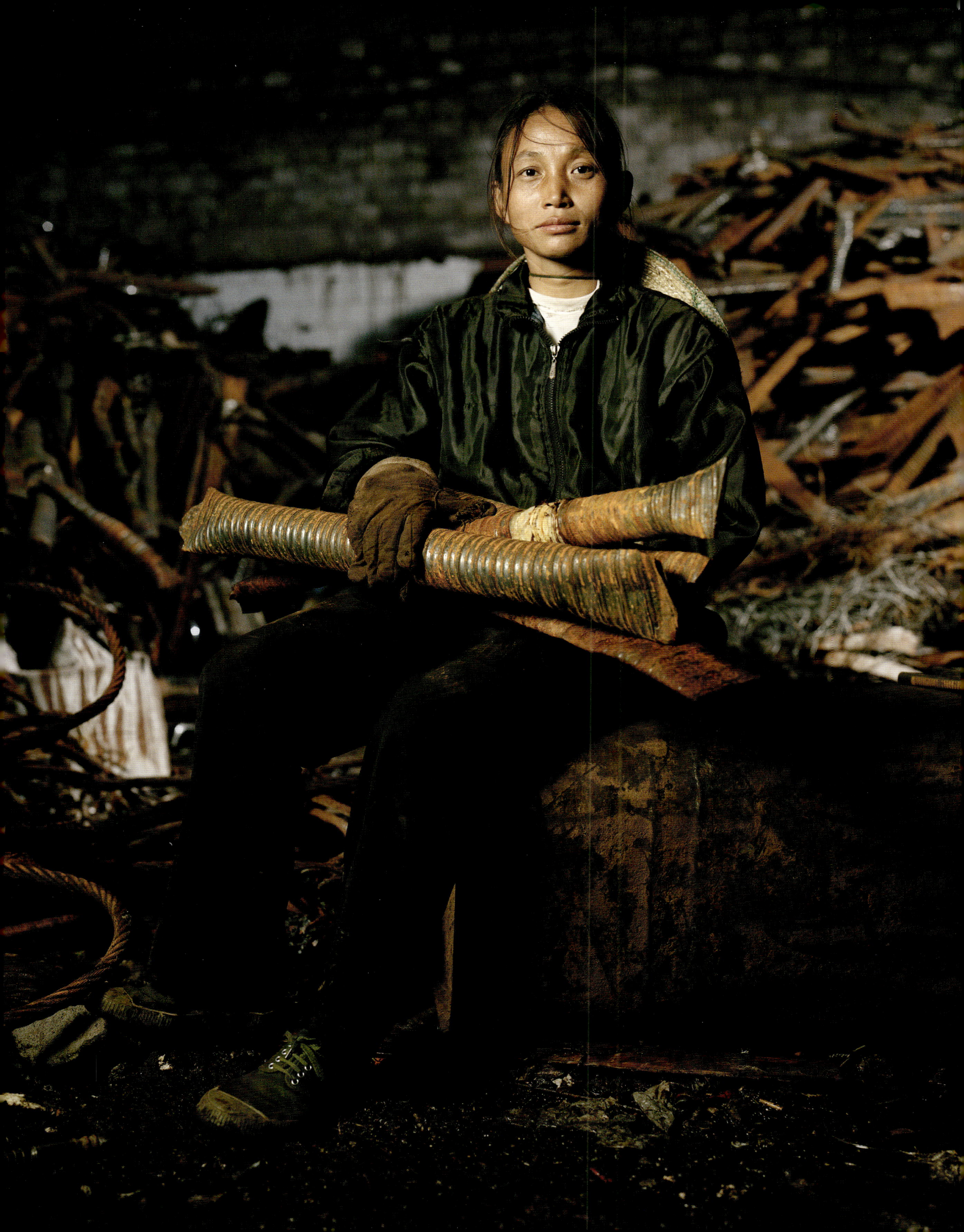

ཆོས་སྐྱབས་

Chokyab (55)
Yak-Bauer
Yak farmer
Lengshen, Qinghai

Chokyab, ein tibetischer Bauer, der Yaks hält, lebt mit seiner Frau und seinen sieben Kindern in einem abgelegenen und sehr einsamen Teil der Provinz Qinghai. Viele Tibeter in dieser Region haben in den letzten Jahren ihre Pferde gegen Motorräder eingetauscht.

Chokyab, a Tibetan yak farmer, lives with his wife and seven children in a remote and lonely corner of Qinghai Province. In the last couple of years many Tibetans in this area have traded their horses for motorbikes.

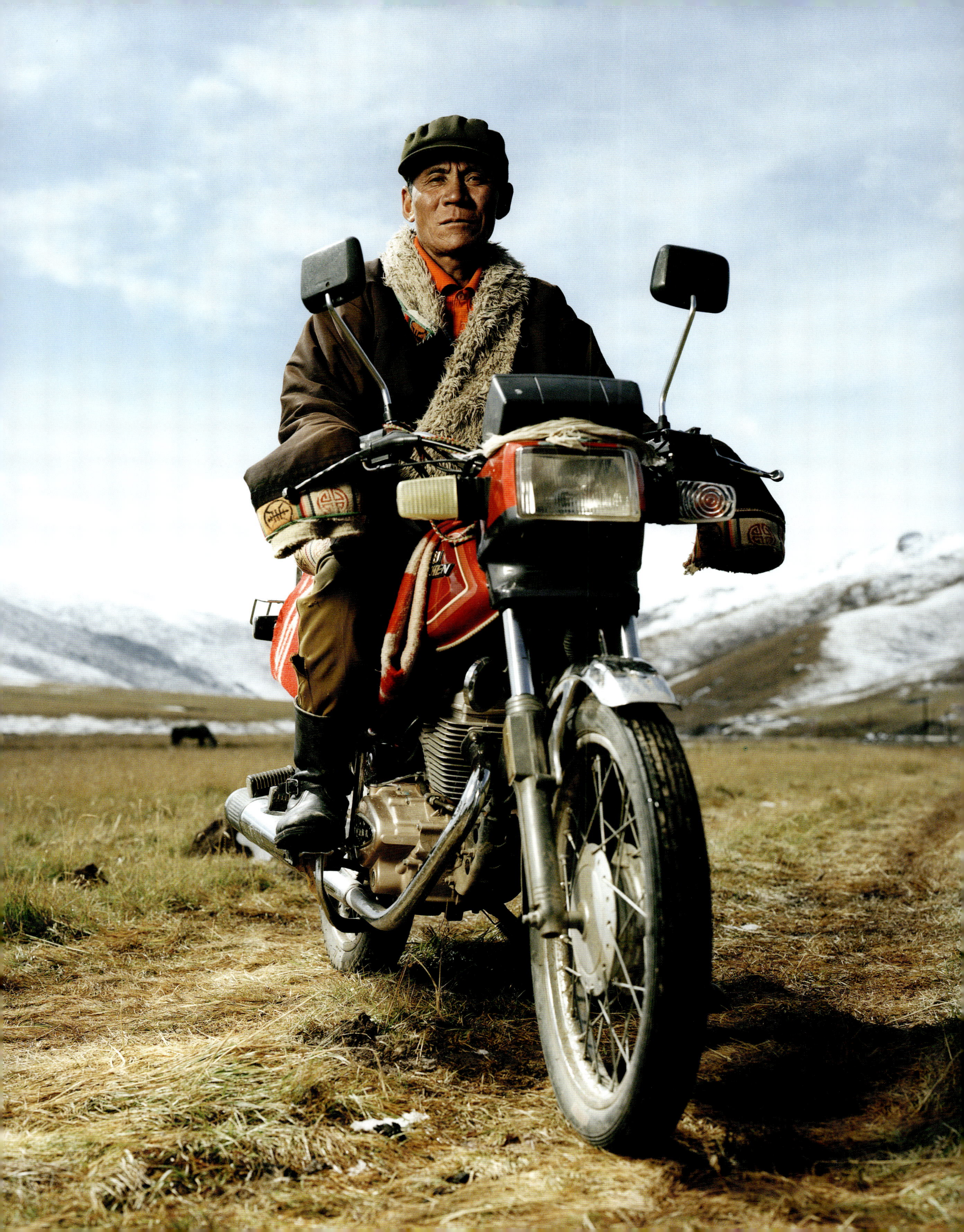

张希庆

Zhang Xiqing (29)
Militärpolizist, Forstabteilung
Military Armed Police Forest Division
Jingdong, Yunnan

Leutnant Zhang Xiqing ist Offizier der Forstabteilung der Militärpolizei. Er ist Kommandant des Stützpunkts Jingdong. Offiziell schützt diese Spezialeinheit der Volksbefreiungsarmee den Wald und hilft, Waldbrände zu verhindern. Aber Mitglieder dieser Elitetruppe werden häufig bei Aufständen oder Demonstrationen eingesetzt.

Lieutenant Zhang Xiqing is an officer in the forest division of the military armed police. He is the commander of the Jingdong base. While officially it is a special unit of the People's Liberation Army that protects the forest and looks out for fires, members of this elite troop are often deployed when riots break out or demonstrations take place.

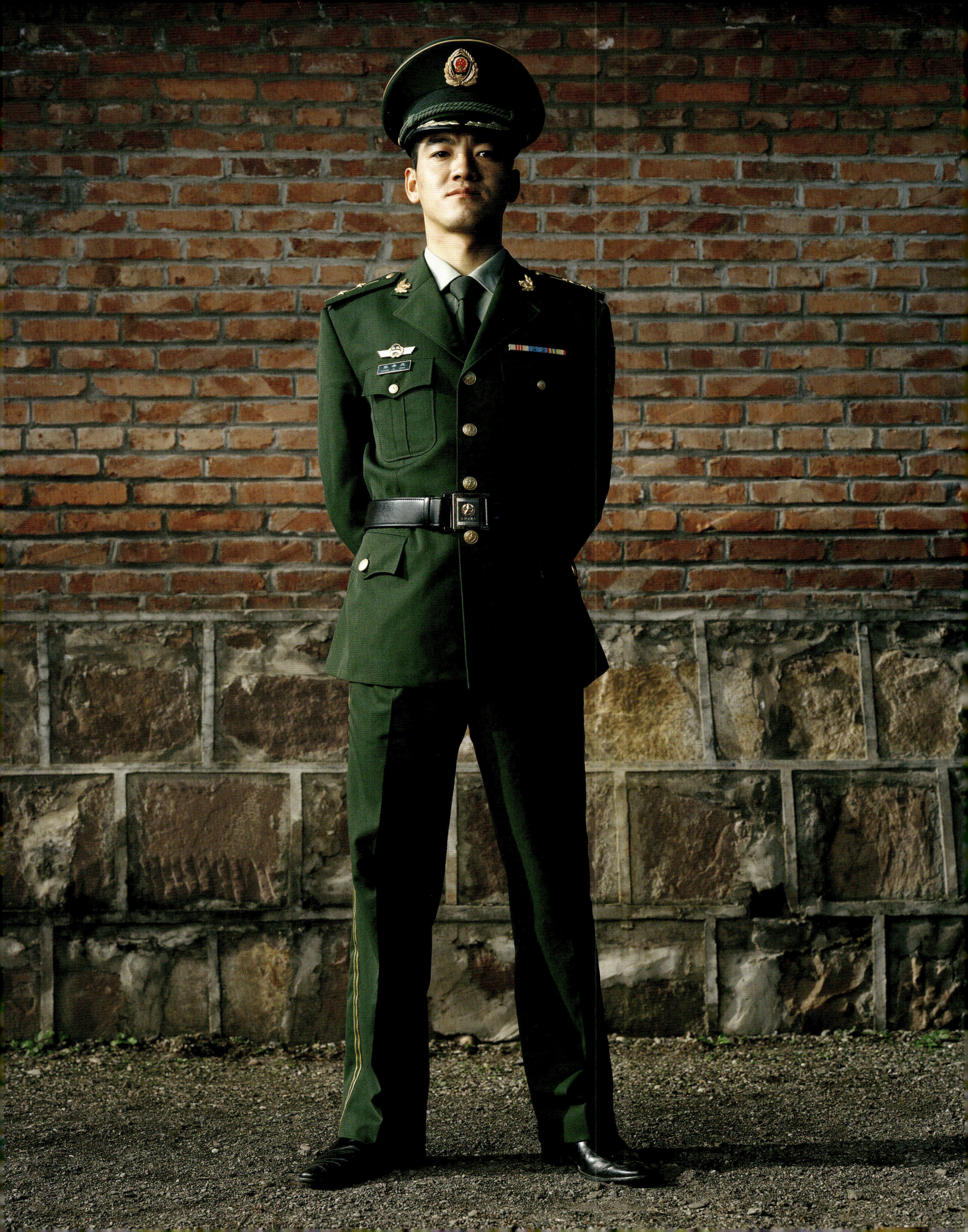

杨金玺 宾兵

Yang Jinxi (21) und / and Bin Bin (21)
Brautpaar
Wedding couple
Wangzuizi, Gansu

Die Hochzeit von Yang Jinxi und Bin Bin, die im sechsten Monat schwanger ist, findet in einem entlegenen Gebiet der Provinz Gansu statt. Ihre Verbindung wurde nicht, wie eigentlich üblich, arrangiert. Sie verliebten sich in Peking in dem Restaurant, in dem beide arbeiteten. Zur Hochzeitsfeier wurde das ganze Dorf eingeladen.

Yang Jinxi and Bin Bin, six months pregnant, are getting married in a remote area of Gansu Province. Theirs is not a customary arranged marriage. They fell in love in Beijing, where they both worked in a restaurant. The whole village was invited to celebrate their wedding.

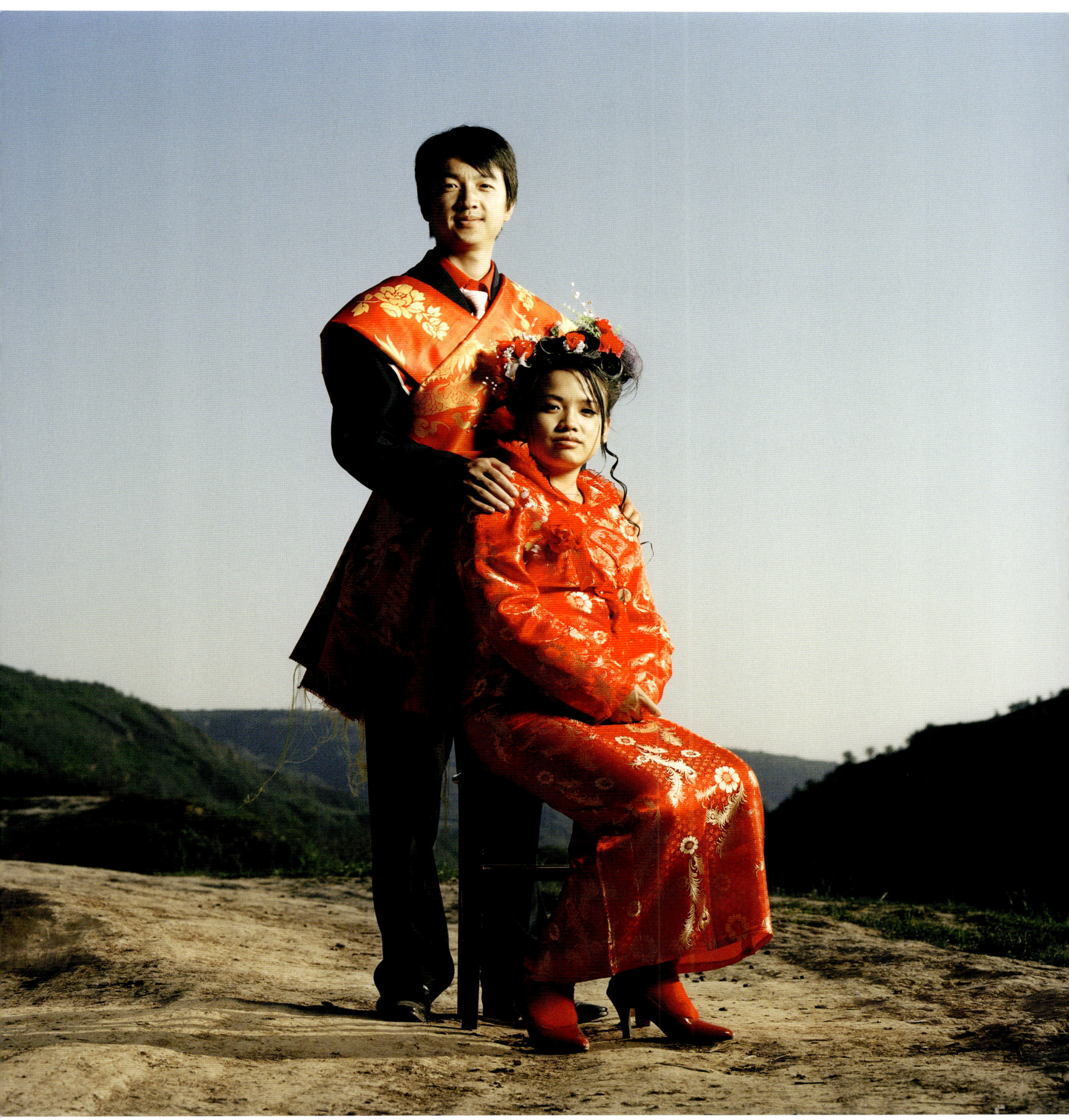

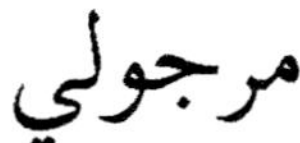

Mirguli (21)
Dorfschönheit
Town beauty
Kumusi, Xinjiang

Die Uigurin Mirguli liebt es, in ihrem besten Outfit die Hauptstraße entlang zu promenieren. Sie könnte sich gut vorstellen, Fotomodell zu werden. Doch außer LKW-Fahrern, die eine Pause machen, hält niemand in der Kleinstadt Kumusi, mitten in der Wüste, an.

The Uyghur girl Mirguli likes to dress up for her walks on the main road and would love to become a photo model, but no one stops in the small town of Kumusi, in the middle of the desert, except truck drivers in need of a rest.

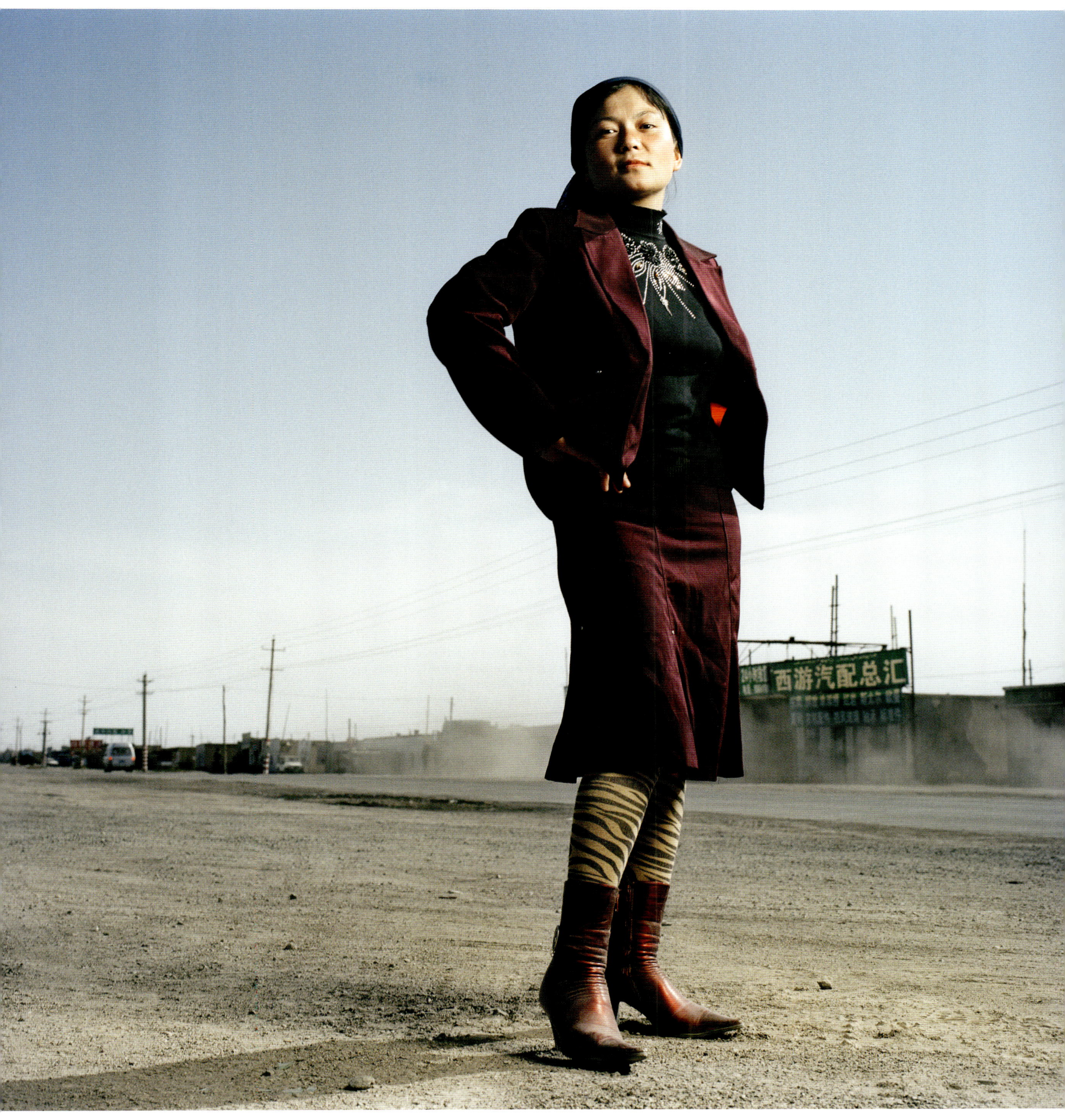
西游汽配总汇

熊富春

Xiong Fuchun (62)
Holzhändler
Wood dealer
Shitan, Jiangxi

In der Provinz Jiangxi in Zentralchina, einer sehr traditionsbewussten Region, kleiden sich viele ältere Männer noch in der klassischen Mao-Art. Während in den Städten die alten Fahrräder langsam verschwinden, sind sie auf dem Land weiterhin das hauptsächliche Transportmittel.

In the province of Jiangxi in Central China, a very traditional area, many elderly men are still dressed in classic Mao style. While old bicycles are disappearing in the cities, they are still the primary means of transportation in rural areas.

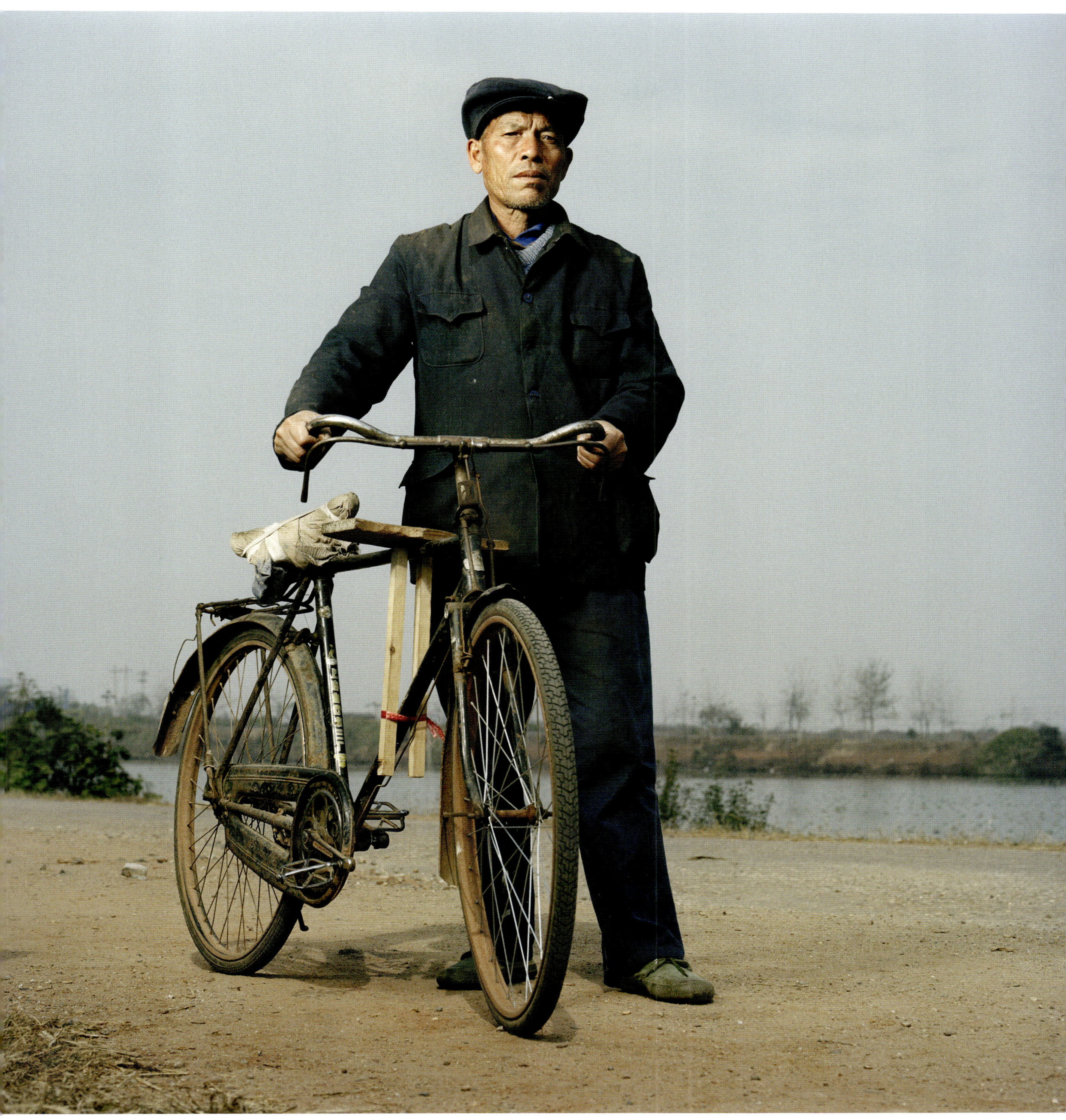

„Chai“ Ricardo Relucio Jr. (33)
Singender Gondoliere des Venetian Casino
Singing gondolier at the Venetian Casino
Macao

„Chai“ Ricardo Relucio Jr. arbeitet als Gondoliere im Venetian Casino in Macao, einer originalgetreuen Kopie des Kasinos in Las Vegas. Wichtigste Voraussetzung für seinen Job ist, italienische Arien singen zu können. Derzeit setzen die Casinos in Macao mehr Geld um als die Originale in Nevada.

"Chai" is proud to be a gondolier at Macao's Venetian Casino, an exact copy of the Las Vegas "Venetian". The most important skill for his job is his ability to sing Italian arias. Today, the casinos in Macao make more money than the originals in Nevada.

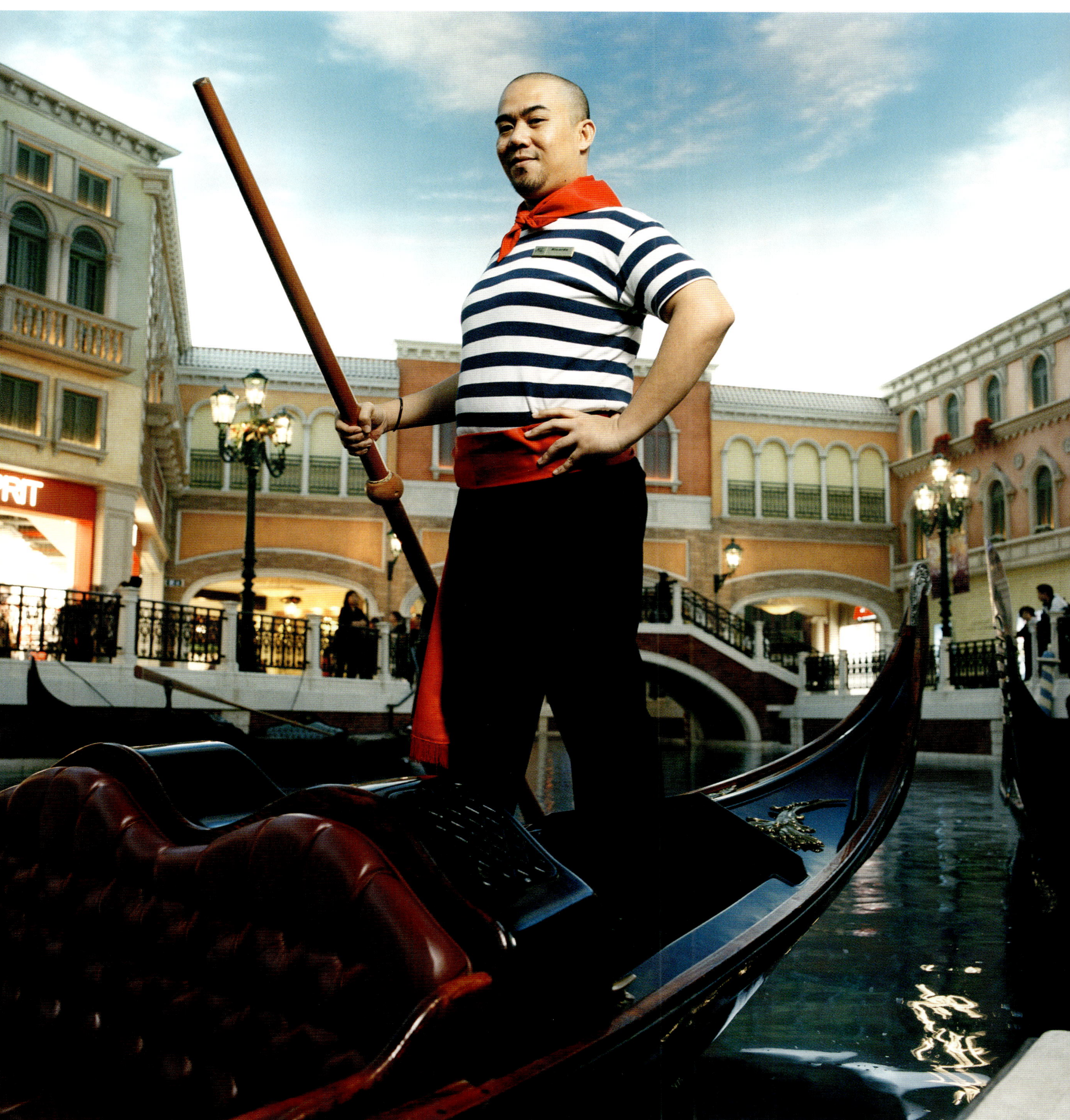

李宝才

Li Baocai (56)
Bauer
Farmer
Habiriga, Innere Mongolei / Inner Mongolia

Li Baocai konnte nie eine Schule besuchen und hat sein Dorf kaum jemals verlassen. Ein weiteres Jahr ohne Regen hat die Dorfgemeinschaft in eine schwierige Situation gebracht und erneut bleibt die Ernte aus.

Li Baocai never attended school or travelled very far away from his village. Another year of drought has again left the village struggling and with nothing to harvest.

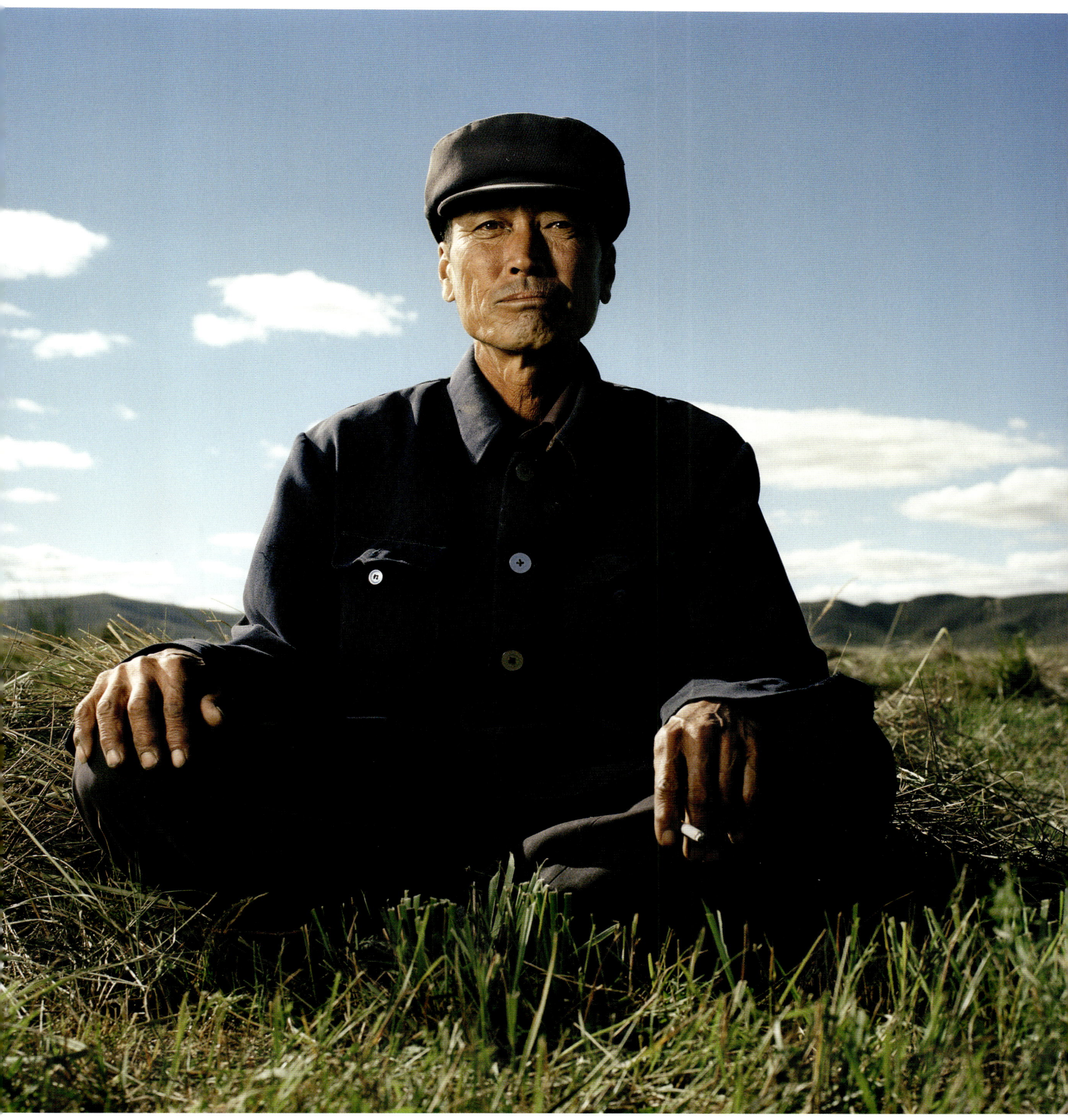

彭辉阳

Peng Yanghui (23)
Student
Student
Guiyang, Guizhou

Peng Yanghui studiert die Schriften von Marx für seine Hochschulaufnahmeprüfung. Er sitzt auf einem Hügel mit Blick über Guiyang, der Hauptstadt der Provinz Guizhou. Sein Ziel ist, chinesische Geschichte zu studieren und Lehrer zu werden.

Peng Yanghui brushes up on Marx for his university entry exam on a hilltop overlooking Guiyang, the capital of Guizhou Province. His goal is to study Chinese history and to become a teacher.

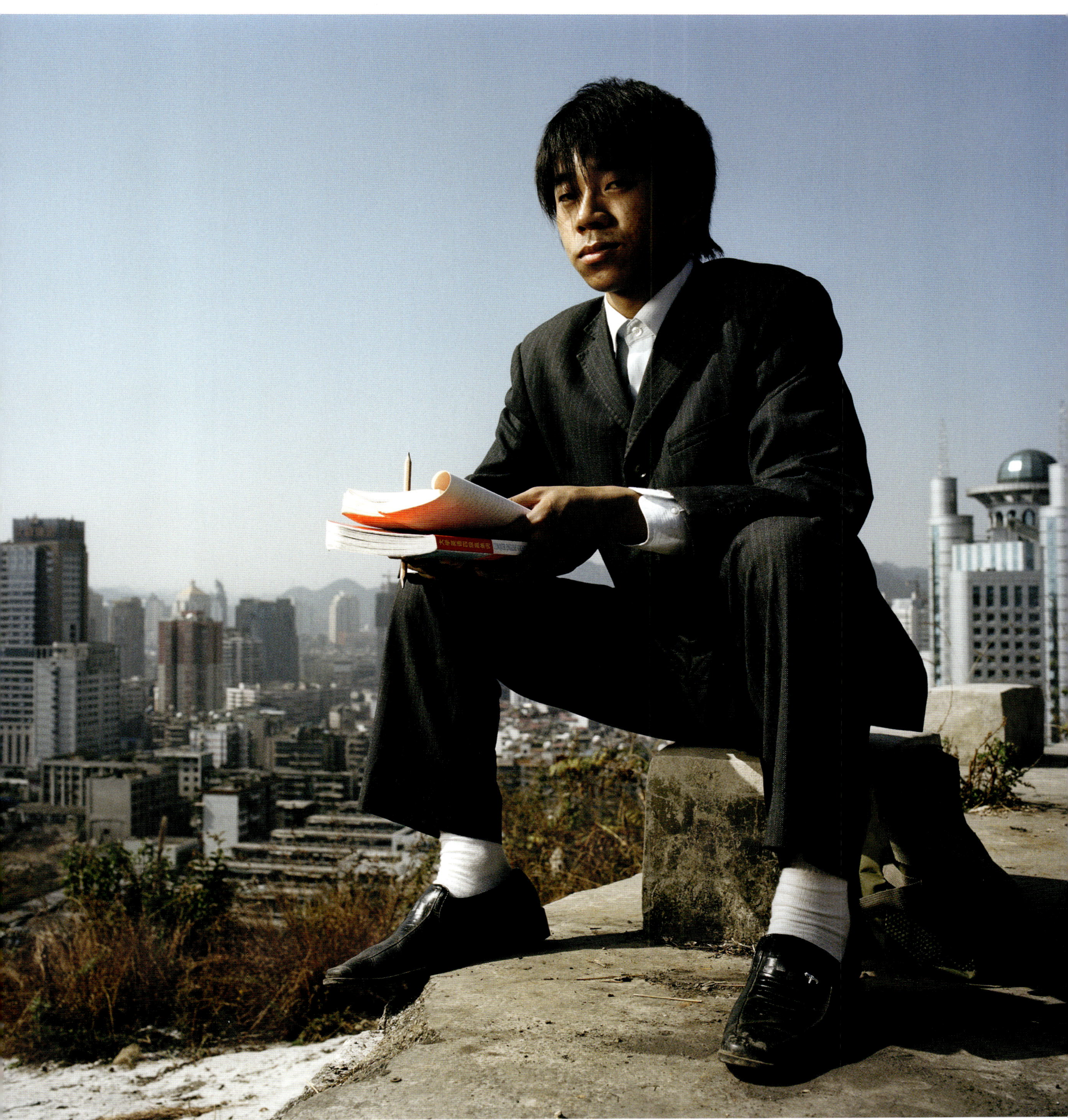

ངག་དབང་
ཧིན་གྲིབ་
ནོར་རི་
ཚེ་བརྟན་

Ngawang (22), Hindrib (21), Nori (29) und / and
Tseten (25)
Pilger
Pilgrims
Sichuan

Ngawang, Hindrib, Nori und Tseten sind tibetische Pilger auf dem Weg nach Lhasa. Sie sind Brüder bzw. Cousins und benötigen von ihrer Heimatstadt aus ungefähr 4 Monate für die Wanderung nach Lhasa. Alle sind in einem kleinen Dorf im Norden Sichuans in einer Region, die größtenteils tibetisch geprägt ist, aufgewachsen. Die meisten Tibeter sind tief religiös. Mindestens einmal im Leben nach Lhasa zu pilgern, ist für sie eine religiöse Pflicht.

Ngawang, Hindrib, Nori and Tseten are Tibetan pilgrims on their way to Lhasa. They are brothers and cousins from the same family on a 4-month walk from their hometown to Lhasa. They all grew up in a small village in the North of Sichuan Province, an area which is essentially Tibetan. Most Tibetans are deeply religious and walking to Lhasa as a pilgrim at least once in their life is a religious duty.

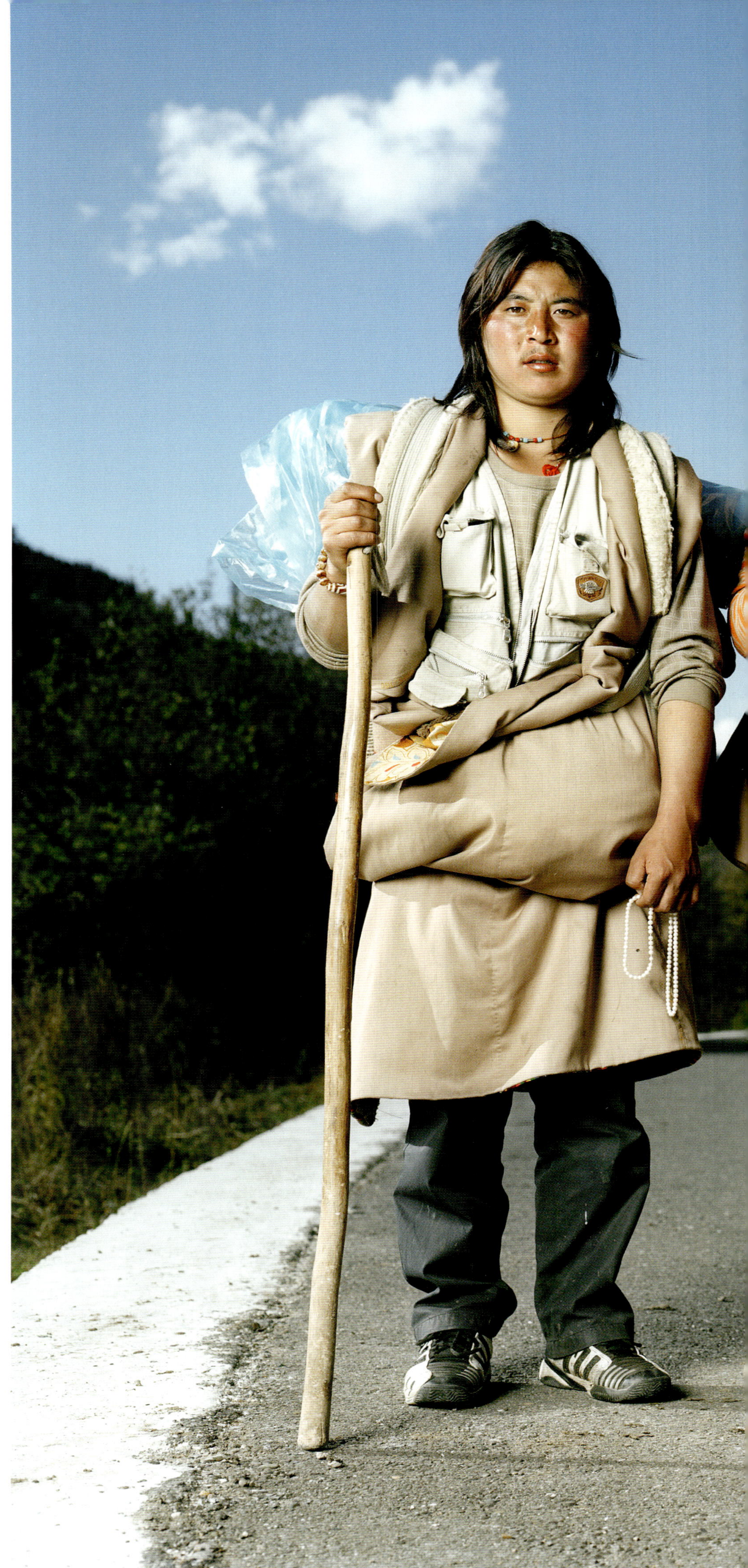

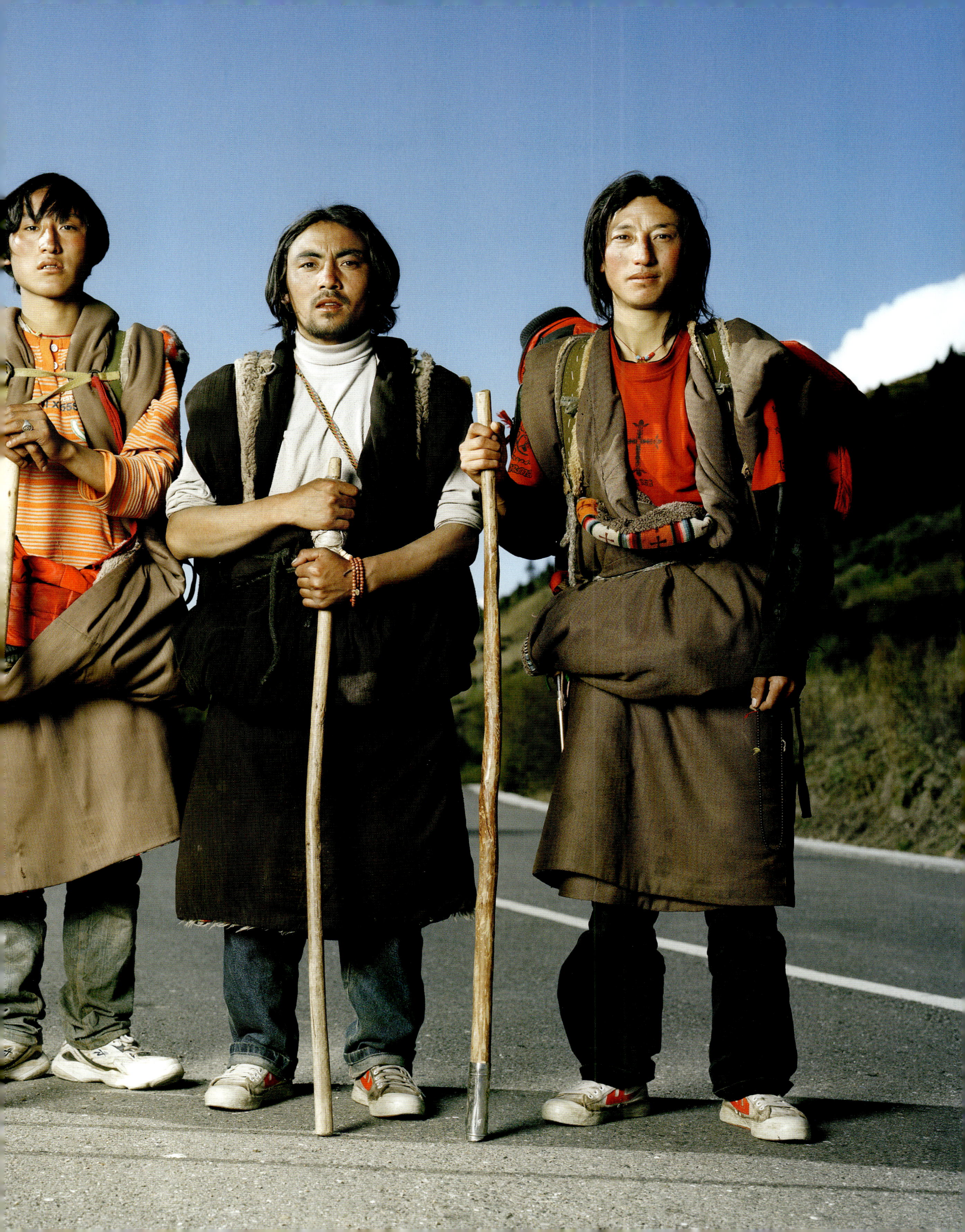

马静　李海峰

Ma Jing (46) und / and Li Haifeng (45)
Besitzer des Penglai Eight
Immortals Geschäftsimperiums
Owners of the Penglai Eight
Immortals business empire
Penglai, Shandong

Ma Jing, die Tochter eines Generals, und ihr Mann Li Haifeng sind als Besitzer eines Geschäftsimperiums die mächtigsten Einwohner der Stadt Penglai. Ihr neuestes Projekt ist der Bau eines Luxus-Hotelkomplexes im imperialen Stil.

Ma Jing, the daughter of a general, and her husband Li Haifeng are the most powerful people in the city of Penglai and the owners of a business empire. Their latest project is building a luxury hotel complex in the style of an old imperial palace.

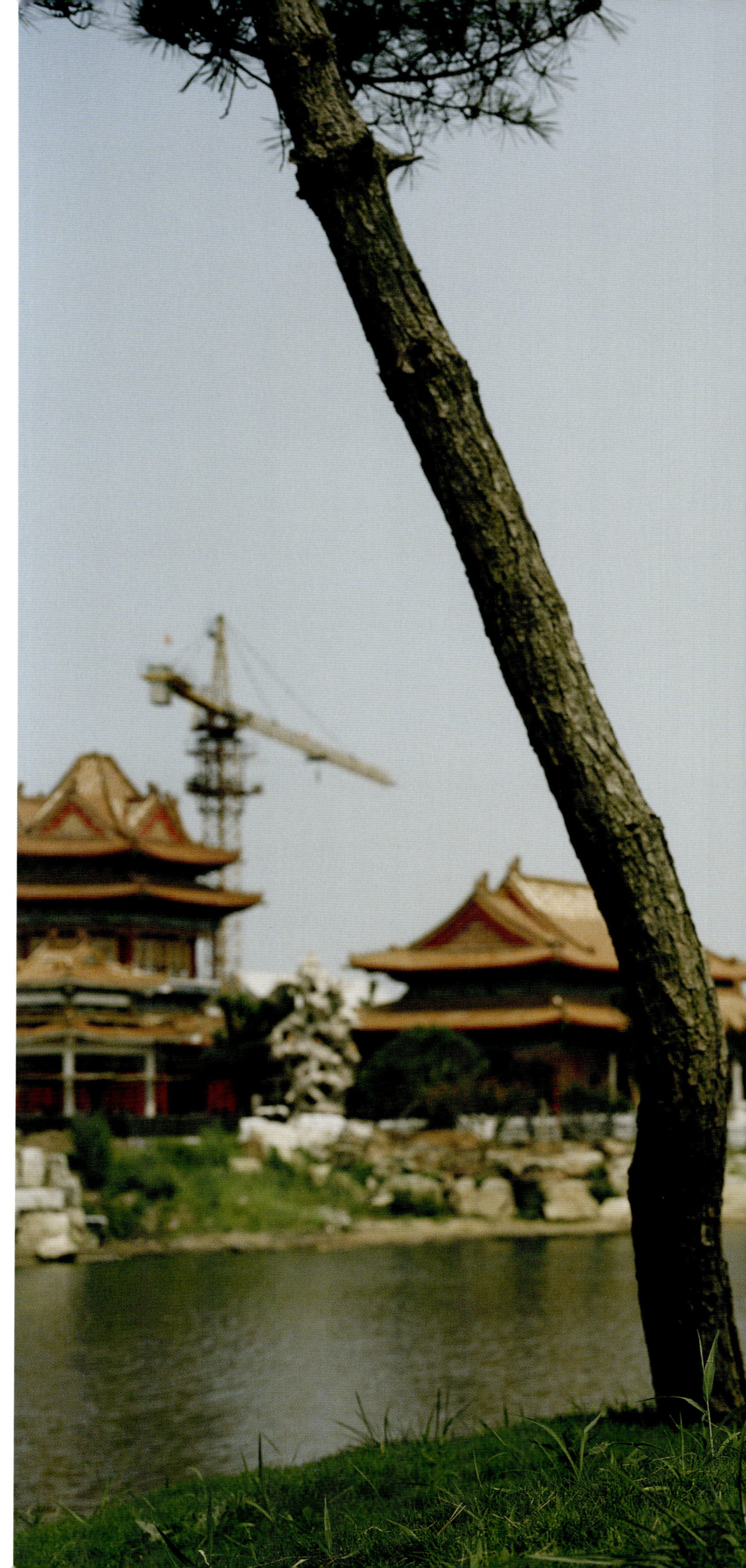

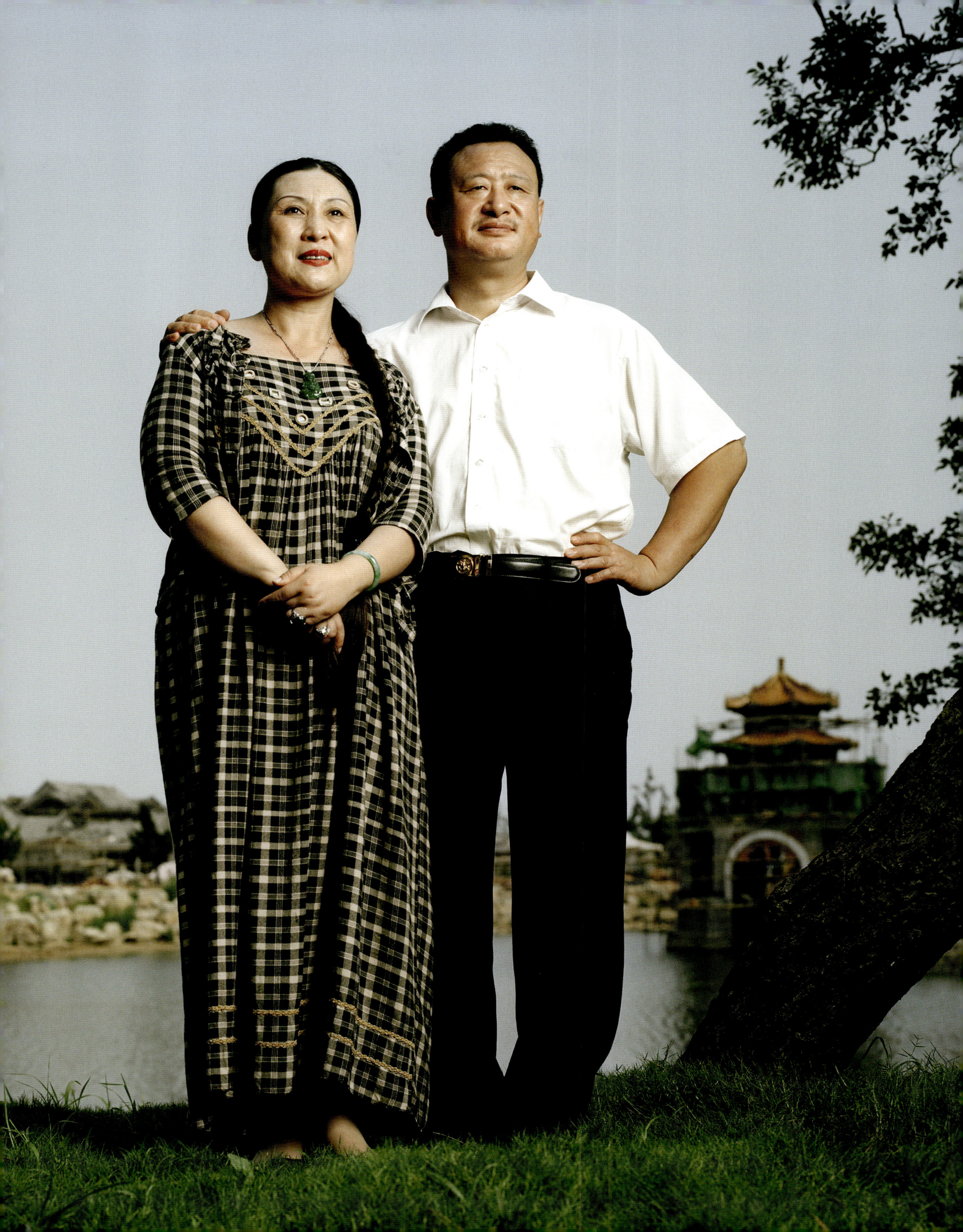

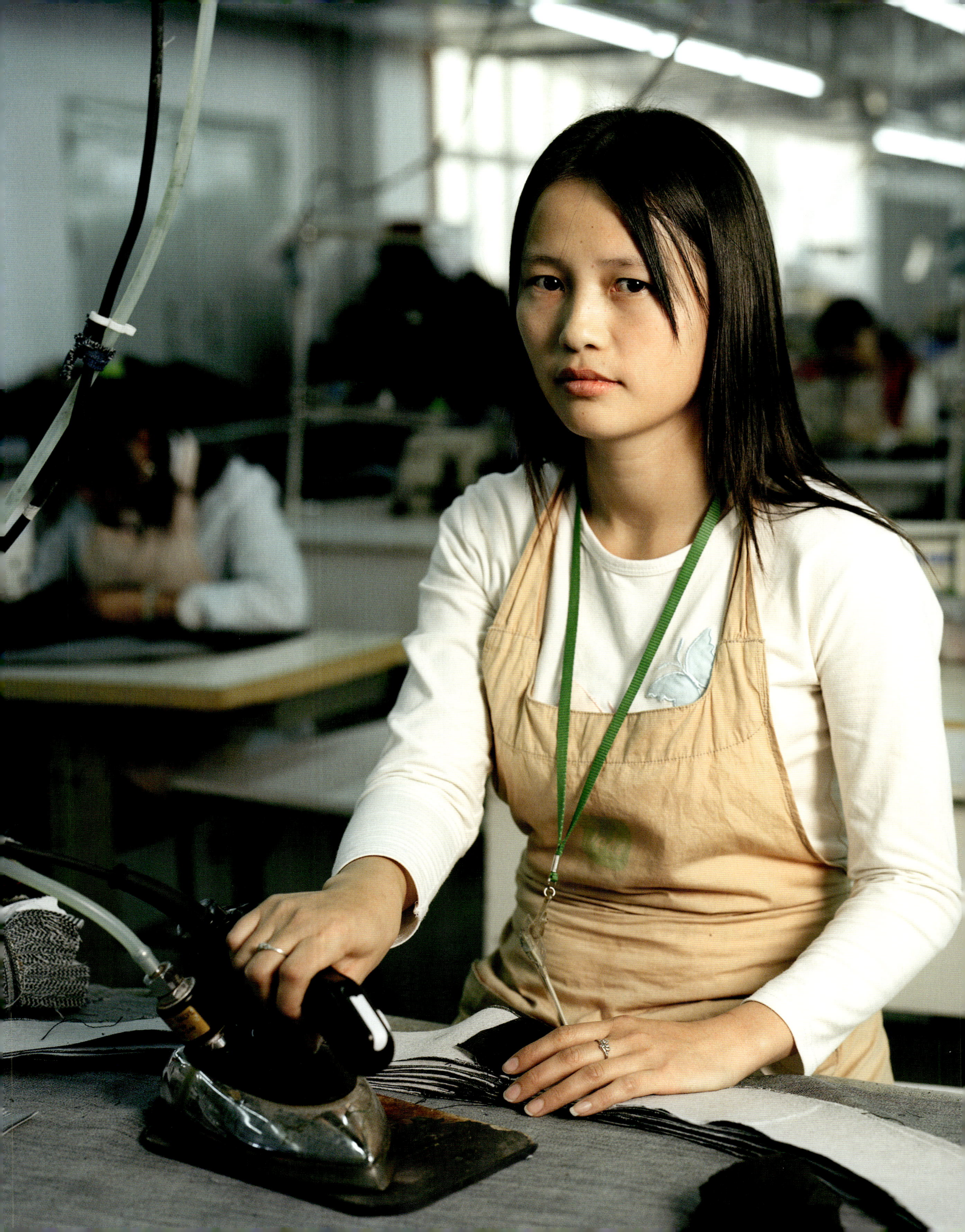

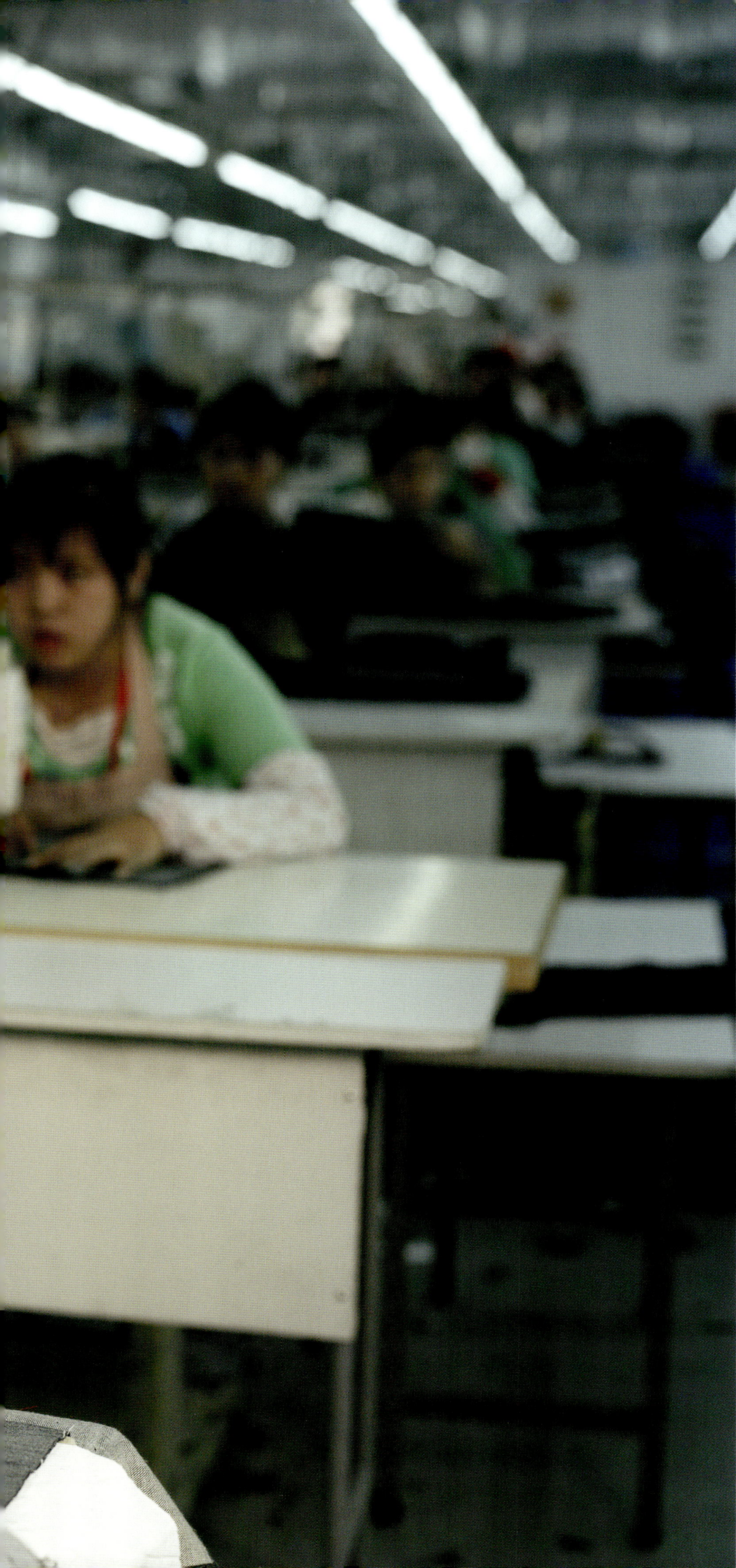

刘宝珠

Liu Baozhu (25)
Arbeiterin
Worker
Nanshui, Guangdong

Liu Baozhu arbeitet in einer Fertigungslinie in einer Textilfabrik. Die überwiegende Mehrheit der in dieser Fabrik produzierten Kleidung wird für den Westen hergestellt und bald in Berlin, London oder Paris verkauft. Liu Baozhu verdient um die 80 Euro im Monat – ungefähr soviel, wie ein Kunde in Europa für das Paar Jeans bezahlt, an dem sie gerade arbeitet.

Liu Baozhu is part of a production line in a textile factory located in Guangdong Province. The vast majority of the clothes produced in this factory is for Western clients and will soon be sold in Paris, Berlin or London. Liu Baozhu makes about 80 euro per month – approximately what customers will pay in Europe for the pair of jeans she is working on.

张文祥

Zhang Wenxiang (32)
Bauer
Farmer
Miaoniaohe, Sichuan

Zhang Wenxiang besitzt zwei Wasserbüffel und ungefähr 100 Quadratmeter Land. Um sein Feld zu bewirtschaften, nutzt er immer noch die gleichen Werkzeuge wie seine Vorfahren vor fünfhundert Jahren, während die Raketenabschussbasis für Chinas Weltraumprogramm weniger als 50 Kilometer von Zhangs Feld entfernt liegt.

Zhang Wenxiang just owns two water buffalos and a piece of land, around 100 square meters in size. Zhang still uses the same tools that were used in ancient times to tend his field, while the rocket launch site for China's space program is located only around 50 kilometers from his field.

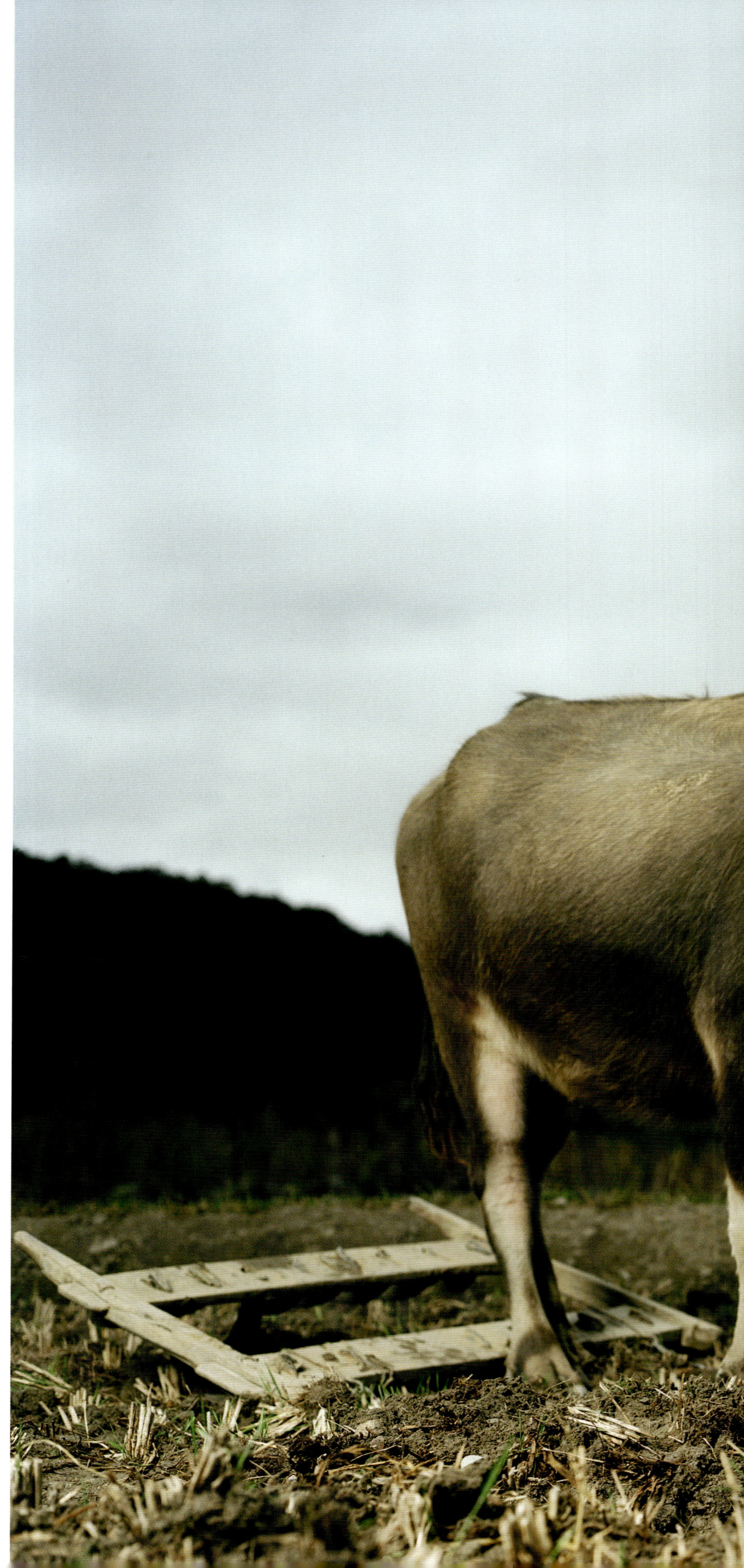

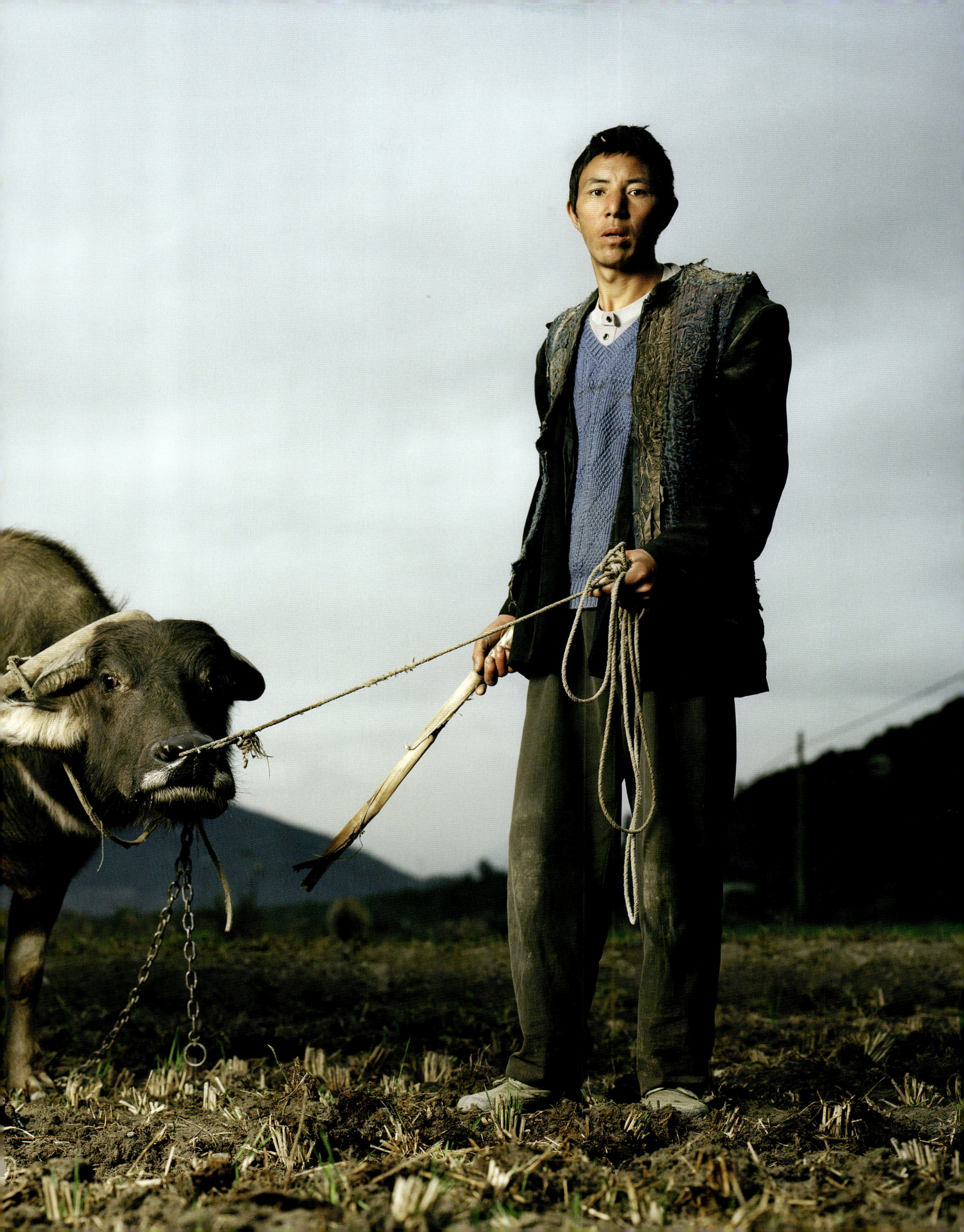

黄淑芬

Huang Shufen (81)
Flaschensammlerin
Bottle collector
Gaojiayan, Guizhou

Jeden Tag nimmt Huang Shufen den langen Weg zu einer Autobahnbaustelle auf sich, um dort leere Plastikflaschen zu sammeln. Der Beutel, den sie trägt, enthält die Früchte eines ganzen beschwerlichen Arbeitstages. Sie bekommt einen Cent pro Flasche. In einem Monat verdient sie zwischen fünf und zehn Euro.

Every day Huang Shufen walks to a highway construction site in Guizhou Province to collect empty PET bottles. The bag she carries contains a long day's work. She gets one cent per bottle and earns around five to ten euro per month.

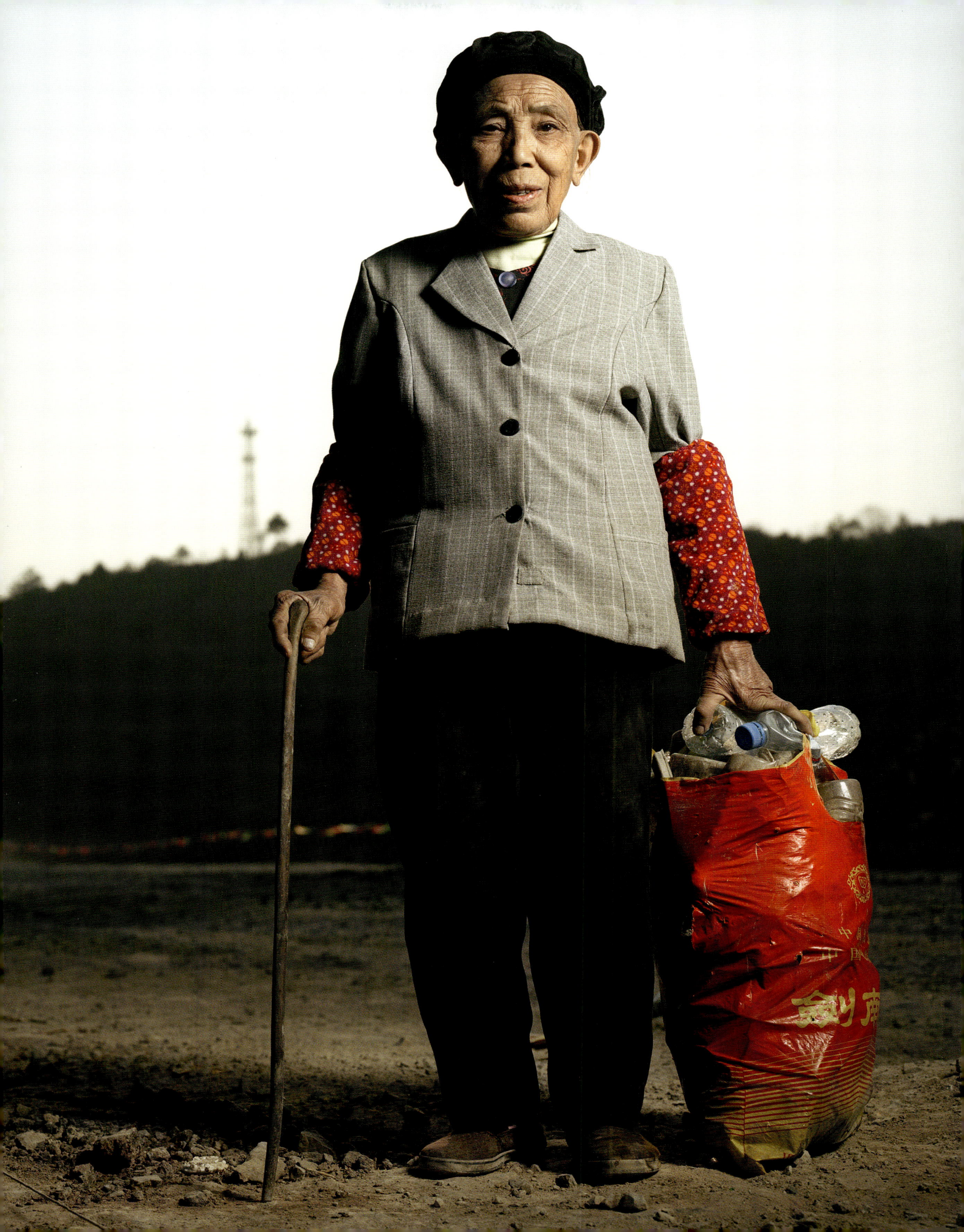

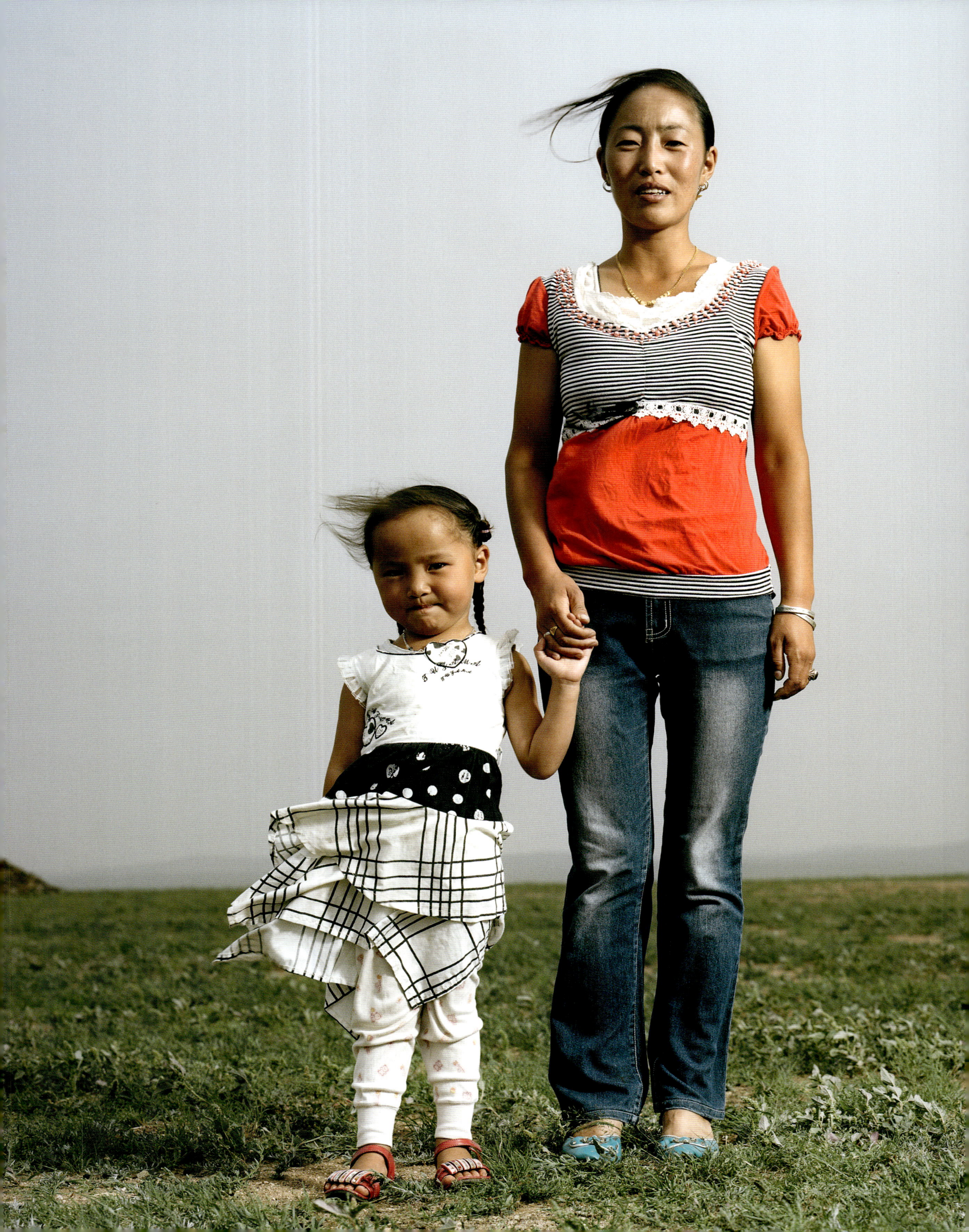

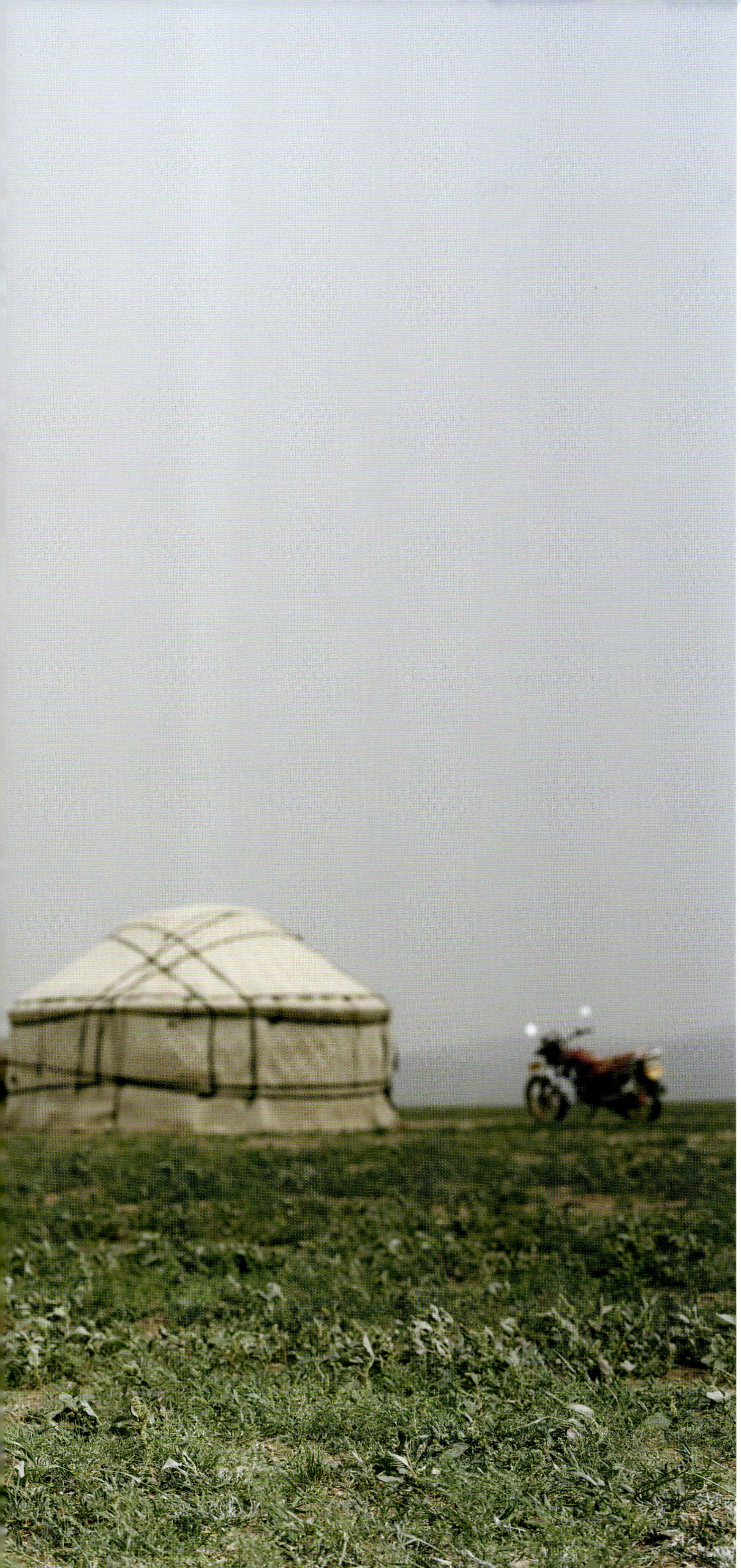

Wuluchua (26) und ihre Tochter / and her daughter
Angerma (4)
Mongolische Nomaden
Mongolian nomads
Donwuzhumuqin, Innere Mongolei / Inner Mongolia

Wuluchua lebt das ganze Jahr über in einer mongolischen Jurte und kümmert sich um die Schafe und Kühe, während ihr Ehemann als Taxifahrer in der nahen Stadt Geld für die Familie verdient.

Wuluchua lives in her Mongolian yurt all year round, looking after her sheep and cows, while her husband makes extra money for the family as a taxi driver in the nearby city.

何光华

He Guanghua (43)
Schmied
Blacksmith
Shuanglong, Chongqing

He Guanghua schmiedet in seiner kleinen Werkstatt im Drei-Schluchten-Tal meist Äxte, die er für 50 Cent pro Stück verkauft.

He Guanghua forges mostly axes in his small blacksmith shop in the Three Gorges Valley, which he sells for 50 cents each.

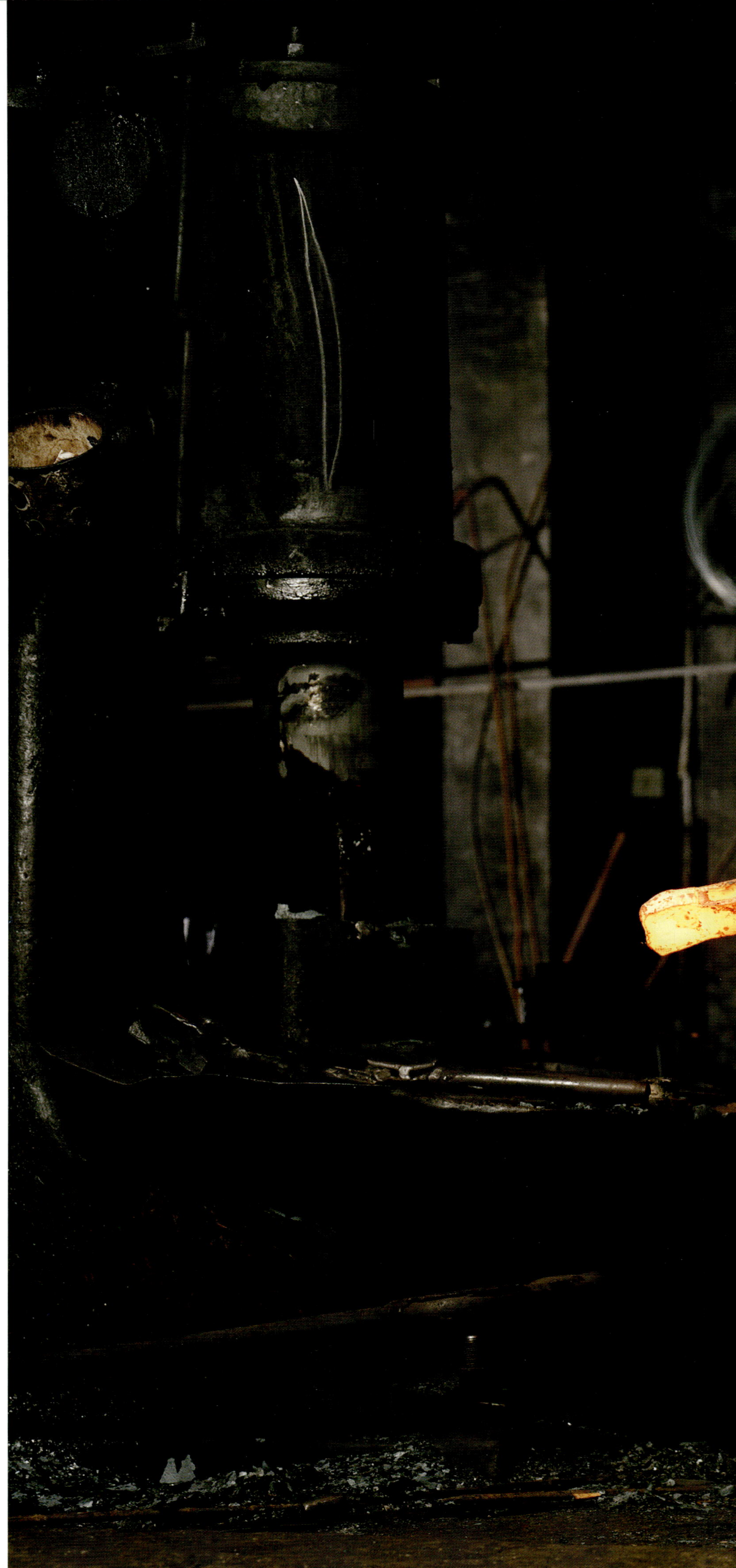

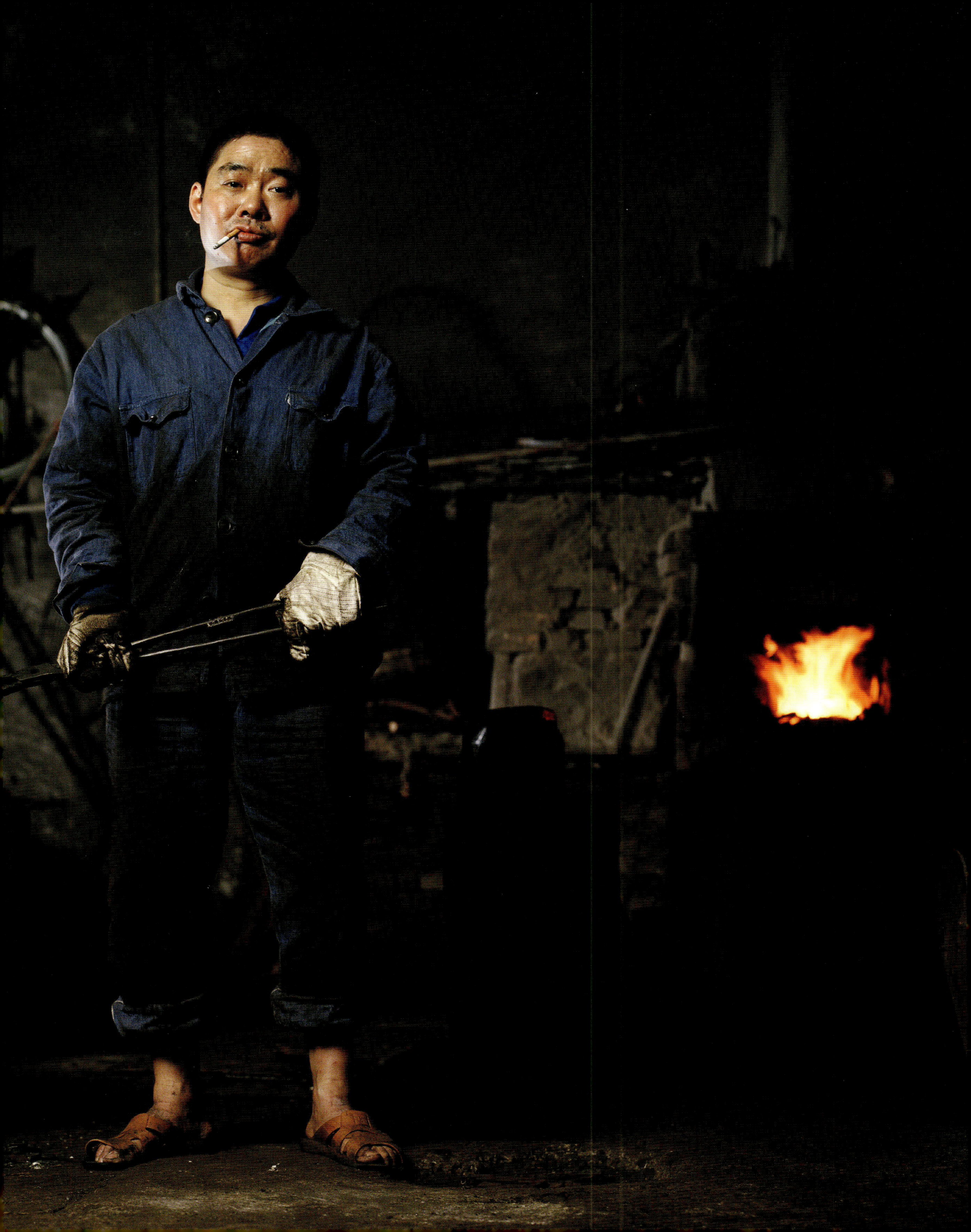

姚冬梅

Yao Dongmei (41)
Projektleiterin
Project Manager
Peking / Beijing

Das von Rem Koolhaas entworfene Gebäude der Central Television Headquarters gilt als eines der prestigeträchtigsten und spektakulärsten architektonischen Wahrzeichen Asiens. Yao Dongmei ist Projektleiterin auf der Baustelle des CCTV-Tower in Peking.

The Central Television Headquarters designed by Rem Koolhaas are considered one of the most prestigious and impressive architectural landmarks in Asia. Yao Dongmei is the project manager at the construction site of the CCTV Tower.

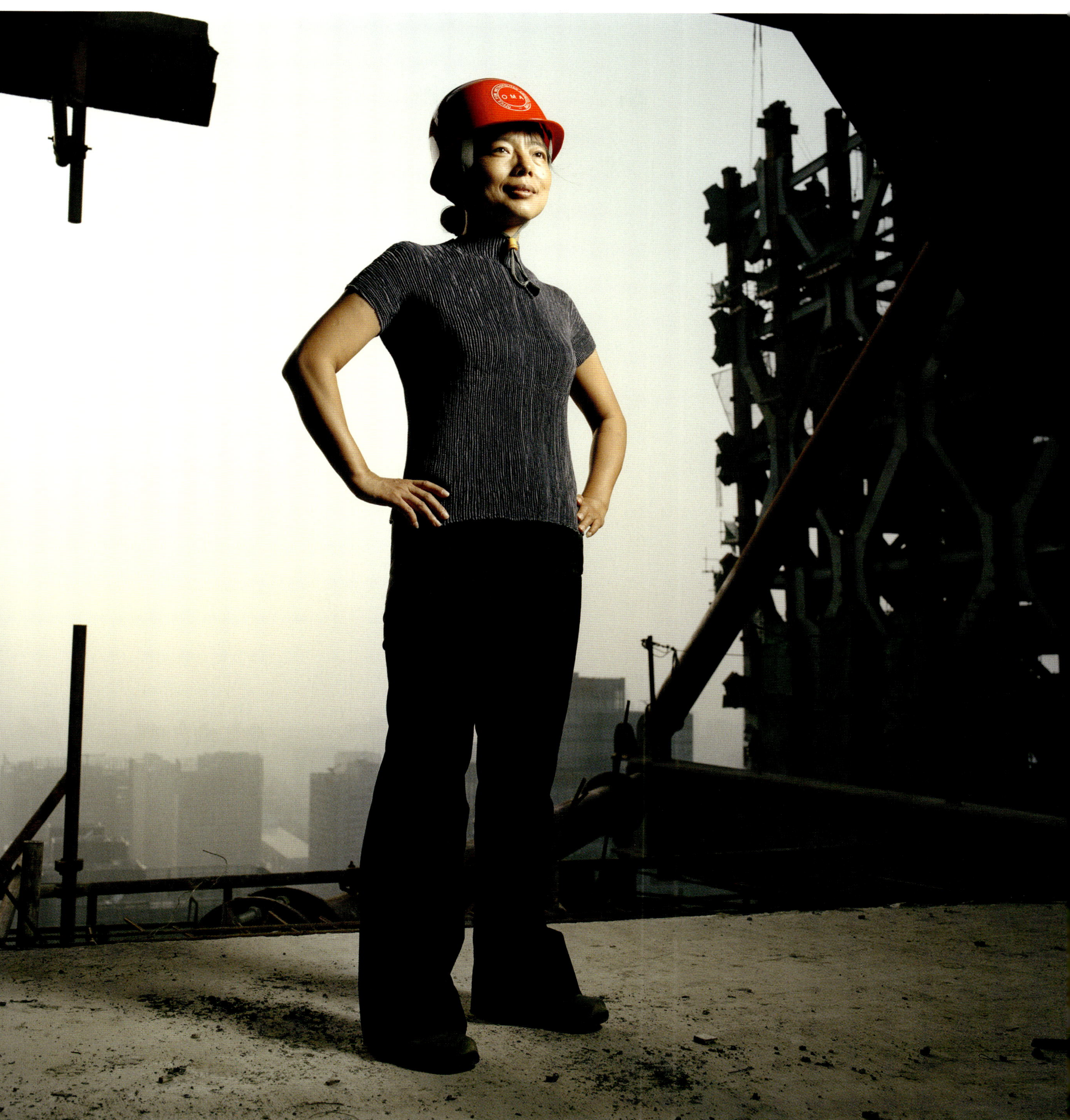
OMA

钟汝芳

Zhong Rufang (41)
Frauenärztin
Gynaecologist
An'ding, Yunnan

Zhong Rufang arbeitet als Krankenhausärztin in einem abgelegenen Tal in der Provinz Yunnan. Als Gynäkologin unterstützt sie Mütter bei der Entbindung ihres einzigen Kindes. Zu ihren Aufgaben zählt auch, die Menschen über die Ein-Kind-Politik zu informieren, wobei sie jedoch nicht immer erfolgreich ist. Manchmal muss sie Zwangsabtreibungen, sogar noch im siebten oder achten Schwangerschaftsmonat, vornehmen.

Zhong Rufang is a doctor in a local hospital in a remote valley of Yunnan Province. As a gynaecologist she helps mothers to give birth to their only child. She is also in charge of teaching the one child policy, but she doesn't always succeed with her lessons. Sometimes she has to perform forced abortions; even late-term, up to the seventh or eighth month of pregnancy.

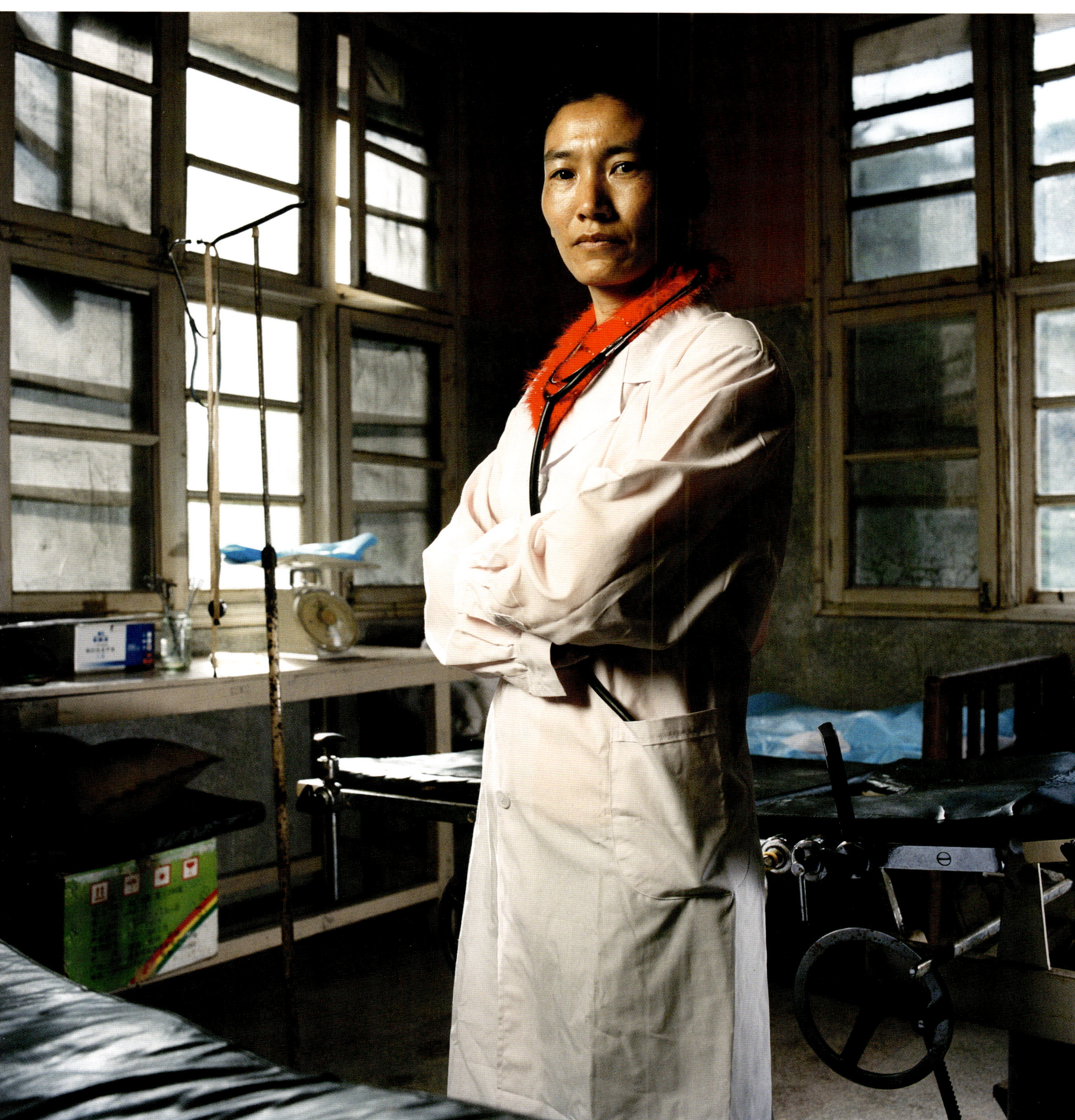

李楚君

Li Chujun (20)
Mode-Großhändlerin
Fashion wholesale trader
Shanghai

Li Chujun geht gerne auf dem Bund, der Uferpromenade vor der berühmten Skyline von Pudong, spazieren. Als junge und trendige Frau aus Shanghai sind für sie eine modische Handtasche, vorzugsweise von Louis Vuitton, und ein glänzendes Handy wichtige Accessoires.

Li Chujun loves to stroll on the Bund, in front of the famous Pudong skyline. For Shanghais' young and trendy a fashionable handbag, preferably from Louis Vuitton, and a shiny cell phone are essential accessories.

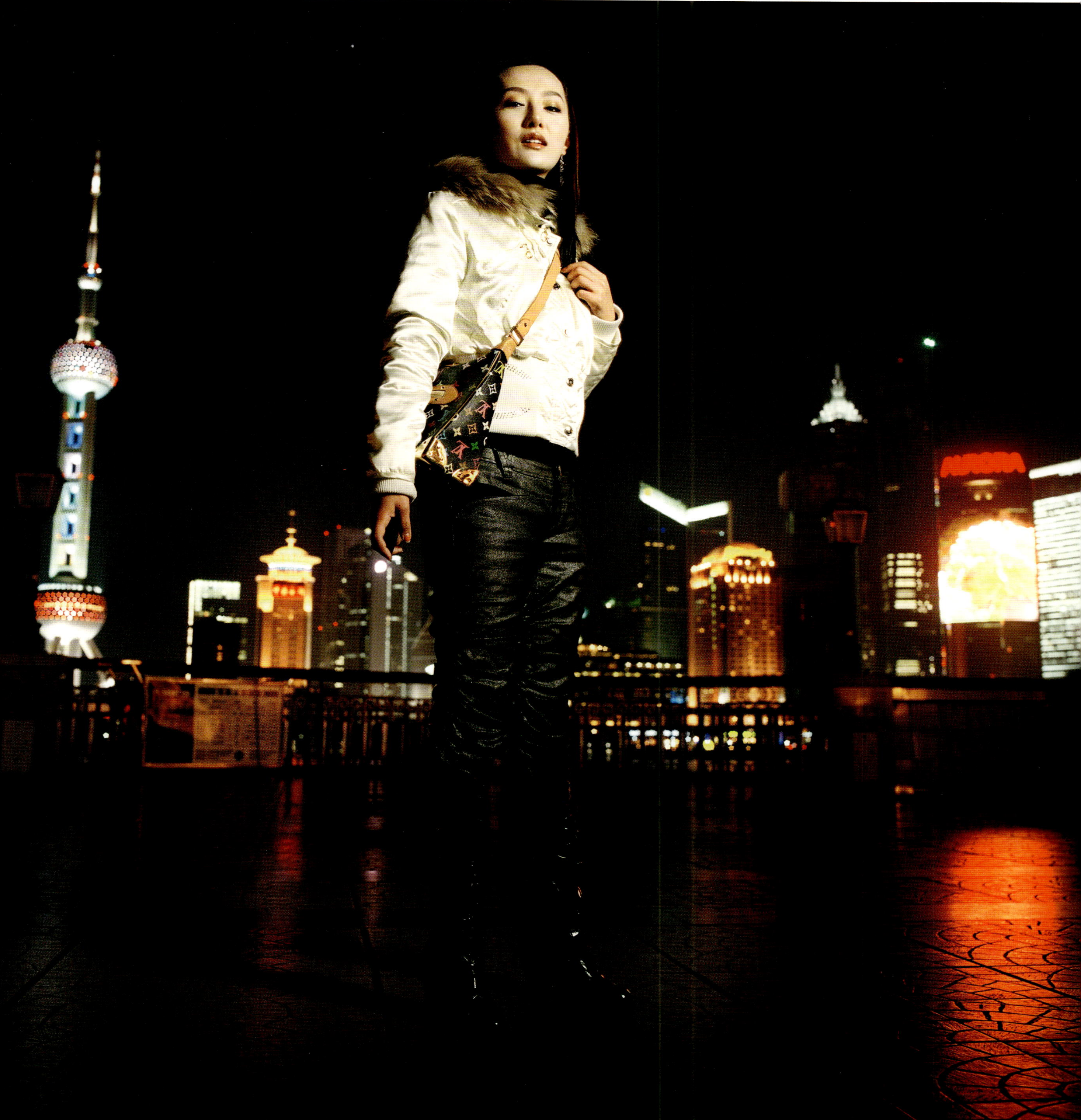

苏青田　苏瑞友　田凤琴

Su Qingtian (80), Su Ruiyou (59) und / and
Tian Fengqin (56)
Bauern
Farmers
Jiangjiagan, Innere Mongolei / Inner Mongolia

Su Qingtian, sein Sohn Su Ruiyou und dessen Frau Tian Fengqin dreschen das Getreide noch genauso wie ihre Vorfahren vor Hunderten von Jahren. Die Familie lebt in einem winzigen Dorf in der Inneren Mongolei, wo noch kaum Ausländer vorbeigekommen sind.

Su Qingtian, his son Su Ruiyou and his son's wife Tian Fengqin still thresh wheat just as their ancestors did hundreds of years ago. The family lives in a tiny village in Inner Mongolia where foreigners hardly ever pass through.

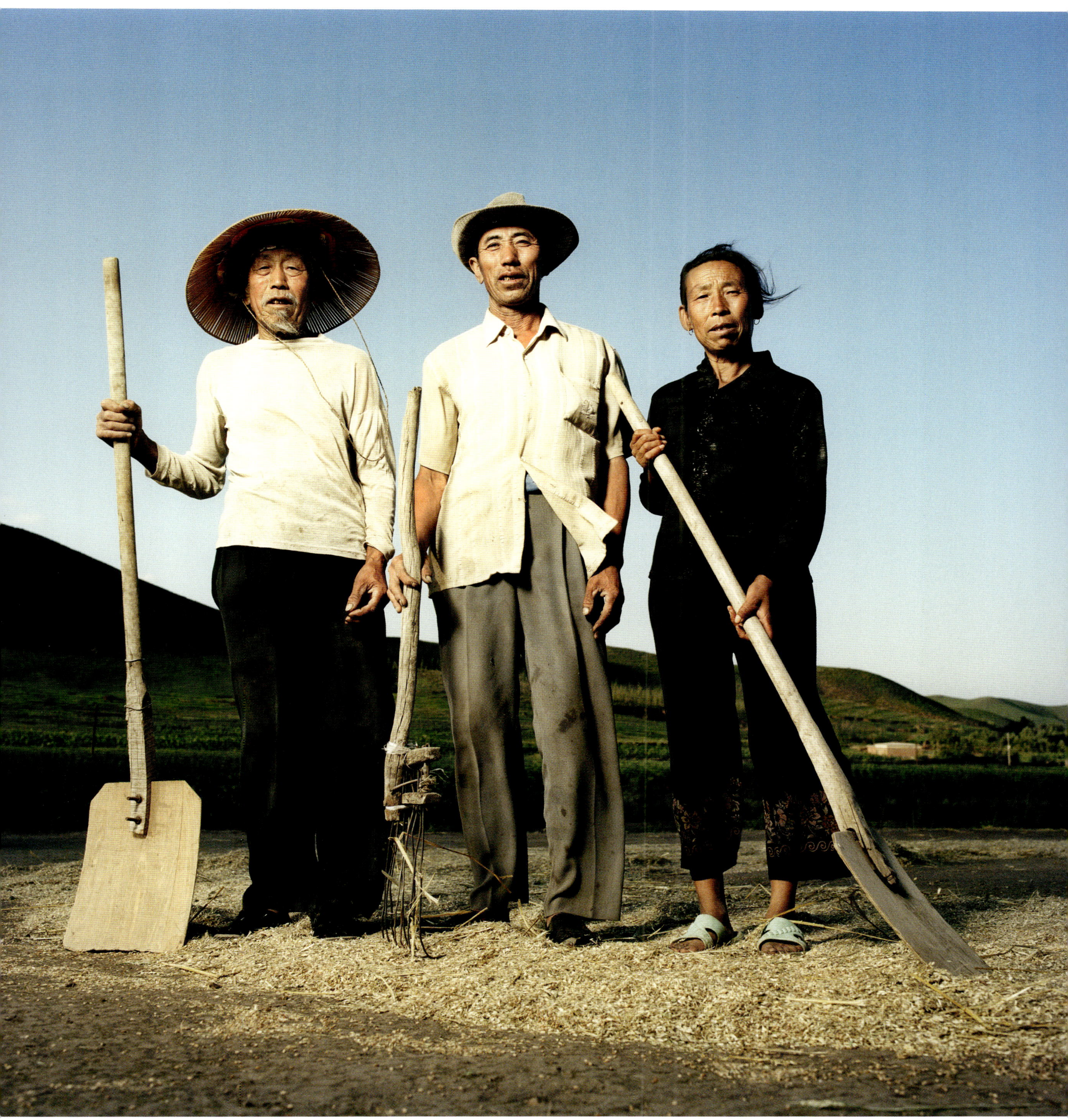

夏阳

Xia Yang (40)
Präsident und Inhaber des Sunny Times Polo-Club, Unternehmer
President and owner of Sunny Times Polo Club, entrepreneur
Kangzhuang, Peking / Kangzhuang, Beijing

Der Tycoon Xia Yang, Gründer des ersten Polo-Clubs im modernen China, führte inspiriert durch Prinz Charles Polo wieder im kommunistischen China ein. Schon vor mehr als 1800 Jahren wurde in China Polo gespielt, aber während Maos Kulturrevolution war dieser Sport als elitär geächtet. Auf Xia Yangs Anwesen außerhalb von Peking werden Dutzende Pferde in hochmodernen Ställen verwöhnt und trainiert.

Tycoon Xia Yang, founder of the first modern era polo club, was inspired by Prince Charles to restore polo to Communist China. Polo first appeared into China more than 1800 years ago, but died out during the turmoil of Chairman Mao's Cultural Revolution. Dozens of horses are pampered in Xia Yang's state-of-the-art stables on his estate outside Beijing.

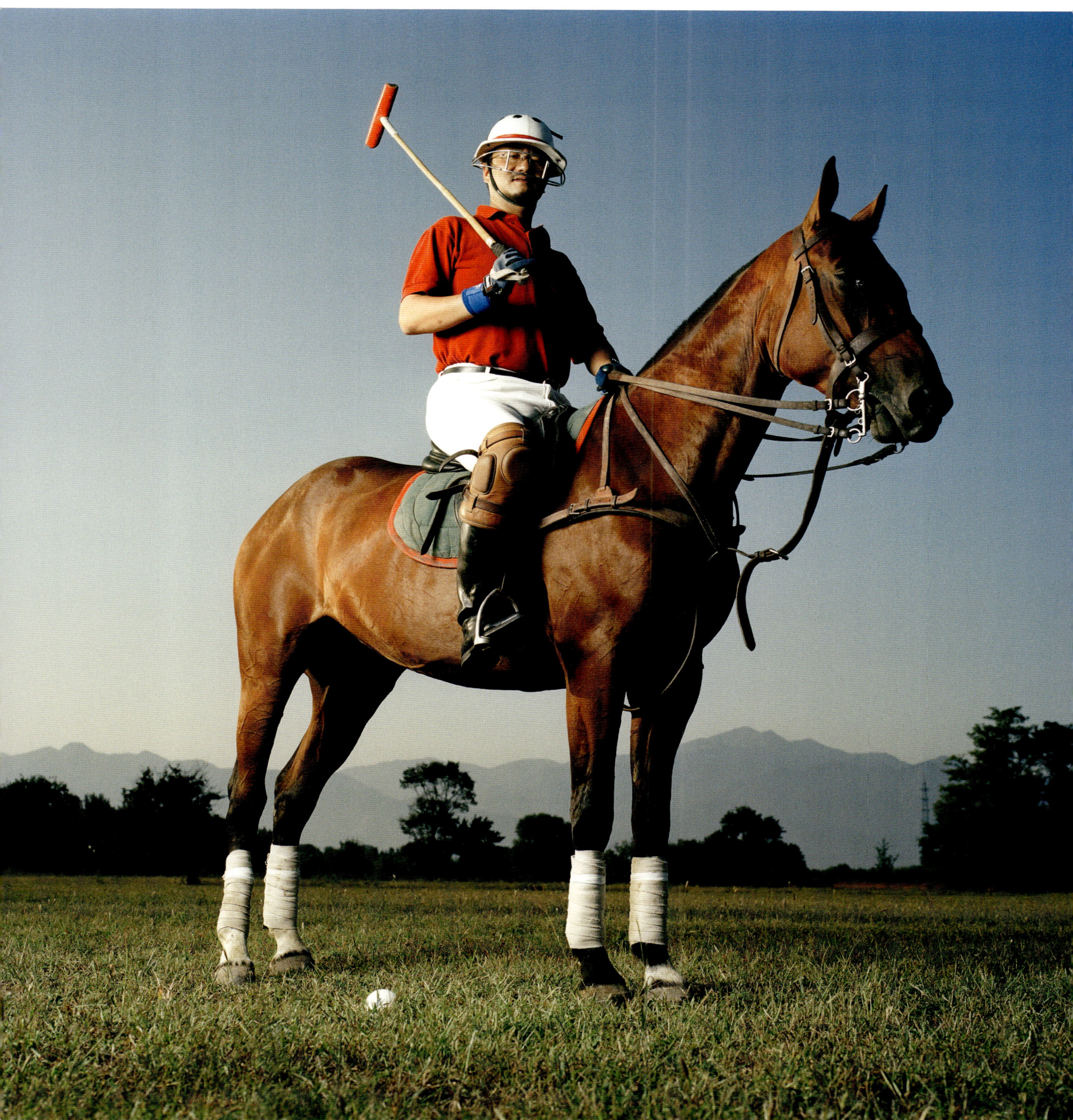

架巴桑

Chabasan (47)
Mongolischer Nomade
Mongolian nomad
Sanggenluoke, Qinghai

Auf dem Rücken seines Pferdes folgt Chabasan seiner Kamelherde weite Strecken durch die Sandwüste. Als mongolischer Nomade lebt er in einem Zelt auf der Hochebene der Provinz Qinghai und ist stolzer Besitzer von 30 Kamelen, 25 Yaks und 7 Pferden.

Chabasan follows his camel herd over great distances through a sandy desert on horseback. As a Mongolian nomad, he lives in a tent on the high plateau of Qinghai Province and is the proud owner of 30 camels, 25 yaks and 7 horses.

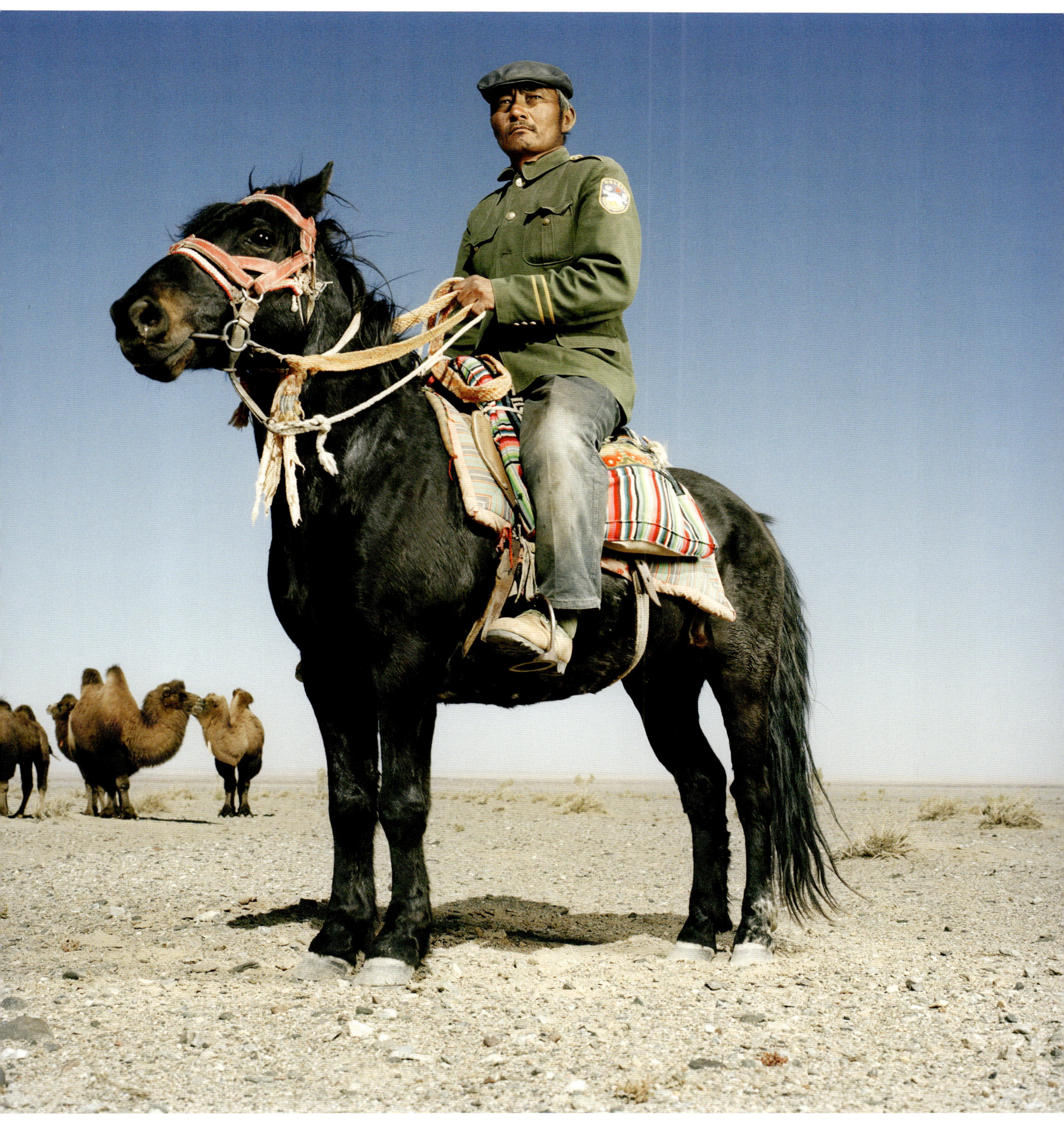

张正祥

Zhang Zhengxiang (58)
See- und Umweltaktivist
Lake activist, environmentalist
Kunming, Yunnan

Zhang Zhengxiang ist ein Umweltaktivist, der sich für die Rettung des Dian-Sees in der Provinz Yunnan einsetzt. Er hat sein ganzes Leben und seine gesamte Energie diesem See gewidmet. Der Dian-See ist tot, verseucht durch hochgradig giftige Algen, die fast den ganzen See in einem giftgrünen Licht schimmern lassen. Fabriken und Gärtnereibetriebe entledigen sich ihrer Industrieabfälle und Abwässer, indem sie sie in den See leiten.

Zhang Zhengxiang fights to rescue Lake Dian in Yunnan Province. He dedicates his life and all his means and energy to this one purpose. Dian Lake is dead, polluted by highly toxic algae that make nearly the entire lake glow bright green. Factories and market gardens dispose of their industrial waste and sewage by discharging it into the lake.

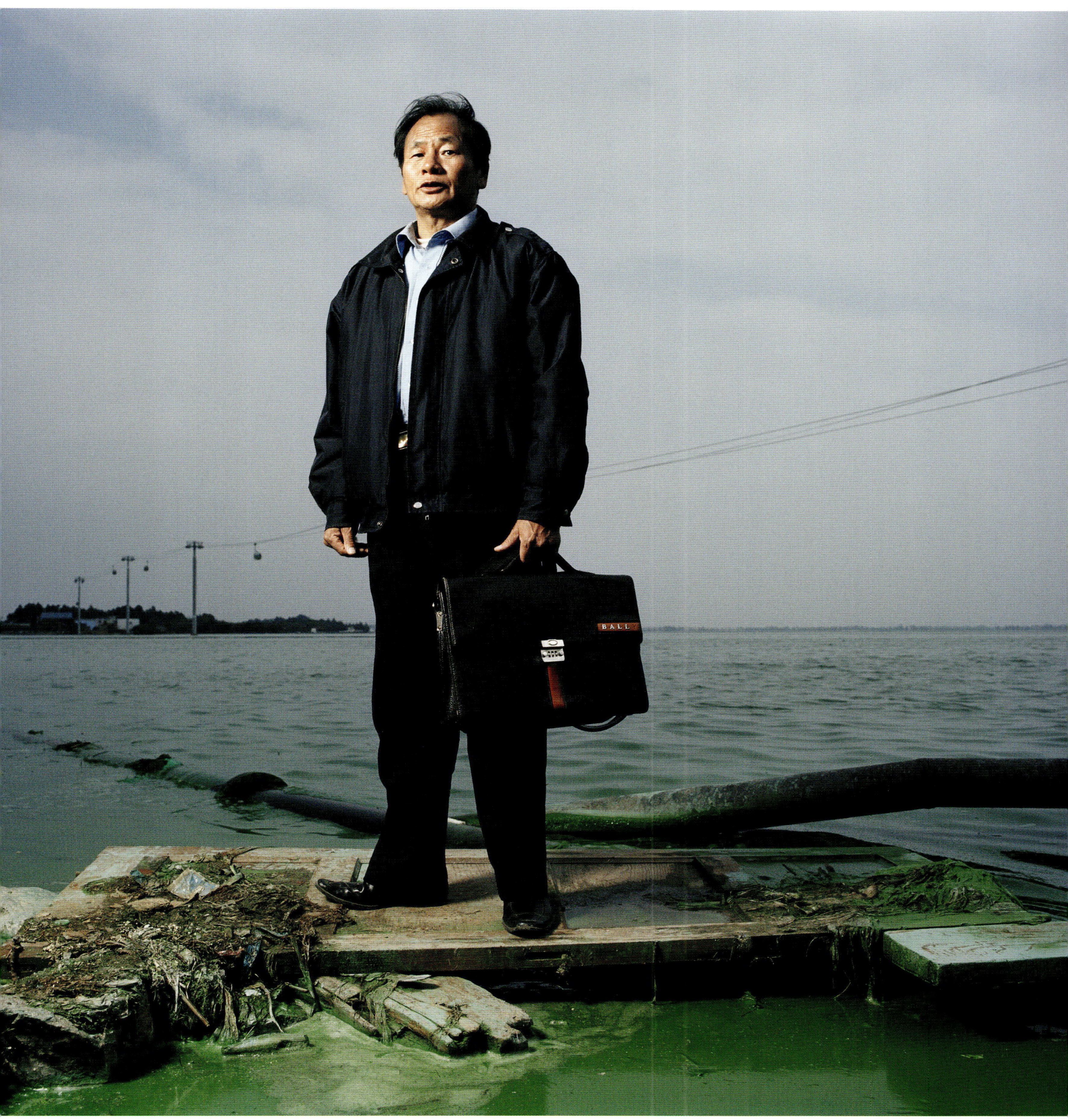
BALL

李美香

Li Meixiang (40)
Arbeiterin in der Kohleaufbereitung
Coal screening worker
Huolinguole, Innere Mongolei / Inner Mongolia

Li Meixiang arbeitet den ganzen Tag an einem Förderband, um unterschiedliche Kohlequalitäten zu sortieren. Ihre Arbeit ist schmutzig, gefährlich und schlecht bezahlt.

Li Meixiang separates various qualities of coal at a conveyer belt all day long. Her work is dirty, dangerous and poorly paid.

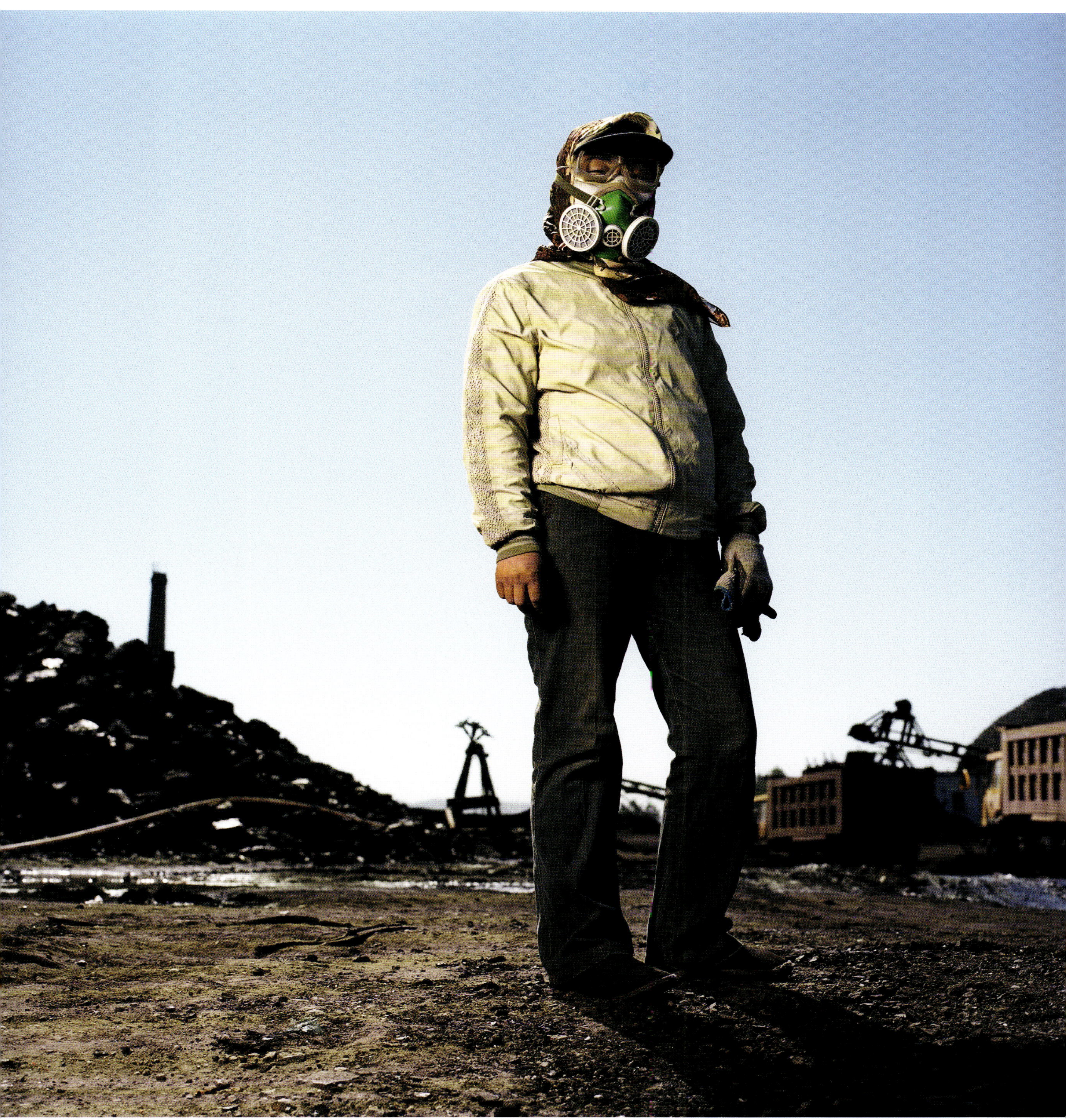

李云山

Li Yunshan (50)
Wander-Straßenarbeiter
Migrant road worker
Wutumeiren, Qinghai

Li Yunshan ist einer der vielen Wanderarbeiter, die in Westchina mit atemberaubender Geschwindigkeit neue Straßen bauen. Die Baustellen, auf denen Tausende von Menschen aus ganz China arbeiten, sind oft mehrere hundert Kilometer lang. Li Yunshan lebt, wie alle anderen Wanderarbeiter, in einer improvisierten Zeltstadt, in der Alkohol und Glücksspiel die einzigen Ablenkungen darstellen.

Li Yunshan is one of the many migrant workers building new roads in Western China at breathtaking speed. Construction sites can be hundreds of kilometers long with thousands of people from all over China working there. Like all the other migrant workers, Li Yunshan lives in an improvised tent town, where the only distractions are gambling and drinking.

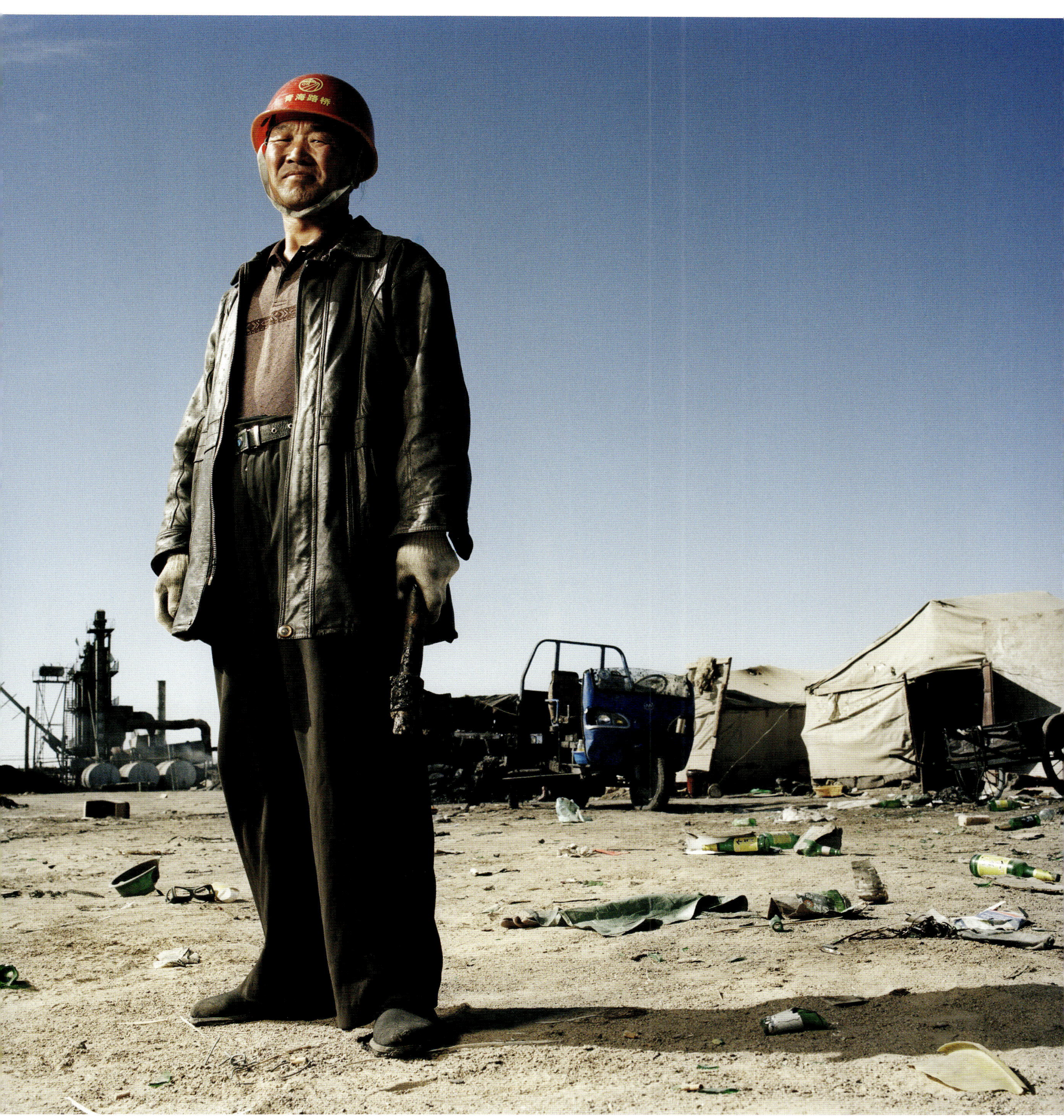
青海路桥

赵玲曦

Zhao „Helene“ Lingxi (22)
Bankangestellte
Bank employee
Beidahe, Hebei

Beidahe ist ein Badeort, der früher ausschließlich von Parteifunktionären besucht wurde. Bei den Mächtigen ist Beidahe immer noch sehr populär, aber heutzutage sieht man auch die neue obere Mittelschicht an Beidahes Stränden. Wenn die Hitze in Peking unerträglich wird, fährt Zhao „Helene“ Lingxi gerne mit ihrem Freund nach Beidahe.

Beidahe is a beach resort that used to be exclusively frequented by party functionaries. It is still very popular among the powerful, but these days the new upper middle class is also seen on its beaches. Zhao “Helene“ Lingxi loves coming to Beidahe with her boyfriend when the heat in the capital becomes unbearable.

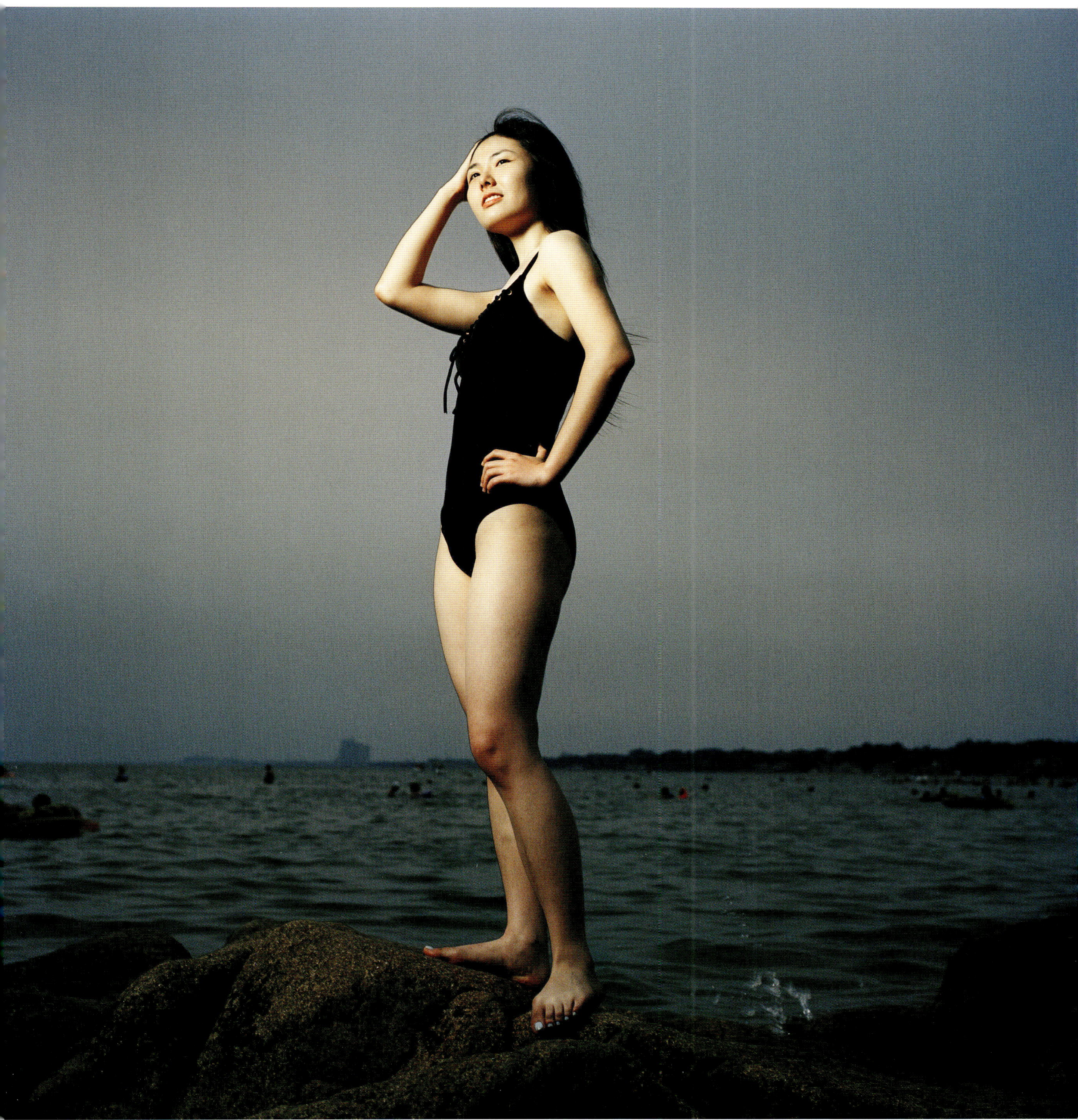

吴相兵

Wu Xiangbing (39)
Leiter der Golf-Akademie im Mission Hills Golf Club
Director of the Golf Academy at the Mission Hills Golf Club
Guanlan, Guangdong

Wu Xiangbing ist Leiter der Golf-Akademie im Mission Hills Golf Club, Chinas renommiertestem Golfclub. Er war früher Profi-Golfer und ist viermaliger chinesischer Meister.

Wu Xiangbing, now the director of the Golf Academy of the Mission Hills Golf Club, China's most prestigious golf club, used to be a professional player and is a four-time Chinese national golf champion.

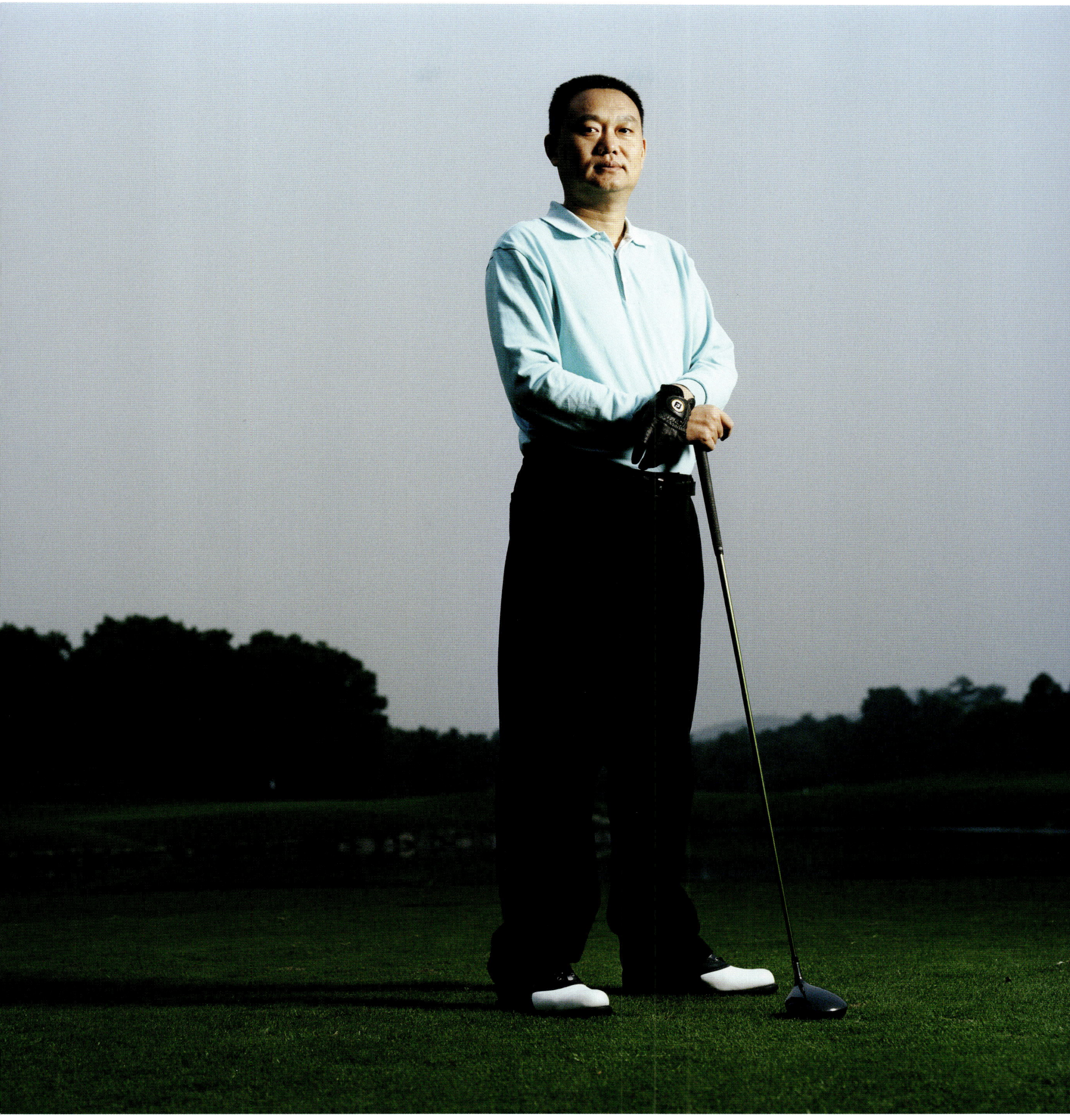

周华建

Zhou Huajian (37)
Fensterputzer
Window cleaner
Xingguangdadao, Chongqing

Zhou Huajian ist Fensterputzer in der Peripherie von Chongqing, der am schnellsten wachsenden Stadt der Welt. Bis zu dem Tag, als er enteignet wurde und sein Land für den Bau neuer Wolkenkratzer genutzt wurde, waren er und seine Frau Bauern. Heute putzt er die Fenster des Wolkenkratzers, der genau dort steht, wo sich früher seine Felder befanden.

Zhou Huajian is a window cleaner in the periphery of Chongqing, the world's fastest growing city. He and his wife used to be farmers until the day their land was taken away to make room for new skyscrapers. Today he cleans the windows of the skyscraper located on the very piece of land where his fields used to be.

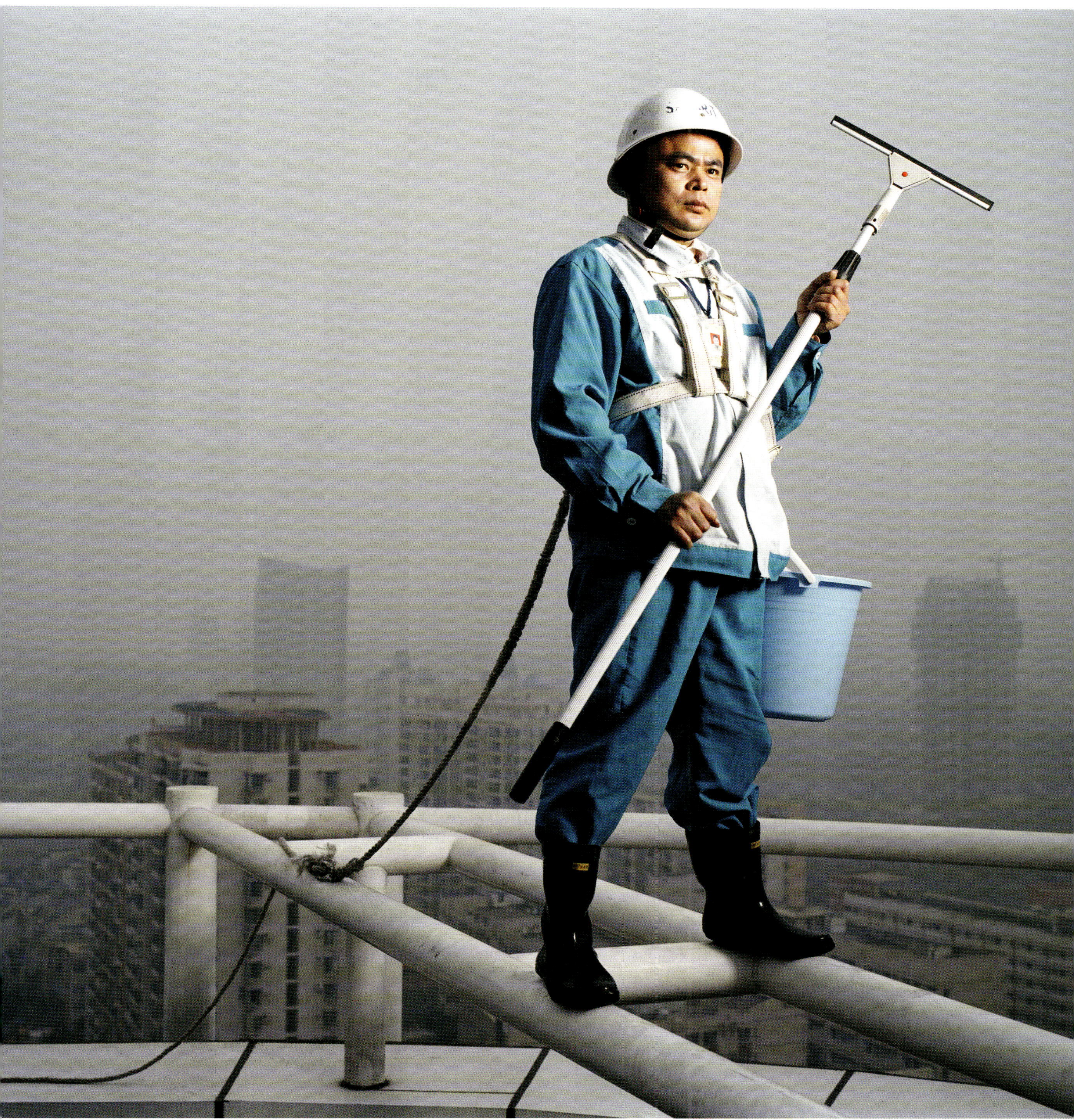

孙荣寿

Sun Rongshou (56)
Enten- und Geflügelhändler
Poultry and duck dealer
Baijiahou, Chongqing

Sun Rongshou läuft jeden Tag sechzehn Kilometer zu Fuß, um lebende Enten und Hühner auf einen lokalen Markt im Drei-Schluchten-Tal zu tragen.

Sun Rongshou walks sixteen kilometers every day to carry live ducks and chickens to a local market in the Three Gorges area.

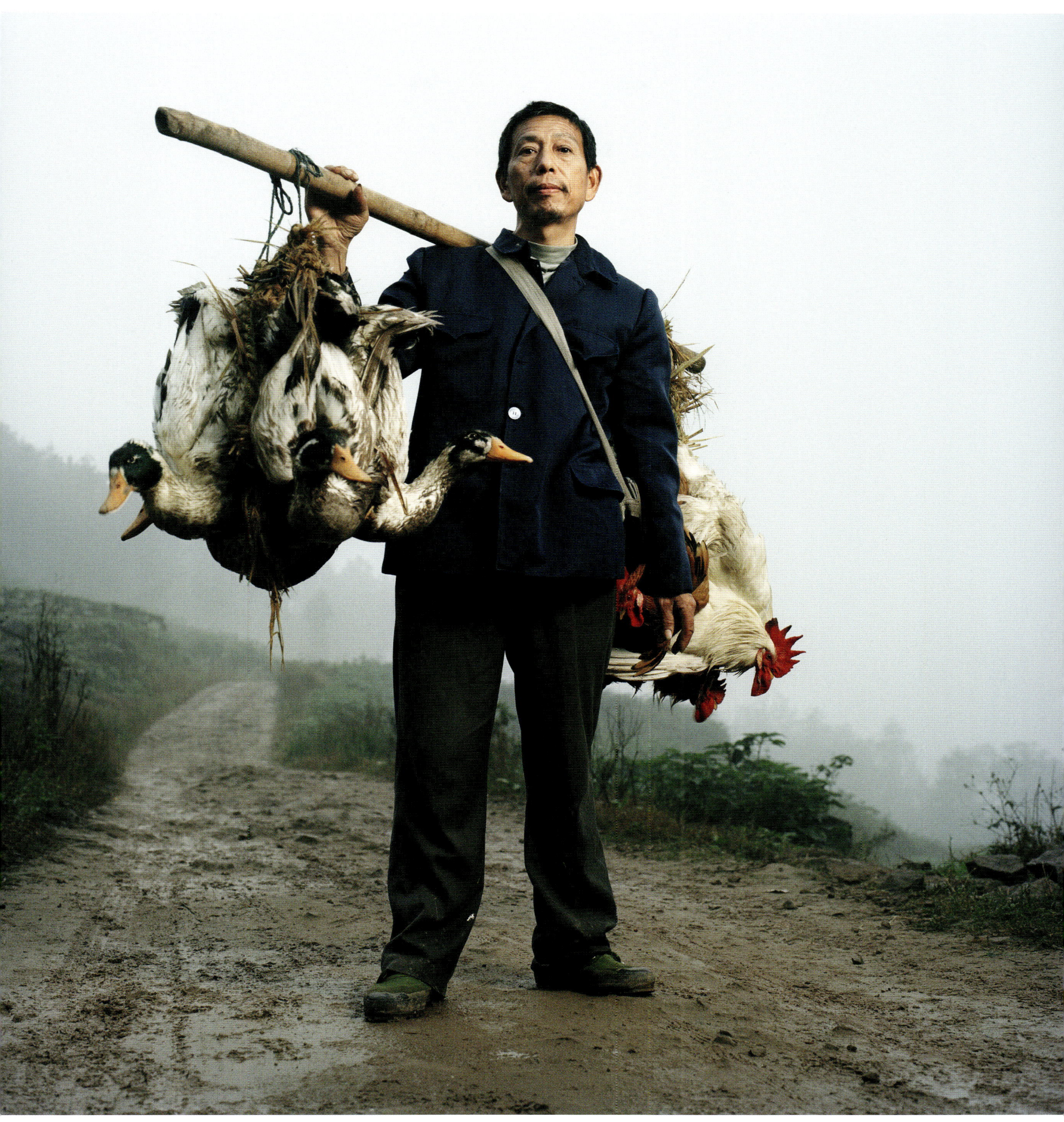

罗金权

Luo Jinquan (27)
Bauer
Farmer
Duoyijing, Yunnan

Leider befinden sich Luo Jinquans Schafe und der von ihnen produzierte Dünger auf der einen Seite des Flusses, sein Feld aber auf der anderen. Es gibt keine Brücke, was für Jinquan bedeutet, dass er den Schafsmist auf seinem Rücken durch die Strömung des reißenden Flusses tragen muss, um sein Feld auf der anderen Seite zu düngen. Bei einem Transport tragen seine Schultern ungefähr 30 Kilogramm. An diesem Tag musste er den Fluss – trotz des starken Regens – zwanzigmal überqueren.

Unfortunately, Luo Jinquan's sheep and their collected dung are on one side of the river and his field on the other. There is no bridge, which means, he has to carry the dung on his back through the rushing waters to fertilize his field on the other side of the river. On every trip, he shoulders about 30 kg. This particular day, in spite of heavy rain, he had to cross the river 20 times.

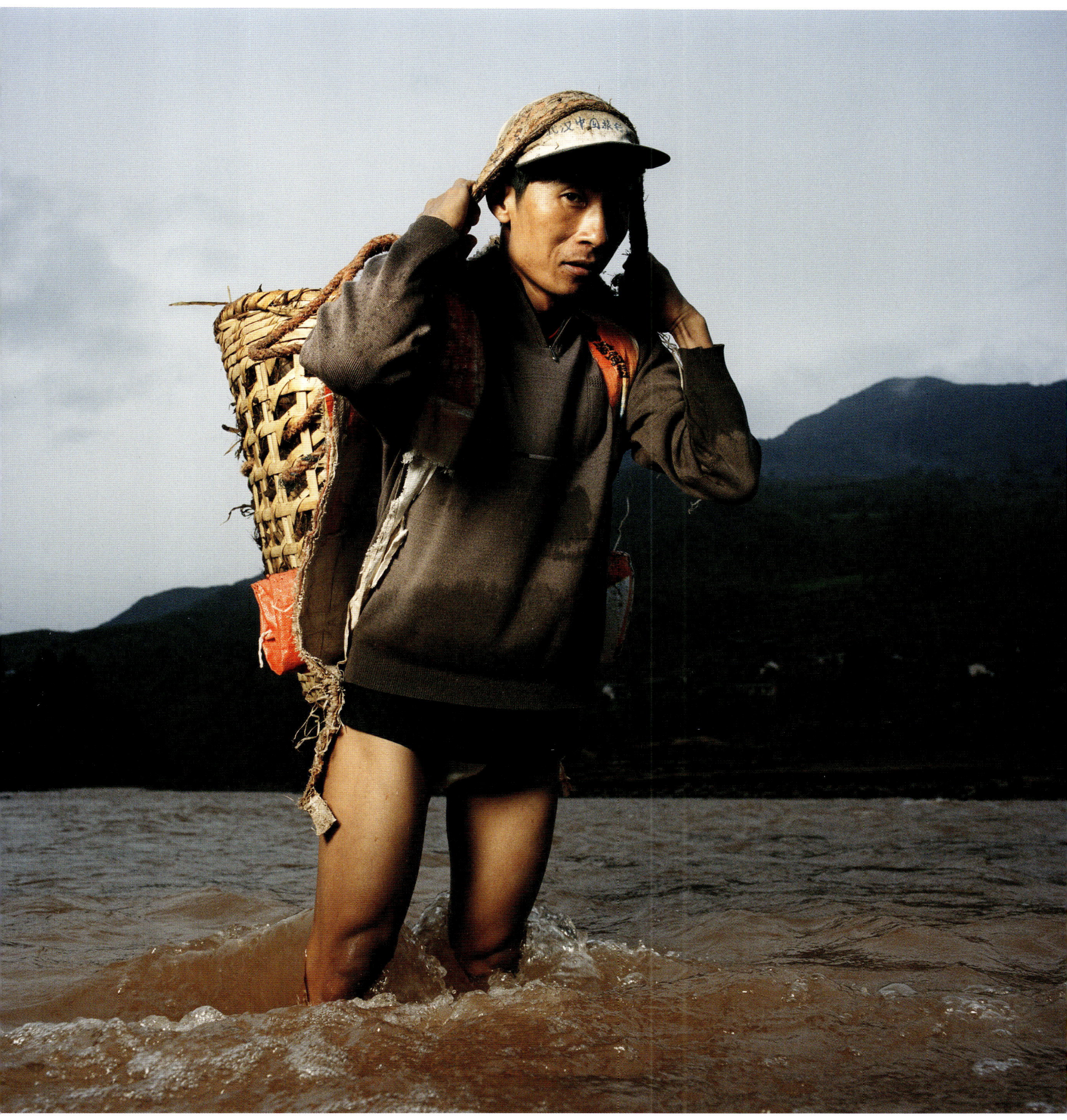

陈婷

Chen Ting (20)
Tänzerin
Dancer
Chongqing

Chen Ting arbeitet als Animationstänzerin im O2, dem neuesten Club in Chongqing. Als besondere Attraktion tanzt sie in einem am Eingang des Clubs platzierten Käfig. Viele mittellose Wanderarbeiter genießen die kostenlose Outdoor-Show. Die Gäste im Inneren des Lokals gehören zur neuen chinesischen Elite, die sich das entsprechende Outfit, die Markenaccessoires und die teuren Drinks leisten kann.

Chen Ting performs as an animation dancer in the O2 club, the latest night club in Chongqing. As a special attraction, she dances in a cage next to the entrance. Many migrant workers enjoy the free entertainment outside the club. The customers inside belong to the new Chinese elite that can afford the necessary outfit, the fancy accessories and the expensive drinks.

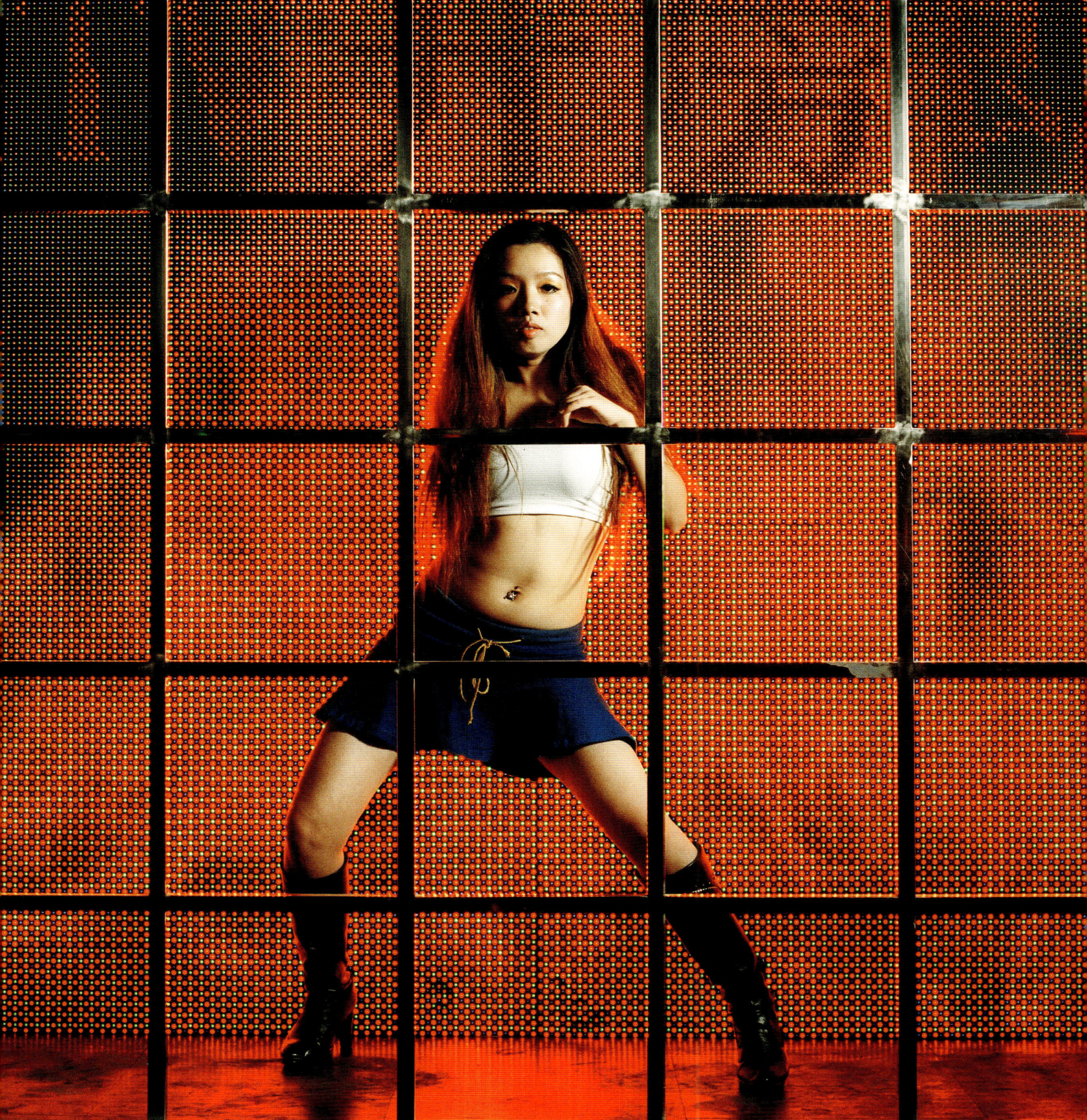

楚薇薇

Chu Weiwei (35)
Offizierin der Volksbefreiungsarmee
Foreign Affairs Officer, Military Forces
Peking / Beijing

Oberstleutnant Chu Weiwei ist Offizierin für auswärtige Angelegenheiten der Volksbefreiungsarmee in Peking. Sie ist verantwortlich für die Region Osteuropa.

Lieutenant Colonel Chu Weiwei is an officer with the Foreign Affairs Office of the People's Liberation Army in Beijing. She is in charge of the Eastern European Section.

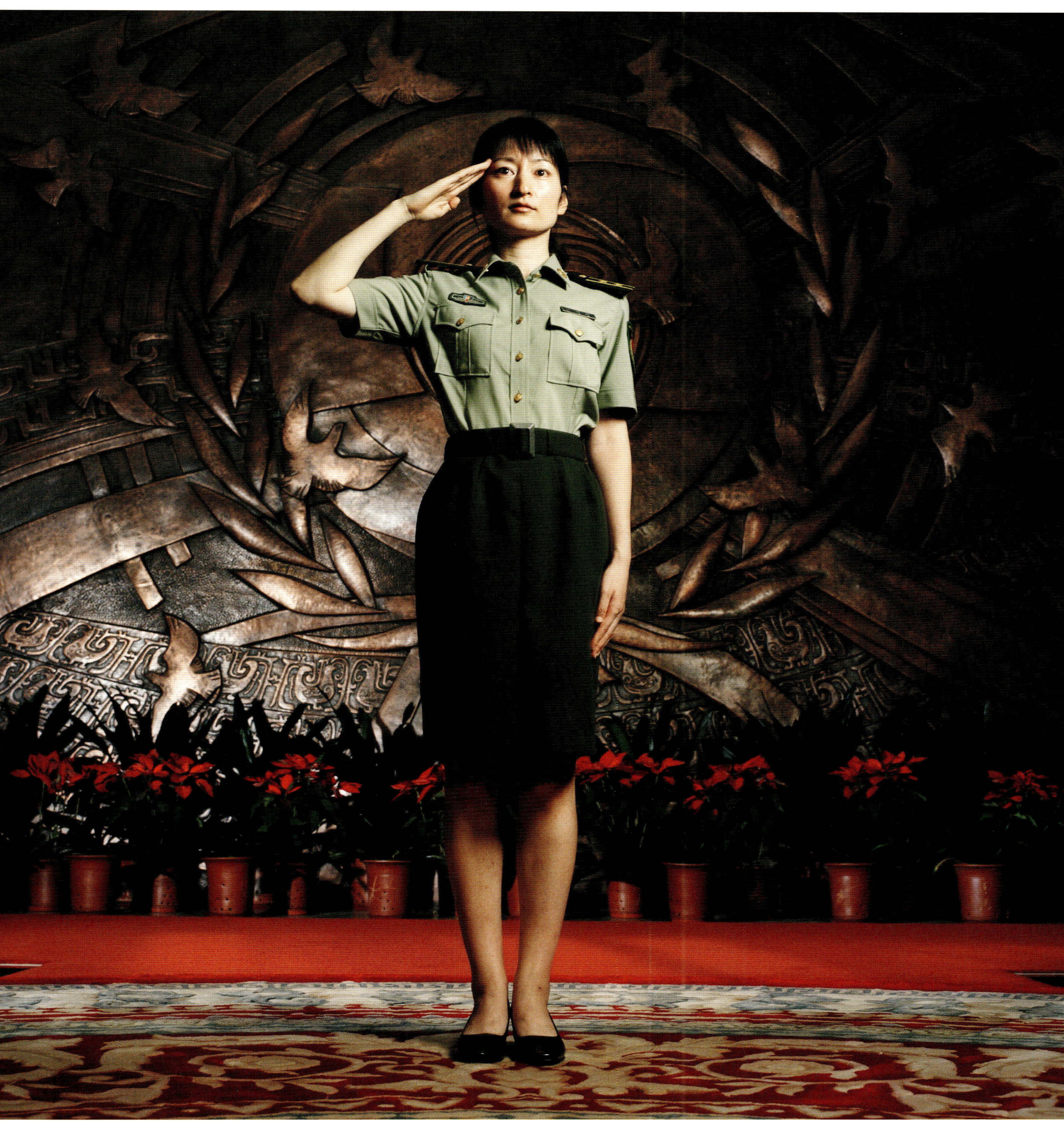

郝汉

Hao Han (8)
Kung-Fu Schüler und Kinderschauspieler
Shaolin Kung Fu student and child actor
Dengfeng, Henan

Hao Han will der nächste Jackie Chan werden. Dafür trainiert er jeden Tag hart im Shaolin-Kloster. Seine Eltern überwachen sein Training, um seinen Erfolg sicherzustellen. Er hatte schon einen Auftritt in einem Kung-Fu-Film. Rund um das Shaolin-Kloster bilden verschiedene Schulen mit jeweils unterschiedlichem Ruf Tausende Schüler aus.

Hao Han wants to be the next Jackie Chan. He trains hard every day at the Shaolin Monastery. His parents monitor his training to make sure he doesn't fail. He has already appeared in a Kung Fu movie. Various schools with different reputations drill thousands of students in the vicinity of Shaolin Monastery.

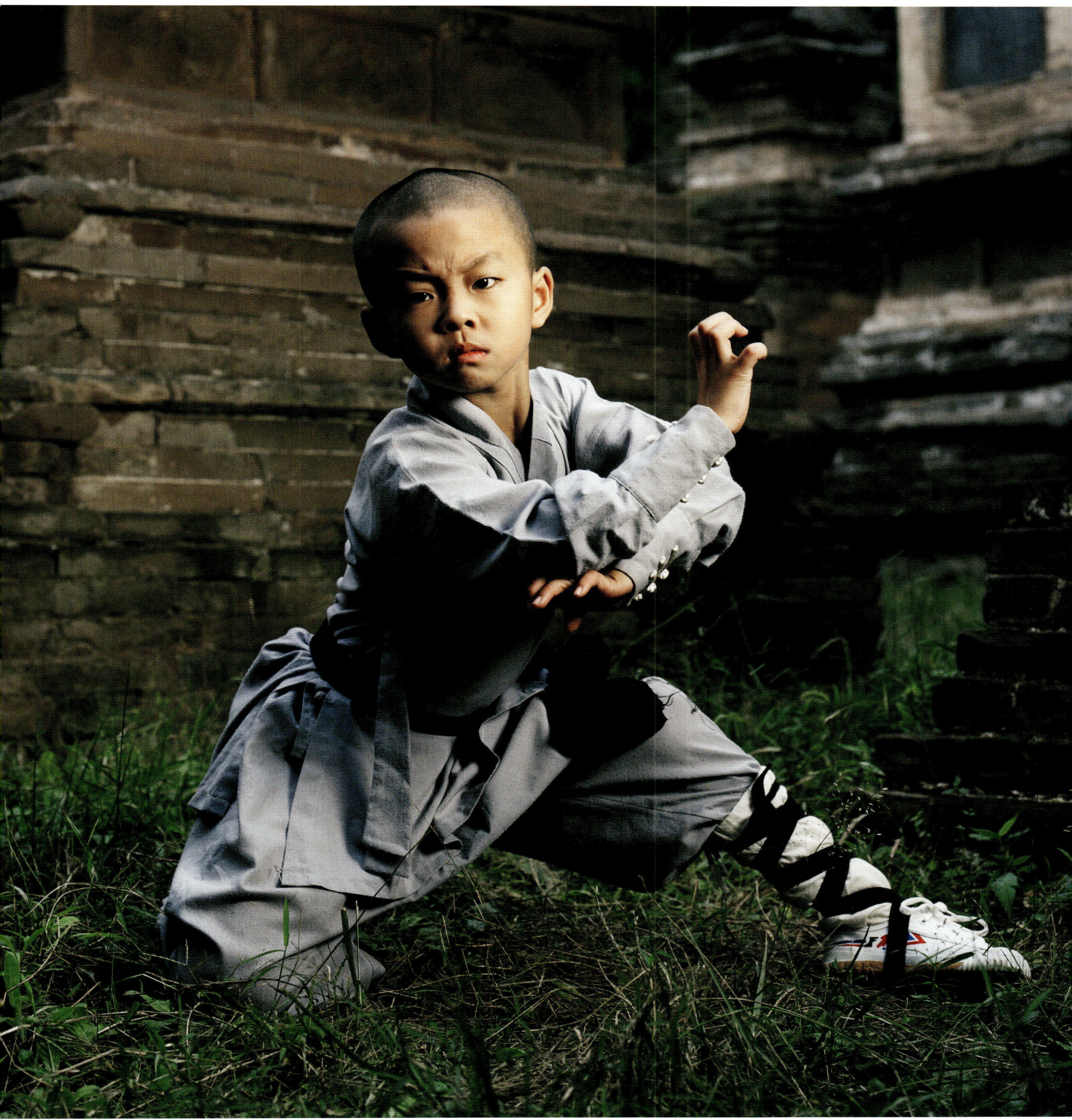

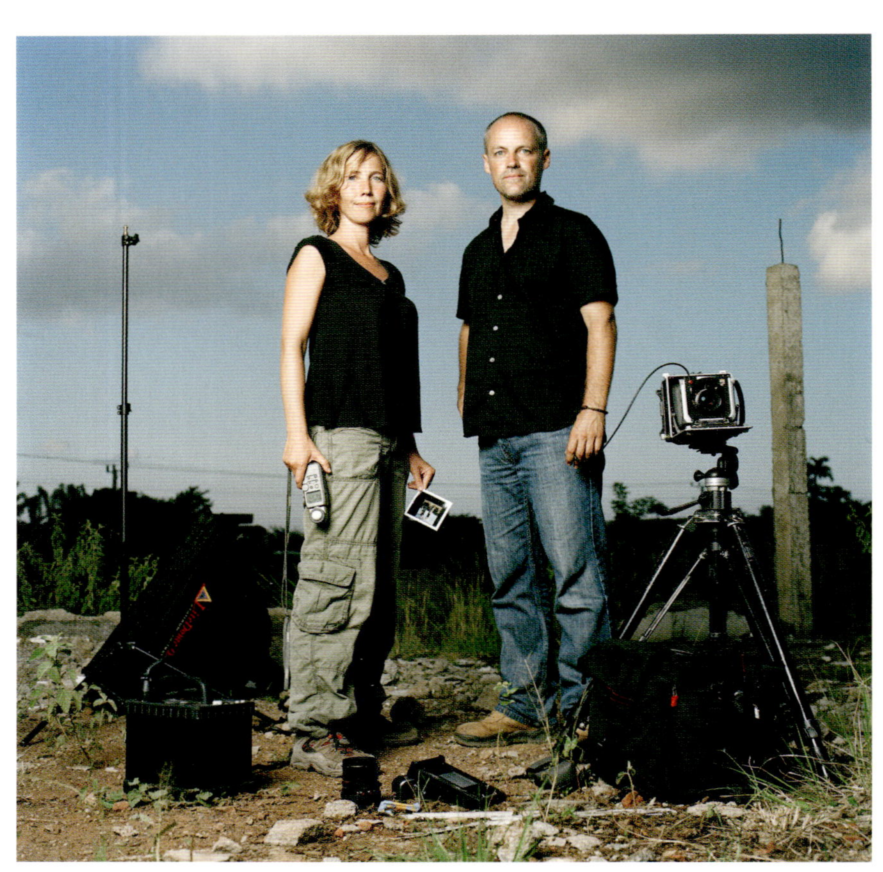

Mathias Braschler wurde 1969 im Aargau geboren. Er studierte zwei Jahre Geographie und Moderne Geschichte an der Universität Zürich, bevor er 1994 seine Karriere im Bereich Fotografie als Autodidakt begann. Er war für verschiedene Magazine und Zeitungen in der Schweiz tätig. 1998 zog er nach New York, um sein erstes Buch „Madison Avenue" zu realisieren. Die folgenden Jahre lebte und arbeitete er in New York.

Monika Fischer wurde 1971 im St. Galler Rheintal geboren. Bereits während ihres Studiums der Romanistik und Germanistik an der Universität Zürich nahm sie eine Tätigkeit als Dramaturgie- und Regieassistentin am Opernhaus Zürich auf. Mehrere Jahre arbeitete sie mit verschiedenen bedeutenden Regisseuren zusammen. Neben der erfolgreichen Kooperation mit Mathias Braschler hat Monika Fischer von 2003 bis 2005 ein Nachdiplomstudium in Szenografie an der Hochschule für Kunst in Zürich absolviert.

2003 begann die enge Zusammenarbeit des Fotografenteams Mathias Braschler und Monika Fischer anlässlich des Portrait-Projektes „About Americans", das die beiden quer durch die Vereinigten Staaten führte. In den Jahren 2005/2006 arbeiteten sie am Projekt „Faces of Football": Mit der ideellen Unterstützung der FIFA fotografierten sie 30 Fußballstars unmittelbar nach wichtigen Spielen. Ein Jahr vor Beginn der Olympischen Spiele in Peking starteten Mathias Braschler und Monika Fischer eine siebenmonatige, epische Reise durch ganz China. Auf ihrem 30.000 Kilometer langen Roadtrip schossen sie Portraits von Chinesen aus verschiedensten sozialen Schichten und aus allen Regionen dieser immensen und gegensätzlichen Nation. Im Jahre 2009 realisierten sie eine viel beachtete Serie über Menschen, die schon heute direkt vom Klimawandel betroffen sind.

Mathias Braschler und Monika Fischer wurden mehrfach ausgezeichnet, unter anderem erhielten sie einen World Press Photo Award und einen ADC Bronze Award in Deutschland. Ihre Fotoprojekte werden in unzähligen internationalen Magazinen publiziert, erscheinen als Fotobücher und werden in Galerien und Museen in Europa, Asien und den USA ausgestellt.

Heute leben und arbeiten Mathias Braschler und Monika Fischer in Zürich und in New York, wo sie von Vaughan Hannigan repräsentiert werden.

www.braschlerfischer.com

Mathias Braschler was born in Aargau, Switzerland, in 1969. He studied geography and modern history at the University of Zurich for two years before launching his career as autodidactic photographer. He worked for various newspapers and magazines in Switzerland and then moved to New York in 1998, where he published his first book – "Madison Avenue".

Monika Fischer was born in St. Gallen's Rhine valley in 1971. While studying Romance and German languages and literature at the University of Zurich, she worked at the Zurich Opera House as an assistant dramaturge and director, where over the course of several years, she worked with various renowned directors. In addition to collaborating successfully with Mathias Braschler, she completed her postgraduate scenography studies and received an Executive Master of Arts diploma from Zurich University of the Arts.

In 2003, Mathias Braschler and Monika Fischer began working together closely as a photography team, producing a portrait project titled "About Americans", which led the two of them all over the United States. They worked on the project "Faces of Football" in 2005-2006. With FIFA's ideological support, they shot portraits of 30 football stars directly after important matches. One year prior to the opening of the Beijing Olympic Games, Mathias Braschler and Monika Fischer started an epic seven-month journey throughout China. On their 30,000 kilometer road trip, they took portraits of people of various walks of life in most regions of this vast and contradictory country. In 2009, they completed an acclaimed project series on people already affected by climate change.

Braschler & Fischer have been honored with numerous awards, such as a World Press Photo Award and the German ADC Bronze Award. Their photography projects are published in countless international magazines, appear in photo books and are exhibited in galleries and museums in Europe, Asia and the United States.

Today, Mathias Braschler and Monika Fischer live in Zurich and New York, where they are represented by Vaughan Hannigan.

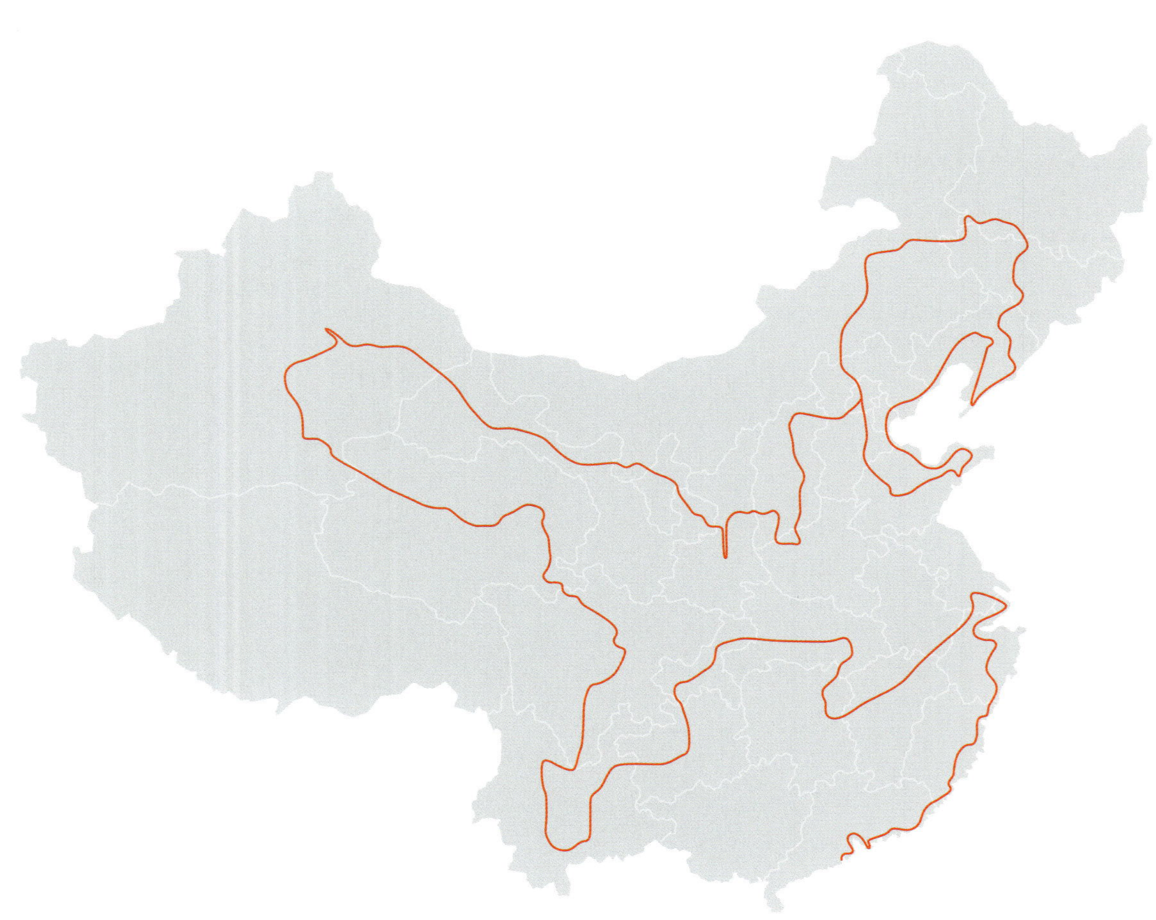

Dank

Wir möchten Fu Yuan, unserem Assistenten, Dolmetscher und Fahrer danken, der uns acht Monate lang, jeweils 7 Tage in der Woche unermüdlich unterstützte. Seinem Talent, annähernd jede Person, die wir ansprachen, dazu zu bewegen bei unserem Projekt mitzuwirken, verdanken wir viel.
Besonderer Dank geht ferner an Jonathan Watts (The Guardian) für seine vielen inspirierenden Tipps. Während unserer fünf gemeinsamen Tage auf der Straße von Yunnan war Jon ein hervorragender Reisebegleiter und Kollege, der unsere Arbeit mit seiner außergewöhnlichen Kunstfertigkeit als Autor und Filmer ungemein bereicherte. Chen Shi, Jons Assistentin, möchten wir für ihre Hilfe danken und dafür, dass sie viele unserer Probleme mit ihrem Charme und ihren Sprachfähigkeiten zu lösen verstand.
Dank gebührt auch Adrian Geiges (Stern, Peking) und seiner Assistentin Ellen Deng für ihre tatkräftige Unterstützung bei Visa- und anderen organisatorischen Fragen.
Ein Projekt dieser Größe konnten wir nur dank der Zusammenarbeit mit einigen der führenden Zeitschriften und Magazine in Europa realisieren: Stern, The Guardian Weekend, Figaro Magazine und Vanity Fair Italien. Wir verdanken ihnen und speziell ihren Bildredaktionen viel. Besonders erwähnen möchten wir die Redaktionsleiter Kate Edwards (The Guardian), Cyril Drouhet (Figaro), Marco Finazzi (Vanity Fair Italien) und vor allem Andrea Gothe (Stern). Sie haben immer an uns und an unsere Arbeit geglaubt. Ganz spezieller Dank geht an Thomas Osterkorn und Andreas Petzold, die beiden Chefredakteure des Stern, die es möglich gemacht haben, dass diese Arbeit auf 30 Seiten ihres Magazins veröffentlicht werden konnte.
Die Schweizer Botschaft in Peking hat uns ebenfalls hervorragend auf unserer Chinareise unterstützt. Besonderer Dank geht an Térence Billeter, den Kulturattaché in Peking, der sich mit großem Einsatz um all unsere vielfältigen Anfragen kümmerte und es ermöglichte, dass die erste Ausstellung dieser Arbeit in China selbst stattfand.
Auch gegenüber Oberst GS Christoph Gertsch, Verteidigungsattaché der Schweizer Botschaft in China, und seinem Stab, der das (fast) Unmögliche möglich machte, möchten wir unsere Dankbarkeit ausdrücken: Wir durften ein Mitglied der Volksbefreiungsarmee ablichten.
Vielen Dank an Maria Fischer und Dominique Brentano für ihre Hilfe in medizinischen Fragen.
Bei den Vorbereitungen zu unserer Chinareise steuerten viele Experten ihr Wissen über das Reich der Mitte bei. Sie halfen uns dabei, diese gewaltige Nation mit offenen Augen und wachem Verstand zu bereisen. Unser Dank geht an Peter Achten, Ulrich Sigg, Marianne Keller, Klaus Littmann und viele weitere Ungenannte.
Danke sagen möchten wir auch Simon Maurer, der uns mit dem Buchdesigner Peter Zimmermann bekannt gemacht hat, Loten Dahortsang für seine Hilfe bei der Schreibung der tibetischen Namen, Ayman Shahin vom orientalischen Institut der Universität Zürich für die Unterstützung bei den Namen der Uigurenminorität und unserer Nachbarin Jinghan für die Prüfung aller chinesischen Namen.
Der Hatje Cantz Verlag, Ostfildern, und die Edition Stephan Witschi, Zürich, verdienen unsere tiefste Dankbarkeit dafür, dass sie an dieses Projekt geglaubt und dieses Buch ermöglicht haben. Herzlichen Dank auch an Roger Zoller, der uns unermüdlich während der Buchproduktion unterstützte.
Peter Zimmermann möchten wir für die Buchgestaltung danken. Und vielen Dank auch an Michael Brewer und Sabine Walter, Word+Image AG, für das abschließende Korrekturlesen des englischen und deutschen Manuskripts.
Nur dank der liebevollen Unterstützung und Motivation seitens unserer Familien sind wir in der Lage, überhaupt so zu arbeiten und zu leben! Heidi und Alex Braschler, Elisabeth und Alex Fischer ganz herzlichen Dank!
Am wichtigsten sind natürlich alle Mitwirkenden in China gewesen: Ganz speziellen Dank dafür, dass sie uns ihre kostbare Zeit geschenkt und uns gestattet haben, sie kennenzulernen und zu portraitieren.
Ganz zum Schluss danken wir außerdem noch allen anderen, die – auf welche Art und Weise auch immer – einen Beitrag zu diesem Projekt geleistet haben.

Acknowledgements

We would like to thank Fu Yuan, our assistant, interpreter and driver, for both his untiring support and his talent to convince almost everyone we asked to participate in our project, seven days a week, for a period of seven months.
Special thanks to Jonathan Watts (The Guardian) for his inspiring input, for being a great travel and work companion for five days on the road in Yunnan and for enriching our work with his outstanding expertise in writing and filming. We would also like to thank Chen Shi, Jon's assistant, for her charm and language skills, which helped us solve many problems.
Thanks to Adrian Geiges (Stern, Beijing) and his assistant Ellen Deng for their crucial support with visa and other organizational matters.
Producing a project of this scale was only possible thanks to the collaboration of some of Europe's leading magazines: Stern, The Guardian Weekend, Figaro Magazine and Vanity Fair Italy. We owe our thanks to these publications and particularly to their photo departments, with their directors Kate Edwards (The Guardian), Cyril Drouhet (Figaro), Marco Finazzi (Vanity Fair Italy) and Andrea Gothe (Stern), who deserves special credit. She has always believed in us and in our work. Very special thanks to Thomas Osterkorn and Andreas Petzold, Stern magazine's chief editors, who made it possible for this work to be published over 30 pages.
The Swiss Embassy in Beijing offered us outstanding support while we traveled through China. Special thanks to Térence Billeter, Cultural Attaché in Beijing, who took great care of our many concerns and helped to make it possible for the first presentation and initial exhibition of our work to be held on Chinese soil.
We want to express our gratitude to Colonel GS Christoph Gertsch, Defense Attaché of the Swiss Embassy in China and his staff, who made the seemingly impossible come true: taking the portrait of a member of the People's Liberation Army.
We very much want to thank Clint Groom, Charmaine Chow and Julia Ni who made it possible for us to visit and shoot at Chinese textile factories.
Many thanks to Maria Fischer and Dominique Brentano for their help with medical issues.
When preparing our Chinese endeavor, many experts shared their knowledge about the Middle Kingdom with us. They helped us to travel this vast nation, both with open minds and open eyes. Thank you Peter Achten, Ulrich Sigg, Marianne Keller, Klaus Littmann and many more.
Thanks to Simon Maurer, who introduced us to our wonderful designer Peter Zimmermann, to Loten Dahortsang for his calligraphic help with all the Tibetan names, Ayman Shahin of the University of Zurich's Oriental Institute for helping us with the Arab names of the Uyghur minority and thanks to our neighbor Jinghan for proofreading all the Chinese names.
To Hatje Cantz Verlag, Ostfildern, and Stephan Witschi Edition, Zurich, we owe deepest gratitude for believing in this project and making this book possible. Many thanks also to Roger Zoller for his tireless support.
We would also like to thank Peter Zimmermann for his creativity and for spending countless hours to find the best possible design for this book. And thank you to Michael Brewer and Sabine Walter of Word+Image Inc. for the final proofreading of the English and German manuscripts.

Only with the loving support and motivation of our families are we able to work and live this way! Heidi and Alex Braschler, Elisabeth and Alex Fischer, thank you so much!
Most importantly, very special thanks to all the participants throughout China who spent their precious time with and had their portraits taken by us. And – of course – to everybody else who contributed to this project.